THE
POWER
OF
FLEXING

THE
POWER
OF
FLEXING

**How to Use Small Daily Experiments
to Create Big Life-Changing Growth**

SUSAN J. ASHFORD

HARPER
BUSINESS
An Imprint of HarperCollinsPublishers

HarperCollins books may be purchased for educational, business, or sales promotional use. For information, please email the Special Markets Department at SPsales@harpercollins.com.

FIRST EDITION

Designed by Nancy Singer

Library of Congress Cataloging-in-Publication Data

Names: Ashford, Susan J., author.
Title: The power of flexing: how to use small daily experiments to create big
    life-changing growth / Susan J. Ashford.
Description: First edition. | New York: Harper Business, an imprint of Harper-
    Collins Publishers [2021] | Includes bibliographical references and index.
Identifiers: LCCN 2021018562 (print) | LCCN 2021018563 (ebook) | ISBN
    9780063011571 (hardcover) | ISBN 9780063011588 (ebook)
Subjects: LCSH: Self-actualization (Psychology) | Goal (Psychology) | Habit. |
    Interpersonal relations. | Success. | Leadership. | Soft skills.
Classification: LCC BF637.S4 A748 2021 (print) | LCC BF637.S4 (ebook) |
    DDC 158.1—dc23
LC record available at https://lccn.loc.gov/2021018562
LC ebook record available at https://lccn.loc.gov/2021018563

21 22 23 24 25   LSC   10 9 8 7 6 5 4 3 2 1

To all the people who stay in the game, finding the courage and the competencies to keep growing throughout their lives

CONTENTS

THE
POWER
OF
FLEXING

INTRODUCTION

What would you do if you discovered—after spending twenty years helping to lead a successful and widely respected business—that you needed
to learn how to lead all over again.

That's what happened to Maggie Bayless.[1] And to make matters
worse, Maggie found herself facing not one but three equally daunting
challenges, in her work and personal life, all at once.

Bayless's first challenge grew out of a major change at her workplace. Bayless had been a cofounder and a co–managing partner of
a well-known business-to-business training firm. She loved the work
and the company was successful, steadily adding clients, growing its
staff, and expanding its revenues and its profitability. But the funny
thing was that Bayless, though one of the chief officers of the company,
had somehow avoided having too many direct reports. "Every time we
hired someone new," she recalls with a chuckle, "I'd say to my partner,
Stas, 'That's fine—as long as they report to you.'"

It worked great . . . until the day when Stas announced his retirement. "I was so happy for Stas," Bayless says. "And then I realized,
'Uh-oh, that means everyone here is going to report to *me* now.'" Suddenly the business veteran—a gifted adviser who had helped many in
the company cope with their own difficult leadership challenges—would
have to start managing the whole team herself: guiding them in making
tough decisions, helping them cope with thorny client issues, resolv-
ing conflicts among members of her team, making fair decisions about
how to allocate resources, and balancing conflicting strategic demands.

For the first time in years, Bayless found herself wondering whether she had what it took to be successful on the job. Were her leadership abilities and her interpersonal skills up to par?

It didn't help that two personal challenges had simultaneously popped up in Bayless's life. One was expected, but it still involved the stresses that often accompany change: her youngest daughter left for college, leaving Bayless and her husband with an empty nest for the first time in more than twenty-five years. The other was unexpected and deeply traumatic: a serious health scare that required emergency surgery, two additional operations, and the risk of long-term complications that could hamper Bayless's ability to work at all.

For Bayless, this triple-threat year would test her in unprecedented ways. Could she develop the new range of skills—in leadership and in personal effectiveness—that she would need to master the business, family, and physical difficulties she suddenly faced? Could she make these difficult and emotional experiences work for her and her personal growth?

The answers to these questions would have a huge impact on Bayless herself. But they would also affect her family, her colleagues, her clients, and the long-term success of the company she had cofounded and the people who were counting on her to shepherd it into the future.

While Maggie Bayless's circumstances were uniquely her own, we all face unexpected, unfamiliar experiences that call for new talents, new insights, and new abilities. In fact, almost everyone can expect to be in Bayless's shoes, suddenly needing to change and grow, at some point in their life. Especially in today's unpredictable world, we all have times when we face unexpected change and the anxiety it can create; we all know what it is like to have many difficult things on our plate all at once. By practicing the Power of Flexing, you not only learn more about yourself but develop a resilience muscle that will help you get through these tough times.

WELCOME TO THE POWER OF FLEXING

This book is about how people like Maggie Bayless—and like you and me—can develop the "soft," interpersonal skills we need to manage and control our emotions, communicate well, lead effectively, adapt to changing conditions, and solve complex problems. And while we refer to these skills as "soft," they're vitally important. In fact, 92 percent of respondents in Deloitte's Global Human Capital Trends report rate these skills as critical to employee retention, better leadership, and a more meaningful culture. Such skills are needed to overcome the challenges we face in business and to be a better leader within a company or, for that matter, within any kind of group—a nonprofit, a church, a community organization, a family. It explains a system anyone can use to continually grow and develop by getting better at gathering insights and learning from the raw material we all have access to—the experiences we encounter simply by being alive. That system is the Power of Flexing.

Flexing is a particular method for increasing your own effectiveness and, for those in organizations, your effectiveness in influencing and leading others. It was developed based on my work with students, emerging leaders, and senior leaders over the years.[2] It draws on a range of research that suggests ways in which individuals can manage their own personal development, and is based on more than seventy-five interviews that my students and I have conducted with leaders and others we admire. All these inputs are woven into this book. Flexing is an approach to growing your effectiveness that is unique and has several notable attributes.

First, it's *proactive*: it puts you in the driver's seat in guiding your own growth. You decide when, how, and why you want to grow, and develop your own plan for learning and self-development. You never need to wait for someone else to provide you with the tools, activities, or opportunities needed to grow.

Second, as the name implies, it's *flexible*: it lets you pursue personal growth in ways that suit your needs and resources. You can flex at work, in your relationship with your boss, in a short-term project in the community, or as a parent, spouse, or church member. You can use flexing to enhance your personal effectiveness, then maybe drop it for a while and pick it up again when you feel moved to do so.

Third, it's *manageable*: it provides you with methods for learning and growing that can fit comfortably into most people's daily schedules. Developing important new skills is often treated as a major undertaking and a substantial commitment: you go to grad school, you sign up for therapy, you hope to be designated as "high potential" by your company and sent off for a challenging overseas assignment. But why wait for opportunities like these? Flexing lets you get started on building your personal skills *now*, using the everyday experiences you're having anyway. To borrow a term from the world of agile software development, it's a sprint—or a series of sprints—rather than a marathon.[3]

Fourth, it's *playful and fun*. Personal development doesn't need to be a grim or painful endeavor. Flexing is about experimentation: trying new ways of doing things, seeing what happens, thinking differently (and more positively) about failure and mistakes, and then trying something else. Most likely, no single experiment will be life altering (although you never know!). But, cumulatively, the experiments you try may provide you with fresh ideas, approaches, and skills that will help you achieve surprising new successes in your daily life and work—all while having fun exploring sides of yourself you may not have known existed.

For all these reasons, many of those who've tried the Power of Flexing—from the day MBA students using it to frame their consulting work, to the hundreds of executive MBA students who have learned it as a lifelong strategy for owning their leadership development, to those who have engaged these ideas in their company settings—have found it to be a surprisingly helpful, enjoyable, and powerful method for building their personal effectiveness and their leadership skills simply by approaching and thinking about the activities of their daily lives in a creative new way.

To glimpse how it works, let's look at how Maggie Bayless used the Power of Flexing to tackle her year of three-problems-in-one.

Bayless started by setting some specific *flex goals* that she hoped to achieve in order to survive and thrive in her "new normal." Having thought about the challenges she faced and how she wanted to come out on the other side, she first developed goals that would help her deal with the new leadership tasks she'd been handed. To address a couple of personal leadership weaknesses that she was particularly worried about, she set one goal of learning to be more open to input from others, and another of improving her ability to manage her immediate reactions to stressful situations. Then, to deal with the personal challenges she faced—including the intense stress she felt over her unexpected health crisis—she set a third flex goal of developing a daily mindfulness and gratitude practice.

Bayless knew that each of these three goals would be difficult to achieve. But she also knew that, unless she named them and committed herself to pursuing them, she would almost certainly fall short. That's why choosing one or more flex goals is the essential first step in practicing the Power of Flexing.

Now, how did Bayless go about developing the skills needed to reach her three goals? She planned to conduct a number of *experiments* to test specific ways of acting and interacting. These were behaviors she could practice while carrying out the activities of her daily life—new, *flexed* behaviors that she suspected might enable her to achieve one or more of her flex goals.

One of her first opportunities to experiment arose when a valued longtime employee announced that she would soon be leaving the company. This was the kind of leadership challenge Bayless dreaded. She'd always found it tough to cope with bad news, and the particular circumstances made this case especially difficult. Even though the employee did everything right, gave appropriate notice, and was committed to the end, it initially felt unfair: Why did this trusted associate choose *this* moment to abandon her? Everyone knew that Maggie was still getting her sea legs as the company's solo leader. It initially hit hard—the kind of painful experience that might once have sent Bayless into a tailspin of denial and resentment.

Bayless understood that she needed to try a different approach. Rather than reacting as her emotions dictated, she instead planned and tested a new, more measured way of responding. She experimented with deliberately refraining from taking any immediate action in response to the news, such as quickly promoting another associate to fill the empty position. Emotionally and mentally, she stepped back from the challenge, considering it in the broader context of the organization's overall human resources strategy. In her most important experiment, she took time to discern and make use of the positive opportunities created by the change. Working with her whole team, she developed a plan to redesign the job's description and to recruit a talented new staff member quickly so she could be trained by the departing employee.

Through these behavioral changes—all driven by Bayless's intention to practice flexing—she transformed a potential disaster into a talent upgrade for the organization.

Bayless also solicited *feedback* from team members and others to gauge the impact—positive, negative, or mixed—of her new behaviors. She engaged in *systematic reflection* to extract meaning and insights from the experiences she was having along the way. And throughout the process, Bayless kept an eye on the mindset she was bringing to her experiences—pushing herself to stay in a learning mode rather than getting anxious about failing or working to prove that she already was great at these skills that were actually new to her. She also practiced *emotional regulation*—observing, thinking about, and controlling her emotions—to ensure that her feelings, good or bad, didn't get in the way of the learning and growth she was determined to achieve.

These processes—setting flex goals, planning and conducting experiments, gathering feedback, engaging in systematic reflection, managing mindset, and emotional regulation—are the basic building blocks of the Power of Flexing.

Of course, like practically all worthwhile endeavors, learning via the Power of Flexing usually involves bumps in the road and occasional setbacks. But, for Maggie Bayless, flexing has made a big, positive difference. Today her firm is doing better than ever, and Bayless's own leadership skills have flourished, thanks to the insights and knowledge she has developed through her experiments and through her reflections on her experiences.

In the chapters that follow, I'll describe the concepts behind the Power of Flexing and show you how it works, step by step. I'll illustrate the ideas and techniques using stories from people in many walks of life. They include people new to management roles who have struggled to develop novel leadership skills that are intricately intertwined with their personal effectiveness; CEOs who've already climbed to the pinnacle of their organizations but are committed to continual learning and improving on the job; a lawyer turned diplomat who had to develop strategies for coping with international crises—all while logging 400,000 high-stress travel miles; a young mom with kids whose developmental problems triggered the most important personal growth challenge of her life; and a Silicon Valley hotshot who found herself having to relearn how to lead while tackling a tough new assignment at the Pentagon.

What do they all have in common? They all share the universal need for continual, lifelong learning and increasing their personal effectiveness—a need that flexing has helped them to meet.

GROWING YOUR PERSONAL AND INTERPERSONAL EFFECTIVENESS

The Power of Flexing is about how we grow, particularly how we grow to become more personally and interpersonally skillful. Becoming personally effective is quite different than learning to code in Python, cook better, rebuild motorcycle engines, or knit sweaters. While learning these skills can be tough, they are fairly straightforward endeavors and there are many books to guide you. It's tougher to try to grow yourself, to become a better listener, or to be a better leader at work or in the community. These activities are more art than science, and learning them requires art as well.

This is, in part, because personal and interpersonal effectiveness is evaluated subjectively by others, suggesting the need for perspective taking and empathy. It is also highly dependent on circumstances, calling for sensitive awareness of conditions both internal and external— your own moods and biases, the needs and values of other people, the power dynamics of your relationships, the surrounding corporate culture, and so on. What's more, your personal effectiveness and your leadership abilities are deeply intertwined. Most everything you do to be more effective as a person will help you to be more effective as a leader.

Furthermore, developing personal effectiveness is just that: intensely personal. When you try new things and fail, or elicit negative feedback from those around you, it's hard not to feel hurt, embarrassed, or angry. And it's never a one-and-done experience. Learning to be a more effective individual is a lifelong process, with new lessons continually waiting to be learned and old lessons needing to be refreshed or applied in new ways to unfamiliar circumstances.

Finally, building your personal effectiveness and your leadership skills involves risk. In the words of personal coach Jerry Colonna, growth is painful; that is why so few choose to do it.[4] It demands that we consciously choose to move out of our comfort zones, and to do so not just once but, as the famous psychologist Abraham Maslow observed, "again and again."[5] Yes, it is scary. Yes, it can hurt. But it has to happen if we want to grow. As IBM's CEO Ginni Rometty puts it, "Growth and comfort will never co-exist . . . [A]nd it's the people and organizations willing to constantly take risks that will be successful now and into the future."[6]

Motivations for growth are as varied as people themselves. Psychologists love to divide the world into "two different kinds of people." One of those dichotomies defines people as having either a *prevention focus* or a *promotion focus*.[7]

My oldest brother, Steve, had a prevention focus. The deepest psychological drive he brought to his career was the desire to avoid loss and to protect his family and the benefits he and they enjoyed. He worked on continually learning and growing as a way of defending himself against the possibility of having his work outsourced or being replaced by someone with more up-to-date knowledge (the fate our father had experienced). It worked: Steve managed to make it through an entire career in one aerospace organization—a very rare achievement these days—by continually improving his skills to such an extent that he was perceived as indispensable.

By contrast, my daughter Allie has the classic tendencies of a promotion focus: she sees upsides and gains everywhere and goes after them. She loves to learn because she continually wants to explore new facets of her mind and personality. While working at a hospital that offered free courses for employees, Allie signed up for classes in gardening, emotional intelligence, and crucial conversations, and paid on her own for a course in anatomy just because she wanted to learn more about it. Later, while happily ensconced in a position in quality control at a start-up compounding pharmacy, she decided to learn JavaScript—not because it had anything to do with her work (it didn't), but just because she wondered whether she could master the art of computer programming, about which she'd heard so much.

Maybe you identify with one of these tendencies. Does your interest in growing derive from your desire to protect yourself from falling behind in today's ultra-competitive world, or is it driven by a passion to create a new and better you? Either motivation can be worthwhile. As the stories in this book will attest, people grow from both mundane, everyday difficulties and dramatic, once-in-a-lifetime experiences. For example, you're standing at the finish line of the Boston Marathon in 2013 when a bomb goes off and you suddenly need to relearn how to walk, or you are in an auto accident that changes your capability to do work. Growth is sometimes thrust upon you.

That is how it was for Jon Horwitz. He was six months into a brand-new job working for Jim, an organizational psychologist who was a sole proprietor. One day Jim brought him into his office and told Jon, "I'm going on vacation for two weeks in the east of France. You're working out really well. I'm fifty-two years old and I am planning to work eight more years and then the business will be yours." He went to France, very sadly was hit by a car, and passed away the next day. Suddenly, Jon found himself in experiences he never anticipated as he tried to keep the business going. He had to grow and grow quickly.

But it doesn't always take trauma or a powerful change to lead to growth. Rather, researchers who examine growth in organizations remind us that it "may be part of the everyday sense making that happens as you take on discretionary work, respond to bosses' directives, and so forth."[8] Growth sometimes is also something you seek out. You might sense a bad fit between who you are and what the environment seems to want from you and become motivated to address that misalignment. Or the environment itself may change sometimes, as it did for Jon Horwitz, in ways that are uncomfortable, and prompt flexing. You also might observe an attractive role model and think, "I want more of that in my life," thereby prompting this process. Growth is possible if you remember to look for it—and no matter which motive operates in your case, you'll find that flexing can be a helpful tool for achieving your learning goals.

One definition of the verb *to grow* is "to come to be by degrees (as in *growing old*)." For the purposes of this book, that definition works well. This book is about how you "come to be by degrees" more of the person you want to be, the professional you need to be, and the influencer the world cries out for you to be. Such growth is a complex process that requires thoughtful action, examination of the results, reflection on successes and failures, time to process the emotions produced, and the development of a plan for further action. In short, it requires the Power of Flexing.

WHY I BELIEVE IN FLEXING

My life and career path to this point has led me to a deep appreciation for individuals' potential to grow, change, and become more effective.

For the first eight years of my career as a business educator, I taught Interpersonal Behavior, a popular second-year elective in the MBA program at Dartmouth College. Working closely with these students gave me the opportunity to watch people learn more about themselves and to put continuous learning on their agendas as they started their careers.

At the same time, I had the chance to participate in an unusual consulting opportunity: a program the faculty teaching in it informally called Interpersonal Boot Camp. This was a three-day intervention conducted in the woods of New Hampshire and provided for business leaders who were struggling to improve their personal effectiveness. The exercises we led these executives through saved at least one from being fired—his improvement was that great.

When I moved to the University of Michigan's Stephen M. Ross School of Business, I taught negotiation, a much-sought-after skill that actually involves all sorts of personal effectiveness skills, from creating influence and making connections with others to communicating empathy. And then I took on a leadership position myself, becoming the business school's senior associate dean. I moved from a lonely faculty office into a highly interconnected team-management setting in which personal effectiveness was suddenly a very high priority for me. I discovered that I, too, needed to work on my personal and interpersonal effectiveness, and I began using many of the processes involved in the Power of Flexing. The result was four very generative and growth-filled years for me.

Finally, eager to return to the classroom, I left the dean's office and began teaching leadership across a variety of programs. This was a new role that had me centrally involved in helping people prepare for leader roles that demand a wide range of soft skills. Such roles draw on the entirety of who you are; your thought processes, experiences, biases, emotions, and behaviors all help to shape your leadership. And leadership, like so much of life, is a contact sport: you have to do it with others, which means you can't succeed as a leader without being personally effective.

My career has been dedicated to helping people develop just this in a variety of ways. I've had the chance to explore questions like: *How do people become better versions of themselves? Why do some people stop growing? Why and how do others continue to grow throughout their lifetimes?* and *What can people do to nurture their growth in the midst of busy, challenging lives?*

My journey to help develop leaders has helped me formulate a set of ideas and practices that help individuals to grow, whether they're in an organization or out; whether they want to learn to lead others or just to collaborate more effectively; whether they're experiencing problems in their work or simply have aspirations to get better and go further. The focus is on the complex endeavor of becoming personally effective—building the so-called soft skills that are so essential to being successful—and using the Power of Flexing to do so. In my experience, the practices that form the core of this book are differentiators in people's career and life success. They are also actionable—things you can easily target and work on to improve. The experiences I described above led me to identify these practices and do research on several of them. But the catalyst for bringing them all together stems from the insight that, as we will discuss in chapter 1, these are the kinds of things best learned from experience rather than by reading a book (ironic, I know). This book is about how you can, on your own, better use your experiences to amplify your growth in these critical areas.

MAKE YOUR GROWTH A PRIORITY

So much depends on becoming personally and interpersonally effective: whether you will be able to make that sale, build that team, motivate that colleague, attract those friends, find the right mate, fix that problem, adapt to that change.

Unfortunately, many people don't take personal responsibility for their own growth. Instead, they simply run the race laid out for them. They do well enough in school to keep advancing. Maybe they manage to get a good job at a well-run company. But so many think and act as if their learning journey ends with college. They have checked all the boxes in the life that was laid out for them and now lack a road map describing the right way(s) to move forward and continue to grow.

In truth, that's when the journey really begins. And, of course, that's the point at which your agency becomes critical. When school is finished, your growth becomes voluntary. Like healthy eating or a regular exercise program, you need to commit to it and devote thought, time, and energy to it. Otherwise, it simply won't happen—and your life and career are likely to stagnate as a result.

"Jordan Jeffers" (not his real name), now working for a materials development company, learned this lesson from a professor while studying chemical engineering in graduate school. This professor served as a mentor to Jeffers and to a number of other students. Jordan describes it as a very weird mentorship, because none of the students ever really talked to the professor or hung out with him, nor did the professor offer any specific academic or career advice. But he did emphasize one message, in class and out, with forceful consistency: "You have to do this. No one else can really help you. Teach yourself, and finish the job."

That message of self-reliance and resilience—of *owning your development*—must have been exactly what Jeffers needed to learn. He succeeded in his engineering program—no small feat, since only twenty-three students graduated out of the sixty who started the program—and the professor's message helped him later in life. "It helped set me up to deal with the Great Recession, my mother's death, and the other big challenges of my life," Jeffers says. "It taught me to say, 'I'm gonna have to do something about this' rather than waiting for someone else to take action."

Unfortunately, many people, perhaps because they are afraid or they view change as hard work, prefer to avoid the challenge of growing. Bob Quinn, a colleague of mine at the University of Michigan, characterizes this attitude as "Shut up and stay for peace and pay; don't force the organization to grow, and hopefully it won't ask you to grow, either." Or as the writer Anne Lamott puts it, "This has always been true that with growing and changing . . . it hurts. So my first response is always to resist. I'm not stupid." But either response is a serious mistake.[9] Not only is growth essential to survival and success; it pays enormous benefits to those who embrace it. Researchers find that a sense of growth contributes to psychological well-being by providing structure and meaning to experiences as well as valuable self-knowledge that enhances the ability to function in and adapt to social life.[10] Further, seeing oneself as growing is associated with increased psychological well-being in the form of greater life satisfaction and self-esteem, lower levels of depression, and a sense of coherence in one's life that helps people feel they comprehend the meaning of the challenges they face and can manage the stress they induce.[11]

Don't think the need for self-motivated development is any less important if you happen to work for a big company. It's true that many organizations have traditionally offered employee development programs, both to meet their own needs and to attract and retain talent. But in recent years companies have been reducing their investment in such programs. Those that still exist are usually focused on just a few, supposedly high-potential employees. The rest are left to fend for themselves when it comes to learning.

That's why Ralph Simone, a leading expert in executive coaching and leadership development, says, "I believe it's the responsibility of the employees to develop themselves, and, hopefully, the organization can provide some of the resources that will facilitate that development." His view is echoed by Royster Harper, the vice president for student life at the University of Michigan. When asked, "What advice do you have for younger people for maximizing their personal and professional development?" she responds, "Take responsibility for it. Nobody is going to be as committed to your own development, or should be committed to your own development, more than you are."

I don't mean to say that the organization you work for is completely irrelevant to the personal growth you hope to achieve. Studies show that most individuals' growth is "deeply situated in an organizational context,"[12] meaning that the groups we are part of shape our sense of how we should grow and the metrics we use in measuring our growth. They can also support our growth by affirming and encouraging it, or make it more difficult by undermining and discouraging it. After discussing each of the Power of Flexing practices individually in chapters 2 to 7, I'll explore the institutional and cultural contexts within which we grow, offering ideas about what businesses and other organizations can do to help their team members learn and develop using the Power of Flexing in chapters 10 and 11. The guidance in these chapters should be valuable for leaders who want to encourage growth on the part of their associates, as well as for human resource professionals and others who are responsible for developing healthy, growth-oriented organizational cultures. Chapter 8 describes a variety of circumstances where you can flex in order to grow, and chapter 9 discusses how to help others on their own growth journeys.

WHEN WE ASKED ROYSTER HARPER, whom you met above, "What do you still hope to learn in a future experience," she was in the most senior position she could attain in the university and very senior in her career (and has since retired). But listen to her answer and see how she is still working on herself, still learning, and still growing: "I am trying right now to better understand how my own biases cloud my ability to see things from other people's point of view. I'm trying to better understand that and to keep getting better at the ability to really listen and hear what a person is both saying and not saying: 'What are they really asking me? What is it that they really want to know?'" Her response embodies all that is beautiful about the Power of Flexing. As accomplished as she is, she has identified this thing that niggles at her—something that seems not quite perfect in her demeanor and interactions with colleagues. She is thinking about it and will likely begin planning some experiments to address it, take action, and reflect more on how to improve. I wish this kind of growth-journey-to-the-end for you. You've taken an important first step by picking up this book. Now I invite you to continue the journey by turning the page and beginning your education in the Power of Flexing.

CHAPTER 1

EXPERIENCE IS THE BEST TEACHER . . . BUT ONLY WHEN YOU FLEX

"Jeff Parks" describes himself as "a card-carrying scientist." He loved his high school classes in biology, chemistry, and physics, then went on to become an eager researcher and problem solver in college and graduate school. But it wasn't until he got his first job at a small biotech start-up that Jeff realized he'd never fully developed the skills and sensibilities he needed to be a business leader.

Like many struggling young start-ups, Jeff's company was desperate to bring its first few products to market before its venture capital funding ran out. It had three products in the works, and Jeff was asked to head the team developing the least promising of the three: a particular kind of synthetic molecule with potentially valuable medical applications. Unfortunately, the four people on Jeff's team were the least experienced employees at the company. They were all very smart but really had no idea about how to conduct clinical trials; in fact, one of them had never even studied science in college. They also were given the fewest resources of any working team at the company—the smallest, worst-equipped lab and the skimpiest budget. When Jeff complained about it, the CEO just shrugged and said, "Sure, we can fix the problem. We can shut down your project altogether and the five of you can apply for unemployment. How does that sound?"

Left with no other choice, Jeff set about teaching himself how to be a leader—specifically, how to motivate his team to achieve daunting goals while working with inadequate resources. In the months that followed, he encouraged his team members to think creatively about each of the challenges they faced—for example, how to repurpose dated lab equipment so it could be used to carry out the clinical trials necessary. They held frequent brainstorming sessions, prodding and stimulating one another in the search for outside-the-box solutions. They often had to encourage one another to tackle tasks they'd never tried before. And because their company colleagues lacked the time—and sometimes the expertise—to give them valuable guidance and feedback, they developed information sources by building connections with knowledgeable people from the outside world, including university professors and experts from government regulatory agencies.

In the end, Jeff's team brought their product to market faster than any of the other company teams, helping to save the business and even earning public accolades from their peers throughout the industry.

Jeff describes this assignment as a career- and life-changing experience. He said that, before this job, "I kind of hated working on teams, because I always felt, 'I can get this done better working alone.' Having to lead this team taught me how to value other people's perspectives—and it showed me how we could actually get a lot more done working across disciplines."

Jeff Parks's story resembles that of many other leaders, not just in business but in life. We all hope to achieve great things and to have a meaningful, positive impact on the world. But circumstances often get in the way. In Jeff's case, his job as a team leader at a start-up company created an opportunity for him to create something new and valuable. Yet his company failed to provide him with the resources that would have made his job easier. Jeff was never labeled "high-potential" by the company; he was never given any training in project management, team building, or problem-solving skills; he had no sponsor or ally to advocate for him, no mentor to give him advice, no role model to imitate. Instead, he was thrown into the pool at the deep end, into an experience that stressed him out, challenged him, and taught him. In the end, Jeff figured out how to swim on his own, becoming more personally effective along the way.

LEARNING BY DOING: EXPERIENCE AS TEACHER

Jeff's achievements reflect what is now a truism in the field of leadership development: that most leaders glean their most important leadership lessons not through classroom study, book learning, one-on-one coaching, or other forms of instruction but through direct experience. And what's true of leadership is also true of other kinds of complex personal and interpersonal effectiveness skills.

I can vouch for this based on more than thirty years of experience teaching MBA students the "soft side" of business: the skills needed for interpersonal effectiveness, people management, team building, persuasive communication, and so forth. Early in the course, it's common to hear one of the students interrupt my presentation of one of these skills—for example, listening, influence, or coaching—with a dismissive remark like "Come on, doing these is all just common sense!" (Sometimes they use a less polite expression than "common sense.") The skeptics who take this view aren't wrong. The principles underlying such soft-side skills are fairly straightforward; in classroom discussion, they go down easily. The problem is in the doing. When students try to practice these skills in role-playing exercises or, even better, in real-life on-the-job encounters, they discover that what sounds easy is actually difficult to do. There's simply no substitute for actually *living* these skills in the context of everyday challenges. Those sorts of real-world experiences transform truisms and broad, "commonsense" principles into vivid, concrete lessons that will be remembered and can be applied when future challenges arise.

Practitioners interested in helping people to develop leadership are among the most enthusiastic proponents of this approach to learning. In fact, they frequently invoke what they call the 70–20–10 Rule, which is not so much a rule as an empirical finding. A study of highly successful managers showed that 70 percent of what they'd learned about how to be good managers had been learned from experience, 20 percent from other people (such as mentors and coworkers), and just 10 percent from reading books or attending courses.[1]

Leadership development educators fell in love with this insight. Many set about using it as the basis for new ways of developing the leaders of tomorrow. Organizations that had been sending their high-potential employees off to leadership development courses now had a new tool at their disposal: they could simply put those high-potential employees into job assignments likely to generate experiences from which valuable lessons could be learned.

But this raised a new question: What sorts of assignments, exactly, would be most likely to produce meaningful learning opportunities for high-potential employees? The leadership development professionals assigned themselves the task of answering this question. Academic experts on leadership got to work identifying and validating the qualities of so-called high-challenge experiences that would promote maximal learning. These attributes also are characteristic of the experiences that prompt learning the skills needed for effectiveness in your family, community, civic organization, church or charitable group, and other settings as well. There is even some evidence that they are valid across cultures: studies in India, China, and Singapore identified the same broad categories of experience as leading to opportunities for learning.[2]

The first step to getting better at learning from experience, then, is by identifying experiences that offer the most developmental potential. The qualities the experts identified that make for high-challenge, high-learning experiences are:

Taking on Unfamiliar Responsibilities

Every time you do something new, there's a great potential for learning. Of course, you will probably learn a lot about the specific skills and contents that you've been asked to master: leading a team retreat, handling a major change in your work role, shifting from teaching in person to doing it online, or planning the launch of a new product. But new responsibilities also create opportunities for developing broader effectiveness skills. Because you're dealing with a situation that is new to you, you almost inevitably need to move out of your comfort zone, trying new behaviors, experimenting with different approaches, and incorporating what works into your existing repertoire. For this reason, an experience that involves unfamiliar responsibilities usually offers significant potential for personal challenge and growth.

Leading Change

It has long been said that if you want to truly understand something, try to change it—and countless leaders who have been asked to manage a significant change effort in their organization have learned the truth of this dictum. So whenever you're called upon to lead a change effort—whether it's a reorganization of your department at work, a move by your company into a previously untapped market, or a lobbying effort to convince your town board to expand fair housing opportunities—you are likely to learn a lot. Taking steps to create that change will require you to take a deep dive into the nature of the status quo and the reasons for it. It will also require you to understand and deal with the psychological and emotional reasons why some team members will support the change while others resist it and to explore how you can be most influential with them. For many aspiring leaders, serving as an agent of change is one of the most challenging tasks they'll ever tackle—and one of the most educational.

Addressing a High-Stakes Challenge

Not all job assignments are equally important. Some involve levels of risk and reward that are unusually high, with potentially significant implications for the future of the entire organization. Some jobs bring with them an unusual level of visibility, subjecting the leader to intense scrutiny and creating the possibility of painful second-guessing in the event of a failure or gratifying acclaim in the event of a success. Jeff Parks's role as a team leader in a beleaguered start-up is an example of this kind of assignment. Another was the time a friend of mine was asked to lead a visioning process for a community organization that was racked with dissension and controversy. Such high-stakes challenges inevitably concentrate the mind, focusing your attention and energy and increasing the likelihood that you'll learn a lot from the experience.

Crossing Boundaries

One of the most challenging experiences a young professional can face is having to work across organizational, institutional, or professional boundaries. Imagine, for example, being a middle manager called upon to lead an initiative that requires both support from top management and cooperation from colleagues in other departments of the organization. To succeed, you'll need to learn how to influence people and groups over whom you have no direct authority and who may even have strong reasons to oppose your plans. This kind of assignment will require you to develop your tools for communication, persuasion, and team building, as well as demanding that you master the organizational complexities and cultural nuances of groups other than your own. All of these activities are likely to generate significant opportunities to build skills and knowledge that will be valuable when future challenges arise.

Working with Diversity

Anytime you have to work with people who differ from you and each other in terms of race, ethnicity, gender, culture, background, values, and perspectives, the potential for misunderstanding and conflict increases—while at the same time the potential for creative exchange and fruitful discovery also increases. In an increasingly complex, globally interconnected, and culturally sensitive world, more and more leaders are being asked to manage teams and organizations that are highly diverse. In the mid-1990s I did some teaching work for a Michigan-based company with offices around the world. The organization was eager to help its managers—many of whom had never traveled outside the American Midwest—to develop a global mindset in preparation for taking on overseas assignments. As you can imagine, this work was challenging both for me and for the managers I was training, all of whom had to learn to understand, communicate with, and work with people whose ways of thinking were quite unfamiliar. In the process, they found themselves examining and even questioning some of their own assumptions about life and the world. It was a great learning experience of a kind that countless leaders both inside and outside of business are now confronting. For example, as their communities become more diverse, volunteers and staff and community organizations need to understand the Muslim religion and its various prayer and dietary practices or just how to negotiate in a style effective with Asian counterparts.

Facing Adversity

The final element of experience that offers significant learning and growth possibilities is different from the others in that it is much less immediately attractive to the aspiring leader—namely, being required to deal with serious adversity. This might mean being in charge when the business environment goes south—for example, during the recession of 2008 or the COVID-19 crisis of 2020. It might mean having to deal with a troubled or toxic relationship with an important colleague; it might mean managing a project that is opposed by key influencers higher up in the organization; it might mean leading a community organization that is drastically short of funding, volunteer support, or other resources. Whatever form it takes, adversity really tests your mettle, and if you are awake to the potential for growth as you go through such experiences, you can learn a great deal.

I do an exercise with my executive-level students that many of them find eye-opening. I ask these executives to create simple sketches that depict the high and low points of their lives and careers. They then share their sketches with a small group, discussing those extreme experiences—the emotions involved, the values revealed, and the lessons learned. Inevitably, these executives discover that their most important lessons learned came from their career lows, not the highs. It's ironic, since we spend most of our lives trying to *avoid* those lows! Of course, we often discover the lessons from adversity only later, after the adversity has been overcome, reframed, or resolved.[3]

HR professionals love this list of experiences that spur personal development. Many who learn about it enthusiastically begin placing their high-potential employees in experiences of this nature. Unfortunately, they often do so without really considering the important question that we'll turn to next.

DO PEOPLE REALLY LEARN FROM HIGH-CHALLENGE EXPERIENCES?

Leadership development scholars have continued to develop their thinking about how high-challenge experiences can promote learning. They have even conducted experimental studies to verify the extent to which experiences presenting developmental challenges truly help people in organizations grow as leaders. In two of these studies, researchers asked employees to rate their work experiences in terms of the challenges they posed. They then asked an outside observer, typically the employees' bosses, to rate the employees' development of leadership skills.

In one study, Lisa Dragoni found a positive relationship: the greater the developmental challenges people perceived in their current job assignments, the higher their managers rated their leadership skills. The skills assessed covered a range of abilities, ranging from broad business knowledge and insight to the courage needed to take a stand and the ability to bring out the best in people. Dragoni's results also indicated that it was the level of challenge, not simply the accumulation of years of experience, that made a difference in the employee's skill rating.[4]

A second study offered a bit of a cautionary note. Like Dragoni, Scott DeRue and Ned Wellman found that high-challenge job assignments produced measurable skill-development benefits. However, they also found that the benefits derived seemed to taper off at the highest levels of challenge—as if, at a certain point, the degree of challenge gets to be "too much." DeRue and Wellman suggest that perhaps individuals experiencing unusually high degrees of challenge may tend to retreat from learning as a result of anxiety. The effect seemed to apply more forcefully to interpersonal skills than to cognitive and business skills. Thus, while people may sometimes talk casually about developmental challenges as an unmitigated blessing, in fact there is a point of diminishing returns.[5]

Despite the cautionary note offered by DeRue and Wellman, most experts believe that the more fully an experience reflects the high-challenge elements described above, the more learning potential it offers—provided you approach the experience with the *motivation* to learn.

You might think that the motivation to learn can be taken for granted; after all, most everyone wants to improve their leadership skills and grow their effectiveness. But that thought or desire doesn't automatically translate into a readiness to use new experiences as a platform for such learning. That's where motivation comes in. For example, when a situation challenges your competency while simultaneously holding out the potential for significant rewards, you are likely to feel motivated to close your perceived competency gaps. Jeff's start-up experience represents a clear example of this kind of motivation. Other times, people feel motivated to learn and grow when they find themselves in a situation that feels uncomfortable or even painful. In this case, in which just getting things back to normal would feel great, the desire to avoid a negative outcome provides the necessary motivation.

Provided that the motivation to learn is present, most of those who have studied the matter agree that high-challenge experiences are a good way to develop improved leadership skills; in fact, it is the single best way we know. High-challenge job assignments give working people who are motivated to learn real-life opportunities to develop their leadership and effectiveness skills.

DO-IT-YOURSELF LEADERSHIP DEVELOPMENT

But—and you've probably suspected that a *but* was coming—to turn out great leaders or realize growth in your personal effectiveness, it's not enough to take motivated people and put them in jobs where their skills will be challenged, tested, and enhanced—right?

Not quite.

In fact, scholars of leadership development and the practices they've recommended have addressed only half of the problem. The power of learning from experience lies in the second half of the equation: *Experiences themselves don't teach. People need to learn.* For this reason, two people can go through closely parallel experiences and learn vastly different amounts, a fact that we all know to be true based on simple observation.

This insight is at the heart of the Power of Flexing. So why do some people learn so much more from their experiences than others? And what, if anything, can people do differently as they prepare for, live through, and reflect on their experiences to enhance and deepen their learning?

The fact is that the ability to derive more learning, insight, and skill from your experiences is an important quality in the aspiring leader, and a crucial differentiator between those who are highly effective in their life and work and those who are less effective.

This is one of the crucial leadership insights identified by the man who has spoken with more top-level organizational leaders than anyone else in the world. Adam Bryant, who interviewed a chief executive officer weekly for his long-running "Corner Office" column in the *New York Times*, is often asked, "How do I get to be a CEO? What is the path to the top?" The assumption underlying these questions is that there must be some definable road to the corner office—perhaps a series of tasks or challenges that has been shown to shape the skills needed by a twenty-first-century business leader.

But Bryant's response to the question rejects the assumption. "It is not that there is a 'right' experience or set of experiences," Bryant says. "It is that the CEOs have made the most out of the experiences they've had. A common attribute across the CEOs: Whatever they are doing at the time, they wring meaning from it. They learn."

Today, a growing number of experts are coming to recognize the truth in Bryant's observation. They are beginning to emphasize that the key to personal development—whether your goal is to become an effective leader within an organization or to make positive changes in your community, your family, or the world at large—lies less in the jobs that a company might assign you and more in the ways you pursue personal learning through whatever experiences you have. In the words of Morgan W. McCall Jr., a prominent scholar who has reviewed the recent evidence regarding leadership development:

> The evidence is actually quite convincing that development is significantly enhanced when individuals proactively take charge of their own learning from experience . . . For all that organizations can do to create a climate and context for learning, and despite all the resources and support they may throw at it, it is, in the end, up to the individual to take advantage of the opportunity and grow.[6]

This conclusion may be a bit daunting. It means that growth and learning don't "just happen" automatically as a result of your daily experiences in life and work. But from another perspective it's profoundly empowering. You don't need to wait around for an organization to dub you a "high-potential employee" worthy of being groomed for leadership; you don't need to hope that you'll be tapped for a "high-challenge" overseas assignment or a role directing some high-stakes, high-reward corporate initiative. Instead, you can use your current experiences, whatever they are, to begin growing yourself. Starting from any point in your life—whether you are a student thinking about how to launch a career, an entry-level worker just learning the ropes, a newly promoted manager tackling your first leadership challenges, or an executive—you have the power and the opportunity to improve your work skills and your personal effectiveness using your everyday lived experiences. The only requirement is a determination to learn—to *wring meaning* from your experiences.

Jeff Parks figured out how to wring meaning from his experiences while helping his team in the lab by drawing on a combination of innate personality traits and instincts. But many other people struggle when faced with similar opportunities—for example, the chance to build a business under challenging circumstances and with little support. Some people ultimately succeed after one or more setbacks that cost them years of frustration. Others suffer a failure or two and either give up or are never given another chance to demonstrate what they can do.

Experience *can* be a powerful teaching tool. But we need to stop leaving it to chance. Instead, we need to get more actively involved in our personal learning. That's what the Power of Flexing is all about.

ONE KEY TO LEARNING FROM EXPERIENCE: MINDFULNESS

The process starts by *becoming more mindful.* By *mindful,* I don't mean that you should meditate more often to calm the mind (although it couldn't hurt; meditation is a practice that has benefited many). Instead, I'm focusing on the second element of mindfulness: *being present to experience. Mindfulness* in this sense is an awareness that comes about by paying attention, on purpose and actively, in the present moment. And such mindfulness is much more difficult than it sounds.

You only need to reflect on the state of mind that you bring to everyday life to realize that true mindfulness is often elusive. You probably fall short of being mindful in a variety of ways. Sometimes you may be so preoccupied with planning for the future that you fail to focus on the present. Other times you may be distracted by thoughts of where you have just come from or even by past events that may haunt you. Fantasies, worries, gossip, speculation, trivia, and the news of the day—all these and more can fill your mind and prevent you from paying attention to what you are actually doing in the moment.

In a world that provides an endless list of distractions—starting, of course, with the smartphone in your pocket or purse—all too many people end up living their entire lives somewhat mindlessly. Many people eat mindlessly without thinking about what they're eating, failing to savor the flavors, aromas, and textures of the food. Many people drive mindlessly: Have you ever gotten from one place to another in your car and noticed afterward that you have no sense of how you did it and what happened along the way? Busy people may travel mindlessly, waking up in hotel rooms on business trips or vacations to realize they've momentarily forgotten where they are and why they are there.

We sometimes even interact mindlessly. Harvard psychologist Ellen Langer documented the phenomenon in a series of clever experiments. In one test, she found that a person waiting to use a shared photocopier is more likely to allow a stranger to cut in line if the stranger gives a reason—even if that reason is nonsensical (for example, "because I need to make copies").[7] I have professor colleagues who now incorporate this advice into their tips for having more influence: when you make a request, incorporate the word *because* followed by any tangentially relevant content; you increase your chances of receiving a mindless, compliant response greatly.[8]

While in this book we are interested in the learning cost of going through your experiences mindlessly, the habit of mindless behavior can even lead to danger and death. It led to a tragedy during the construction of a new building at the Ross School, where I teach. At the end of each day the construction workers would routinely take the elevator up to the top floor and then go up to the roof and lock it. In the morning, someone would come in, walk up to the roof, unlock the elevator, walk down one flight, and get on the elevator to use it during the day. One day, a worker unthinkingly walked down two flights instead of one. He opened the elevator door, stepped into the empty shaft, and fell to his death.

There are many forces in life that make it harder for us to learn from our experiences. Most people working in organizations, especially those who consider themselves potential leaders, are very busy. They typically rush from meeting to meeting, receive countless phone calls, text messages, and emails, and are glued to their smartphones; in any given day they interact with a wide variety of individuals and groups and confront an extensive variety of issues, ranging from employee performance problems and budgeting dilemmas to big-think strategic challenges. As a result, most people in business feel they have little time to reflect on or even to be particularly thoughtful about what they are doing. And corporate managers aren't the only ones who struggle with over-busyness. So do people in the nonprofit sector, health care workers and teachers, artists and performers, volunteers and activists. Their situations are not dissimilar from that of a young mom raising kids, working part-time, serving on two community boards, and planning a new nonprofit. She, too, likely runs herself ragged as she goes from role to role, meeting to meeting, taking little time to eat, much less prepare and reflect. For all of them, as important as it is to be mindful in their experiences to enhance their learning, it is not easy. In all spheres, most of us suffer today from the "hustle culture" that leads us to "rise and grind" through our days rather than slowing down a bit and paying more attention to learn from what we are doing.[9]

Management gurus Jim Loehr and Tony Schwartz point out that "great athletes spend a lot of time practicing and a little time performing." If you've ever had a kid who competes in swimming or track and field, you know it's true: they spend hours in practice sessions preparing for an event that often lasts mere seconds. By contrast, Loehr and Schwartz observe, executives (and I would add beleaguered, community-involved parents here, too) "spend no time practicing and all their time performing. It's no wonder that [they] recycle their problems."[10]

When we consider all these realities, we begin to think about the 70–20–10 rule slightly differently. It implies that, if we go through our high-challenge work experiences mindlessly or without a thoughtful plan to convert those experiences into sources of growth, we are giving up

70 percent of our learning. Seventy percent! That's not a resource that any of us can afford to waste!

WHILE LEADERSHIP DEVELOPMENT, OR growth in personal effectiveness more generally, comes from experience, there is growing recognition that it doesn't happen naturally—and what *is* learned is often "happenstance and ad hoc at best."[11] The way to fix the problem is to put some structure into that learning—which is exactly what the six practices of the Power of Flexing that we will take up in chapters 2 to 7 are intended to provide. They will help you to make growth a continual process—a habit that comes naturally to you rather than a rare event restricted to occasional classroom programs or mentorship opportunities. They can empower anyone to develop their own work skills and leadership abilities to the fullest—and to do it throughout their careers—through high-challenge work assignments as well as during other periods when work may be less stressful but can also lead to highly productive and rewarding learning.

The Power of Flexing also offers an opportunity to organizations. If the system is made widely available and implemented consistently, it can help change the organizational culture into one that recognizes that growth can and should be universal rather than exceptional. As David Thomas, the president of Morehouse University, in emphasizing the importance of context and organizational culture, likes to say, "It's the soil that matters," by inviting people to invest in their own development and then equipping them with the tools to do so, organizations can dramatically expedite and enhance the growth of entire teams.[12] As I will discuss in the last section of the book, the benefits that organizations can enjoy as a result, in terms of creating more leaders in more places who offer their proactivity and initiative, are enormous.

CHAPTER 2

MINDSET MATTERS

Framing Experience to
Enhance Learning

Doug Evans knew he had a choice. A talented performing arts admin-istrator with prior state government experience, he now found himself 8,000 miles and twelve hours by plane away from his home, his family, and the culture he knew. He'd accepted the mission of assembling a show on the scale of those produced on Broadway and bringing it to China, where it would tour some twenty-five cities around that vast country. Doug knew show business and had all the skills required to put on a great show for Chinese audiences. But he had zero experience in Asia, didn't know a word of Chinese, and had received just the barest briefing on the country's unique cultural protocols. Now that he'd arrived in Beijing, the daunting reality of it all was sinking in. And it was overwhelming.

Doug could have easily succumbed to the psychological pressure of the situation and become highly stressed, difficult to live with, and an im-possible boss. But he knew he had a choice. Doug describes himself as the kind of person who likes to "flip the paradigm." One of the ways he does this is by thinking about the most stressful experiences in his life as "adventures." When times are tough, Doug's internal mind chatter runs: "This is a learning experience. You're going to grow tremendously, even when it seems impossible." And when he's asked to do something he's never done before, he likes to ask himself two questions: "How hard can it be?" and "Why not?"

Doug had previously found that asking "Why not?" can also be a powerful tool in dealing with other people. His first big job had been working for the governor of Connecticut in Hartford, the state capital. He had the task of turning around a multimillion-dollar performing arts center that was in sad financial shape and whose staff morale was on the rocks. "I was twenty-seven years old," Doug recalls, "and I had no idea what to do first. I really had no choice except to fly by the seat of my pants, reading a lot and trying to figure out what might work."

In that government job, Doug was surrounded by bureaucrats—very experienced, smart people who had mastered all the procedures, protocols, and politics of running complicated government agencies. But because he was facing a novel challenge—something he'd never even thought about doing before—he would propose solutions that made sense to him but that had no connection with traditional government processes. The bureaucrats' most common response was to say, "You can't do it that way."

When Doug asked, "Why not?" the bureaucrats never really had an answer. Instead, they would just say, "Well, because we've never done it that way." Doug now says, "That was a giveaway. I realized that what they were saying was really 'It's not because you *can't* do it that way; it's because no one's ever tried.'"

Doug's experience in Hartford—and the successful turnaround of the arts center that he engineered through sheer experimentation and persistence—showed him the power of "Why not?" Asking that question helped him to think about seemingly impossible problems as adventures to be embraced, survived, and learned from. That attitude enabled him to tackle his China challenge with a degree of equanimity—and to emerge from it with his reputation, his career, and his sanity intact.

One of the most powerful maxims in executive coaching is "What you see depends on the window from which you look." We don't see our world in an unbiased way; rather, we look at the world through a particular frame that colors our understanding of the world around us. Our observations of other people, of unfolding situations and our reactions to those situations, depend importantly on the frame we put around them. Our expectations, assumptions, biases, and the like affect what we see, what we pay attention to, and how we react. How things are framed matters.

The power of framing is well known. We can see it most clearly by observing how others frame things and its effect on us. Politicians do it, leaders do it, and perhaps most prominently marketers—those interested in selling us things—do it. Marketers very cleverly frame how we look at things all the time. We come to equate alcohol with fun because of the money poured into messages creating just this picture. Sometimes framing is based on something as simple as word choices: consumers prefer ground beef that is "95 percent lean" to ground beef that's "5 percent fat"; they'll buy and use a condom that is "95 percent effective" while rejecting one that fails 5 percent of the time. The actual product is the same in both cases; it is just the framing that differs.

But framing is not only something that happens to us; it is also something that we do ourselves. Thankfully, we have some agency in the way we frame our experiences. We can choose the frame that we put around any situation, and that frame will affect our thoughts, feelings, and actions. When Doug Evans frames an experience as an "adventure," it colors every bit of that experience. Thus, how we approach and think about experiences influences the way we think, feel, and act, as well as the benefits we gain—or fail to gain—from our efforts to flex in those experiences.

It comes down, in part, to your mind chatter. We have a story in our family about our youngest daughter, Maddy, who was not a fan of skiing, which is a particular passion of my husband and my oldest daughter, Allie. So we went skiing more than occasionally and Maddy was dragged along.

More than not liking skiing, she hated the chairlift. At age six, she was very afraid not of the chairlift or being up high but rather of getting off. In fact, she spent the whole time riding up in the chairlift saying to herself and to whoever was sitting next to her, "I'm going to fall! I'm going to fall!" As we approached the moment of off-loading, she continued her mantra and, sure enough, she would typically fall.

After a few rounds of this, I asked her, "Maddy, why don't you say over and over, 'I'm going to ski off! I'm going to ski off!' and see how that works?" She tried that all the way up the next lift and, indeed, she skied off.

The frame that you put around an experience—particularly a challenging one—colors that experience. When Maddy changed her frame by changing the story she was telling herself, her experience changed. She did fall occasionally after that, but she interpreted those falls in the context of a more positive story about her growth rather than as proof of her inability to deal with the chairlift. We can certainly change the frame we put around experiences anytime we want.

Jane Dutton is a management scholar who has studied how strategic decision-makers frame the issues facing them as either threats or opportunities. Ironically, she found herself faced with a similar framing choice during the quarantine period of the coronavirus pandemic in 2020. When Dutton had to switch from teaching seventy students in person to teaching them online, her first reaction was a natural one: "Oh, sh*t! I can't believe I have to do this. I dread, dread, dread it."

But then one day she decided to switch her framing. She resolved, "I'm going to try to see myself as making a contribution to the university and to these students." This change made all the difference in the world. It prompted a second mental shift: from focusing on herself to focusing on the students who were disappointed and unsettled by the change to online work. Rather than agonizing over the question "How can I get through this?" Dutton began asking herself, "How can I serve my students and use myself as an example of adaptability and strength?" This framing shift liberated her to try different teaching approaches to make the new circumstances work.

ALTERNATIVE MINDSETS: TWO FRAMES FOR UNDERSTANDING OUR EXPERIENCE

The most common way to frame experiences is through what I call *the performance-prove mindset*. People usually take on tasks and challenges with the goal of demonstrating their effectiveness and skill to others as well as to themselves. In particular, the performance-prove mindset comes naturally in most business settings. It probably helped get you where you are today. But it probably will not get you where you want to go from here. In fact, it often backfires. As we'll see, research shows that the overemphasis on avoiding failure and proving that you are a high performer that comes with the performance-prove mindset often *detracts from* performance rather than enhancing it.

Even more important, in addition to inhibiting performance, the performance-prove frame is *not* conducive to learning. When we are single-mindedly focused on achieving short-term success and impressing others (and ourselves) with our leadership skills and our personal effectiveness, we actually *avoid* many of the behaviors that make learning, growth, and skill development possible. When Doug thinks of his experience as an adventure, it helps him to engage rather than avoid behaviors such as asking questions, seeking information, revealing ignorance, and seeking feedback—behaviors that allow and enable his growth.

Unfortunately, the performance-prove mindset is so widespread in business that most people apply it to new challenges almost automatically, thereby short-circuiting the opportunity to learn from their experiences. Of course, we all want to perform well in our jobs. But the performance-prove mindset is all about wanting to prove to others that we are doing well. That focus may prevent you from engaging in behaviors that will help your long-term effectiveness. You avoid asking a question after a presentation because you don't want to look stupid; you don't ask for feedback because it hurts too much to hear a negative message. As a result, when a setback comes, you are less able to adapt and overcome it.

Instead of remaining stuck in the performance-prove mindset, when facing any upcoming work or career challenge, you should shift to a second way of framing such challenges. I refer to this as *the learning mindset*. It's a way of approaching experience through the frame of learning and development, an approach that sets you up well for the rest of the flexing process.

Psychologist Carol Dweck has been engaged in research on how frames impact our ability to learn and grow for over thirty years.[1] Her research focuses largely on the attitudes that people have toward the nature of their own talents. Whether the subject is intelligence, task ability, negotiation ability, or leadership, some people tend to regard their ability as fixed—that is, "set in stone"—reflecting the idea that a person is either "born with" particular aptitudes or not. Other people see their ability as malleable, something that can be developed. Dweck's research, on everyone from children to working adults, suggests that where you land on that continuum has important impacts. It's so important to your ability to learn and grow from experience that it is our starting point in the flex system.

Your belief about ability creates a particular orientation that affects how you approach performance situations and what you do in them. If you believe abilities are fixed, your focus tends to be on showing that you are great at the ability in question; in other words, you bring a performance-prove mindset to the situations you face. So, if you believe that an ability, or even your basic intelligence, is fixed and unalterable, you tend to approach situations feeling that you need to prove that you can handle them, thereby showing others that you are talented. In a slight variation of this mindset, if you believe that abilities are fixed, you might also approach situations with an intense focus on avoiding failure at all costs.

With this kind of performance-focused mindset, your orientation is to prove you are smart enough, talented enough, and skilled enough to do well in the situation, be better than others, and avoid failure at all cost. Those with a performance-prove mindset are interested in showing that they are good enough and keeping anyone from seeing that they are not.[2]

The contrasting mindset is based on a different belief, one that research has shown to be more accurate: the belief that human abilities are malleable—that they can grow through our experiences, training, reflection, and learning. After all, skills are rarely fixed. It may be true that people have different average levels of skill in, for example, mathematics or expressive writing. Some will always be better than others at activities like these. However, almost everyone can improve their skill levels, especially in the area of personal effectiveness. These skills can be learned and the practices that I focus on in this book are a way to do so.

People with a learning mindset tend to approach situations looking for the learning that they might contain—hence the term *learning mindset.* Here you're trying to improve your skill over time and do better than you did in the past. It's not that those with a learning mindset don't care about performing well in the present; they do. But they approach situations with an interest in growing and improving—an interest in what they can learn from the situation. The learning mindset encourages behaviors that lead to learning and skill development—behaviors like asking questions, trying new things, challenging assumptions, seeking help and advice from others, and taking risks, all of which are necessary for flexing.

Don't be fooled by the fact that one of these mindsets has the word "performance" in its title. All of the people interviewed for this book want to perform well, achieve, and move forward in their lives and careers. The mindsets, rather, describe an attitude that one brings to performing. The performance-prove mindset described above is somewhat of a clench-jawed, intense, and often fearful attitude while those who bring a learning mindset seem to feel freer, have less anxiety, and feel more in control and empowered.

HOW OUR CHOICE OF MINDSET AFFECTS OUR ABILITY TO LEARN, ACHIEVE, AND RELATE TO OTHERS

To clarify the nature of these mindsets and how they might affect learning, let's look at a real-life example. Consider Hannah, my daughter and a graduate of a prestigious college who took a job at Teach for America (TFA), a well-known nonprofit organization that trains high-potential college graduates to teach in underserved schools for a period of two years. These are graduates who don't necessarily want to be teachers or be in education as a career but want to give back, help others, and make a difference in the world.

Hannah joined TFA in July of her graduation year and came home for a visit with her family during the winter holidays in December. Her second day home, she casually commented, "Hey, Mom, the week I get back, two of the school's most experienced teachers will observe me all day in my classroom." She went on to explain that this evaluation represented a high-stakes challenge that every TFA participant is asked to meet—not an easy hurdle for most first-time teachers to overcome. As you can imagine, having this test looming in her near future gave Hannah a lot to think about while enjoying her holiday time with family and friends.

Hannah's mindset will have an important impact on what she will think, feel, and do over those winter holidays prior to returning to her school. If Hannah has a performance-prove mindset, chances are that she will perceive the examiner who will be evaluating her as a possible threat to her career, causing her a significant amount of anxiety. She'll respond to these emotions by orienting her thinking toward proving that she is not merely competent but one of the best TFA teachers ever hired at that school. Most likely she will spend much of her holiday break prepping a special class that she believes will wow the observers. When she returns to school and the big day arrives, she may well suffer a serious case of butterflies in her stomach, exacerbated by weeks of intensive preparation that have heightened her awareness of the stakes involved.

If Hannah were to adopt a learning mindset instead, she would see this upcoming day more as an opportunity than a threat. After all, her examiners will be the school's most experienced teachers, and their feedback is likely to offer valuable insights she can use to improve her teaching for the remainder of her work with TFA. Her anxiety will surely lessen; while she will certainly prepare for the observation and try to do a good job, she won't spend two solid weeks prepping for it. And because her anxiety level is lower, Hannah is likely to do better in the classroom during the observation day, interacting with her students in a more natural, relaxed fashion and adjusting comfortably to unexpected challenges or problems rather than "freezing" due to performance anxiety.

Most important, by adopting a learning mindset for that impending experience, Hannah makes genuine learning much more possible. Focusing on expanding her knowledge more than demonstrating it, she'll be better able to absorb the feedback she receives rather than responding with anger or defensiveness. What's more, she'll be better able to use the feedback to improve her teaching performance because the circumstances of the evaluation will be more realistic. After all, no teacher can spend two full weeks prepping for every class.

As Hannah's example shows, having a learning mindset enables you to perform better, even in the short run. By contrast, being intensely focused on proving how good you are often gets in the way of performing well. Ironically, trying too hard to prove to others your ability to perform at your best tends to make you perform at your worst.[3]

Data backs this up. Psychologists Laura Kray and Michael Haselhuhn conducted a study testing the impact of a performance-prove mindset versus a learning mindset on business students preparing for a negotiation in the context of a course on the topic. Kray and Haselhuhn found that individuals with both mindsets held high aspirations for the negotiation, but those with a learning mindset did much better in the different negotiations and in the course as a whole. The psychologists attributed this effect to the fact that those with a learning mindset persisted longer and handled setbacks better.[4]

Other studies confirm the same pattern. Those who tend to embrace a performance-prove mindset express more anxiety about being in performance situations and show less confidence. And even when that mindset helps their performance, the positive relationship tends to be fairly small. By contrast, those who tend to adopt a learning mindset report learning more as well as far less anxiety and significantly higher performance. The performance level of learning-mindset individuals is especially high when compared to that of people who tend to have a performance-prove mindset with an emphasis on avoiding failure. That focus on avoiding failure is a costly one. It's associated with elevated levels of anxiety, low levels of confidence, and significantly lower performance. Being concerned about avoiding failure ironically brings about more failure.

Note, by the way, that in the studies I'm summarizing, the assessment of performance was done by someone other than the performer. Thus, the results do not arise from the fact that people who worry about failure see themselves as failing. It seems that the diminished performance of those who are focused on avoiding failure is an objective reality as measured by observers whose views are not colored by mindset.

So mindset matters. The more you frame an upcoming experience with a performance-prove mindset, the less you will likely learn from that experience—and, ironically, the worse you will probably perform.

Now a couple of caveats. Recent meta-analyses—studies that evaluate the strength of effects across many studies—have found some important qualifiers to this general statement. First, having a performance-prove mindset tends to impair learning and performance for complex tasks, but not for tasks that are relatively routine and simple.

Second, those with a performance-prove mindset perform equally well as those with a learning mindset if the environment is slow-moving and when things are going along smoothly. Thus, for simple tasks in environments that don't change much or quickly, either mindset is reasonably effective.

However, most people today are typically grappling with challenges that are complex and fast-moving rather than simple and slow. And as we move through our careers, particularly as we move up within companies, a performance-prove mindset is particularly problematic. It's in the nature of things that, when we take on tough new challenges, we tend to make mistakes, suffer setbacks, and experience failures. In such situations, people with a performance-prove mindset tend to crumble. Paralyzed by anxiety and fear of failure, people with this mindset often withdraw their effort, refuse to absorb information on how to improve, and disengage from the challenges they face.[5] By contrast, people with a learning orientation tend to redouble their efforts in such situations, seeking out ways to improve and persisting in their efforts despite setbacks.

These meta-analyses provide additional evidence for the importance of mindset. The learning mindset enhances learning while also controlling anxiety and enhancing performance. People for whom the learning mindset becomes habitual enjoy the best of both worlds: they achieve great things today while also developing new skills and knowledge that will enable even greater accomplishments tomorrow and over the long run.

Your mindset also affects how you interact with others. Megan Furman is a great example of this. Early in her career, Megan held an important position in a tech start-up that created software programs for the U.S. Department of Defense. She had already developed a reputation as a "fix-it person"—the one the organization turned to when an impossible project needed doing. So Megan was asked to guide the implementation of a vital software package used by American troops abroad. She had to manage a team of seventy-five software developers and engineers, as well as service representatives, who would travel to field sites to work with the deployed service members, who needed to learn how to use the software effectively.

Megan brought a performance-prove mindset to this project. As a young manager, she really wanted to prove to her managers that she was great at team leadership. It was a high-pressure assignment, and in retrospect Megan sees that her mindset exacerbated the problem. Eager to control every detail of the project, she micromanaged her associates rather than encouraging them to take the initiative and develop creative solutions. Partly as a result, over her two years in this job, she suffered from exhaustion and extreme anxiety. At one point, overwhelmed by the intensity of the tasks she was taking on, she became so disoriented that she accidentally locked herself in a bathroom at a military base in Jordan. That's the sort of incident that says it's time to ratchet down the pressure a couple of notches!

Megan pulled off the assignment successfully, and she was very proud of how her team provided amazing support to U.S. troops on the front line of national defense. But she also learned from it the importance of shifting her frame from a performance-prove mindset to a learning mindset. She is applying this new insight effectively now that she has gone on to lead even bigger teams for the U.S. government and the Department of Defense. With more of a learning mindset, she has become adept at inviting her team members to propose their own approaches to the challenges that arise rather than swooping in with a solution. And she has given herself permission to learn from those around her rather than focusing exclusively on proving her competence to them as she used to do when operating with more of a "performance-prove" mindset.

CHOOSING THE LEARNING MINDSET

As you read my description above of the two alternative mindsets, you may have found yourself identifying more strongly with one mindset than the other. Due to many factors, from parental influence to school experiences and work histories, most people develop a tendency to adopt either a performance-prove mindset or a learning mindset, which becomes their default response to any new or challenging situation.

The good news, however, is that your choice of a preferred mindset is not set in stone but can be shifted. In experiments, psychologists have been able to induce temporary mindsets in participants and show their effects, suggesting that in life individuals can shift their own mindsets. The Power of Flexing system asks you to decide to do this for a specific challenge, event, or experience by first noticing how you are thinking about the upcoming experience. Are you seeing the experience as a test that might expose your personal weaknesses or as a chance to do your best and learn something new? Then flexing proposes that you take the opportunity to shift your thinking to the more productive learning orientation frame. You can do this by reminding yourself of the potential to learn and the importance of staying open to new ideas.

If you like the results you achieve, you may decide to modify your mindset repeatedly for future events. Over time, the new mindset can become a habitual way of thinking about achievement situations, as you'll see in the story of the next professional we will meet.

Before her work as an executive coach, Karin Stawarky was a management consulting partner and corporate executive who found that her mindset significantly affected her impact. She always excelled at her work. People would comment on her grasp of the facts; they described her as confident, poised, and articulate. But one day a colleague made a comment that helped her realize how her mindset was impeding her effectiveness, particularly when she made group presentations. Her colleague said, "There's a way in which this other persona comes over you when you're in front of the room. It's really smart, but it actually creates distance. A different Karin seems to emerge, someone I can't quite connect with. Your warmth, compassion, and infectious laughter are missing."

Reflecting on this feedback, Karin realized that she was focusing so hard on giving her clients good information that she'd forgotten another important goal: to help them connect to the information she was sharing so that they would want to do something about it. What had caused her to lose sight of this goal? Like many professionals, Karin suffered from the persistent fear of "not being good enough." Her colleague's comment revealed that this fear was leading her to act in a way that actually detracted from her performance. She was so intent on establishing her own credibility with her clients through her intelligence and knowledge that she neglected the need to connect with them personally and emotionally. Thus, her emphasis on performance-prove was preventing her from actually being extraordinary. It required her to be fully *Karin*.

Karin took steps to alter her presence and engagement style. In particular, she consciously worked on shifting the mindset with which she approached client engagements. During the planning process, she realized she was subconsciously focusing on "How can I demonstrate to these clients how smart and knowledgeable I am?" She defined a new frame of "How can I understand the personal and professional challenges these clients face and help them find ways to address those challenges more effectively?" In other words, she deliberately sought to shift from a performance-prove mindset to a learning mindset. "I realized that asking great questions was really my superpower," she says. The new outlook she brought to client meetings helped her become more open-minded, inquisitive, and perceptive. It reminded her to speak a little less, be more curious, and listen a lot more; to think about the underlying messages behind the comments and questions her clients offered; and to seek real-time feedback from them regarding whether or not her key insights were turning out to be meaningful and useful to them.

In Karin's case, the impetus to modify her mindset emerged from a colleague's comment that revealed a shortcoming in her approach to work. Others shift their mindset when they face particularly challenging experiences.

In chapter 1 we discussed the qualities of experiences that scholars have shown are most likely to stimulate learning and personal growth. They involve challenges that have high stakes and high visibility, call for the crossing of interpersonal and cultural boundaries, and demand the creation and facilitation of change. Challenges like these make a learning orientation more important even as they may push us toward falling back on a performance orientation that we find more familiar or comfortable. In such situations, adopting a learning orientation has particular payoffs.

In that chapter, I introduced you to the research of leadership scholar Lisa Dragoni and her colleagues. As you recall, Dragoni studied more than two hundred young people trying to develop their leadership skills. She found that the more they described their current assignments as having these challenge characteristics, the more highly their managers rated them on a variety of competencies associated with leadership. Thus, the challenge of the job brought out qualities in these young managers that helped them to be seen as competent by their bosses.

Dragoni's research also produced two additional findings important to us here. First, Dragoni found that people with a learning mindset reported being in challenging assignments more often than those with a performance-prove mindset. This suggests that, if you are more learning oriented, you are more likely to enter situations that have the most to teach you. Dragoni also found that people with a learning orientation were rated more highly as leaders following their challenging experiences. In other words, their orientation helped them to grow, and their growth in leadership was noticed by others.[6]

In some circumstances, choosing a learning orientation is very difficult. When Megan Furman was managing software implementation with members of the U.S. military, she was constantly being reminded how much her company had on the line. Her corporate supervisors often called to ask whether schedules were being met and to express their displeasure at any slippage. Perhaps as a result of these environmental stressors, she felt so overwhelmed trying to prove that things were okay that she had difficulty processing information and seeking help effectively. Thus, at a time she needed to be more open and inclusive, she felt pressure to be the opposite, which in the end served neither her nor her team very well.

Megan worked in an environment that pushed people into a performance-prove mindset. It was very high-pressure, high-stakes, and intolerant of mistakes and failure. The powerful emotions associated with Megan's experiences trying to be more learning oriented in a performance culture came through clearly when I interviewed her for this book. When she described her experiences in this environment, her whole body tensed, her face turned a little red, and she picked up things on my desk, holding them tightly in clenched hands. By contrast, when the topic changed to her current job and the learning mindset she has adopted there, her whole body loosened up. "It has been very exciting," she said. "There is so much to take in and learn from my colleagues . . . and when I am in that learning space, I am the best leader."

The value of a learning mindset extends beyond situations in which people are trying to learn the complex skills of leadership. At the age of fifteen, Lisa Shalett, a financial industry professional who now devotes most of her time to advising growth companies, developed a learning mindset that came to exercise a powerful influence on her life. Thanks to a competition that allowed her to win a scholarship from an international student exchange organization, she ended up living with a Japanese family in a three-month homestay.

Lisa didn't speak a work of Japanese, and her host family spoke no English. On top of that, there were many little things that made her adjustment difficult. Lisa is allergic to fish, which of course is at the heart of many Japanese meals. She was taller than practically everyone she met in the community. Even seemingly simple things like ordering a meal in a restaurant or adjusting the temperature of the water in the bath turned out to be complicated.

That experience forced Lisa to adopt a learning mindset. She had to learn everything and relearn lots of things that she thought she knew. She had to develop a tremendous sense of humility and a willingness to make mistakes and even to look foolish, because, in an entirely new world, you can't learn anything unless you try.

"Today," Lisa says, "I look back at that journey, and I realize that Japan is where I formed my belief in continuous improvement and development. That realization has helped me learn both on the job and in my personal life ever since. Every experience, no matter how big or small, is a potential opportunity to learn."

A new job can also make people realize they need to alter their mindset.

David McCallum (no relation to the famous actor of the same name) was unexpectedly recruited to become dean of the Madden School of Business at Le Moyne College in Syracuse, New York. He had received personal appeals from the university president, the provost, and even the major donor to the business school.

But David had real doubts about whether he should accept the offer. "I'm not a business guy or a quantitative person," he says. "My background is in adult learning and leadership. So I thought to myself, 'What do I really know about being the dean of the business school?' But then I reflected on the fact that I'd been speaking and writing about leadership for years, and now I was being challenged to actually step up and be a leader.

If I didn't say yes to doing this, my experience would forever remain on the theoretical level rather than being based in actual practice. I realized that if I turned down the offer, I'd probably regret it for the rest of my life. So why not give it a try?"

So David said yes, and plunged into two years of intensive *stretch learning*—the kind of learning that stems from experiences containing a high level of developmental challenge, as described in chapter 1. Putting a learning frame around his new job was critical, because David found himself "flying by the seat of my pants on a daily basis." "I learned every day," he says. "I learned skills, I learned about the management of an academic business program, and I learned quite a bit about myself."

Just like our young skier whose concern over falling contributed to her doing so more often, David also failed occasionally. One key to his success at working through those failures was his mindset. "I went into it with the goal that if I did fail . . . I wouldn't take it to heart. I would be accountable, and I would learn lessons as fast as I could." David even got to the point where he deliberately sought out opportunities to stretch beyond his comfort zone. "Whenever I found myself back in my comfort zone," he says, "I would consciously push myself back out again, trusting that was what I needed to do to keep learning."

Some people make the "new job" challenge into a permanent career description. An example is "Jacob," a serial entrepreneur from the social business space, who speaks about his work this way: "As an entrepreneur, I have the same job my first day with an organization as the last day: I'm always the founder and the ultimate leader. I'm not moving up or down or sideways through new job assignments. But I've come to realize that I actually need to change the nature of my job every year, because the organization itself changes every year. I can never assume that what worked last year will work this year or next year. So I have to frequently check in with my team, getting their feedback and asking, 'What do you need from me now?' It's a constant transition, which requires a lot of learning from me."

WAYS TO MODIFY YOUR MINDSET

It's all well and good to extol the virtues of the learning mindset and to urge you to consider adopting it. But how, exactly, do you go about shifting from one habitual mindset to another?

One tool for accomplishing this is to deliberately change your mind chatter: the way you talk to yourself on a daily basis. Karin, our executive coach, was trying to conquer her perfectionism, which she realized had served to reinforce her "performance-prove mindset" and make it harder for her to be open to new ideas and approaches. Over time, she became more comfortable with trying new things, even if she failed at first. But occasionally her old hunger for perfection popped up inside her again.

Karin's solution was to consciously alter her mind chatter. She found that the more she said to herself, "I'm not perfect. I embrace my imperfection. I am a work in progress," the more she actually believed it. From time to time she even spoke this mantra out loud. "It's like I am waking up my mind to look at the world in a different way," she says. "And one of the ways I want my mind to look differently is how I hold myself and who I am."

Karin goes on to explain that changing your mind chatter can gradually help you to modify a sense of identity that may be holding you back. In other words, how you talk to yourself has a long-term impact on how you see yourself and ultimately on who you are. "Suppose you identify yourself as a master, an expert at XYZ," she says. "That may be what your identity is anchored on. But now you realize you need to develop new skills and behavior that are outside your area of expertise. The need to shift and change can threaten your sense of self-identity, making you become unmoored."

Research on identity change highlights that there's often a *separation stage* triggered by events, work changes, or perhaps trauma, followed by a *liminal stage*—an in-between stage—where people explore possible selves and experience the unmooring that Karin describes. But note that Karin continues: "You need to develop a more expansive sense of self-identity, one that's not so closely tied to a specific role or job. If you can do that, then your resistance to change will be much lower." In these comments she accurately captures the desirable end state identified by researchers, one in which you internalize a new identity that provides a coherent sense of self and allows for growth. Karin says, "It's something I've practiced on myself, and it's something I work on with my clients as well."

Another way to shift to a learning mindset from a performance-prove mindset is to work on developing a greater degree of compassion toward yourself. The learning mindset is particularly important when you encounter a setback or failure. Being kind to yourself when that happens— reminding yourself that this is a chance to learn and grow, recalling past times when you've stumbled, fallen, and recovered—is important for staying in a learning mode and not falling prey to the downsides of a performance-prove mindset.[7]

There is even research evidence to support the value of self-compassion in supporting learning and growth. In a series of experiments, participants who'd been prompted to focus on feelings of self-compassion exhibited an array of positively adaptive attitudes and behaviors. They felt more hopeful about their ability to overcome a personal weakness; they reported greater motivation to make amends and avoid repeating a recent moral transgression; and they were motivated to spend more time studying for a difficult test following an initial failure. Research suggests that interventions as simple as remembering a time of being self-compassionate or taking time to write about an experience of being self-compassionate can make a difference.[8] In short, encouraging yourself to adopt an attitude of compassion toward your own weaknesses or failings, rather than an attitude of judgment or condemnation, can help set you on a course toward self-improvement, growth, and learning.

Don't misunderstand what I mean by "self-compassion." This is not about letting yourself off the hook for avoidable mistakes or failures, or deciding that there's no need to prepare carefully for an upcoming challenge. Aspiring to high performance is important and desirable. But the orientation that you bring to your preparation is crucial. A learning mindset will reduce your anxiety, increase your confidence, and make you more open and willing to explore, therefore helping you learn and grow from your experiences.

So there's no contradiction between the aspiration to high performance and the self-compassionate attitude that enhances the learning mindset. In fact, research has shown that those who have more of a learning mindset are more likely to set themselves specific and challenging learning goals as they consider an upcoming activity. Thus, the learning mindset and high performance go together; they feed and support each other.[9]

THE LEARNING MINDSET IS critical to the Power of Flexing. The ability to see what the situation demands, to let go of some behaviors and take up others, is the hallmark of flexing. Doing so effectively involves staying open to what the situation has to teach you and to the feedback given by others in the situation. It requires a willingness to admit when you have questions, to acknowledge your moments of confusion and mistakes, and to learn through trial and error. And, of course, it helps if you can think of complicated, stressful problems as adventures, the way Doug Evans thought about his "mission impossible" in China—as an opportunity to master new skills and to grow in the process. All of these attitudes and behaviors are aided by having a learning orientation.

One of our interviewees, a university vice president, expressed it well. "The important thing is to be teachable—to stay a student even after your classroom days are over," she says. "It's about staying curious, always ready to learn, rather than rushing to come to a conclusion and then shutting down your mind."

In the chapters that follow, we'll show you some specific techniques you can use to translate this attitude of openness, experimentation, and exploration into valuable insights and behaviors that can greatly enhance your effectiveness and satisfaction in work and in life.

CHAPTER 3

SETTING A
LEARNING FOCUS

Choosing a Flex Goal

If you're like most people nowadays, your life and work are filled with complex, absorbing challenges. Figuring out how to get through the issues of the day—completing a tough assignment for your boss, helping to organize an activity for a community group, straightening out the family budget—is more than enough to occupy your mind. How can you also find the mental and emotional resources to simultaneously work on developing your personal skills?

The Power of Flexing can help. The goals you set for enhancing your personal effectiveness can help you focus on your development even as you strive to master the daily tasks you must perform. And when the situations you face are particularly difficult, using flexing to support that dual focus is especially important. Defining a flex goal as you approach any moment of challenge, change, or potential growth allows you to better use that experience to grow yourself as well as achieve.

"Simon Biel" put this insight into action. A fairly senior HR manager in a consumer products company, Simon used an important new job assignment as an opportunity to grow personally as well as achieve. Simon had been asked to head a prestigious search committee tasked with designing a new position focused on leading innovation within the company and filling it. The committee included a number of senior associates from around the organization. It would be the kind of experience primed to be "growthful," involving an important content goal, high visibility, and the need to work with people across boundaries. In other words, a perfect opportunity for flexing.

Shortly before the first committee meeting, Simon was chatting with a close friend at his company. The friend mentioned a conversation she'd recently had with one of the members of the new committee. "He's a little nervous about working with you," the friend remarked.

"Why is that?" Simon asked.

"Oh, you know," her friend replied, "he's heard about how *formidable* you can be. That's the word everybody uses about you!"

Simon wasn't happy to hear about how people talked about him. Given where he worked and how he most wanted to be with his colleagues, he knew he had to focus on this issue. The word *formidable* suggested that he was standoffish, put up barriers between himself and others, and maybe came across as aggressive—and this in a company that prized collegiality and cooperation! Simon knew that the upcoming work with the committee would be fast-paced, intense, and demanding. But it also seemed like a great opportunity to work on being more approachable. So Simon set this as a flex goal for himself while running the search committee.

Now Simon had both a content goal (to deliver an excellent slate of candidates for the job) and a flex goal (to work on being more approachable). Finding this second focus for an upcoming experience is your mission as you take this second step in the Power of Flexing.

A flex goal arises out of something you want to work on about yourself, some area where you want to grow. For many people the goal will be the very thing that triggered them to start working on the Power of Flexing in the first place, perhaps in response to specific feedback received. For others, the trigger might have been a general desire to improve, but now they need to set a more specific goal. In either case, the important thing is to identify and commit to a goal for an upcoming experience. Setting a goal has what psychologists call a "facilitating effect on behavioral enactment."[1] In other words, once you decide what you want, you're much more likely to take action to achieve it.

The Power of Flexing makes you the author of your own growth journey. Choosing a destination is a crucial step in that journey.

WHAT IS A FLEX GOAL?

Flex goals help you to keep your focus on your personal development in challenging situations so that you can learn lessons from those experiences. While anyone who has worked in an organization knows a lot about goals, flex goals are a bit different. In most companies, goals are ubiquitous: managers set quarterly goals that get translated into weekly and daily aspirations. Research validates goal setting as one of the organization's most important tools for achieving high performance. Decades of research shows that if your boss gives you a specific challenging goal to achieve ("increase sales units by 30 percent," "launch six brand-new products by the end of the year"), you'll accomplish a lot more than if your boss merely tells you, "Do your best."

Common wisdom tells managers to set "SMART" goals for their team members: specific, measurable, attainable, realistic, and time-bound.[2] But flex goals are different from the goals set by corporate managers. While flex goals may have some of the SMART elements, their role in the Power of Flexing makes them differ in important ways.

First, flex goals are *self-set*. In this sense they are less like corporate objectives and more like the goals we pick for ourselves as New Year's resolutions and pursue, with greater or lesser success, throughout the year, although they can be (and often are) work-based rather than the more typical personal goals we set as New Year's resolutions.

Second, flex goals are about *learning, not achievement*. It's likely that you've often set some achievement, or content-oriented, goals for yourself (master a new coding language or land a challenging account); some of these may overlap with the goals your company has set for you. But the Power of Flexing rests on the premise that you can get something accomplished at work, within your family, or in a community organization *and at the same time learn something important about yourself*. Your flex goal will reflect something to be learned, not about a specific task and how to do it better, but about you and the growth and change you want in your own personal effectiveness. Simon's goal of becoming more approachable is a good example of a flex goal.

In my workshops with executives, I keep this goal question simple by asking, "What would you need to do to be the person your dog already thinks you are?" Every dog owner recognizes the look of adoration their pet bestows upon them, regarding them as perfect in every way. Setting a flex goal is about acknowledging the ways you are less than perfect and then picking one as a focus for improvement.

Neither the management literature nor psychological research has much to say about self-set *learning* goals. Management experts, perhaps because they focus on work and work outcomes, have mainly studied whether self-set *achievement* goals are higher than company-set goals and whether they are more or less motivating.[3] Like management experts, psychologists have focused mainly on achievement goals. Until recently, neither group has looked closely at the workings of self-set learning goals, which will be our focus.

Research is beginning to discover the importance of learning goals, including their ability to enhance achievement. When tasks are very simple, a specific, challenging achievement goal creates motivation sufficient to increase performance. But when tasks are more complex, studies show that setting a learning goal—as in one study, the goal of identifying and learning six or more strategies to increase performance on the task—leads to even better performance.[4]

THE POWER OF ASPIRATIONAL GOALS

Although the setting and pursuit of personal goals has long been the stuff of literature, from ancient quest sagas to modern novels, psychologists have only recently begun to research where goals come from and how people choose them. Some come from people's *fantasies about the future*— for example, an aspirational vision of the kind of brave, open, strong, or influential person we might become. This type of goal is driven by our desire to move toward something. Others come from the *pain of the present*—our aversion to the pain caused by our lack of bravery, openness, strength, or influence in the present.[5] Goals are thought to be nested, with higher-order, values-driven goals such as "be a good person" or "be there for family or neighbors," prompting lower-order goals such as "work on my relationship with Joe at work" or "help out more in my neighborhood."[6] So Simon, being an HR person in a collaborative company, held the higher-order goal of being a friendly person and felt the "pain of the present" when he heard comments suggesting that he came off as "formidable."

The aspirational goals we set based on fantasies about the future can be compared to the inspirational visions that corporate executives are expected to set forth for the teams and organizations they lead. Consider Ari Weinzweig, the CEO of the Zingerman's Community of Businesses in Ann Arbor and the author of several books on leadership.[7] Ari, his partners, and the team at Zingerman's built their successful business by periodically visualizing where they wanted it to be several years down the line—by creating a word picture, a detailed description of where the company should end up. He believed so strongly in the power of picturing the future and writing it down that he, along with the leadership team at Zingerman's, became a passionate advocate of goals based on envisioning of the future. They developed a series of visions over the years, picturing the goals they were determined to achieve—including, specifically, the launch of a collection of community-based small businesses organized and managed according to a set of socially beneficial principles, including racial and ethnic diversity, civic engagement, and support for local educational and health initiatives.

Today, most of their vision has come to pass. Weinzweig considers this envisioning practice essential to everything that Zingerman's has collectively achieved so far and to everything they hope to achieve in the future. Today, whenever people working at Zingerman's launch a new project, they start by creating a vision that allows them to picture the future they are trying to shape. As Weinzweig explains when young people ask for advice, "When you don't have that engagement with the future, it doesn't work."

Ari Weinzweig is on to something. Imagining a desired future is a critical step in bringing about human change. And, Ari would add, writing it down so that it sticks. In doing so, the language you use is critical. The more evocative the language and the more vivid the images of that imagined future, the more compelling the vision. It needs to be inspiring. For those who have ever built a house, the difference here is like the difference between a monochrome blueprint of the house you're building and a full-color, computer-generated rendering that shows your future home in three dimensions. The former provides basic data; the latter evokes an intense feeling of desire for the finished product that is powerfully motivating. The best corporate leaders are skilled at producing visions of the future that are both positive and draw a specific picture of where they want the company to go.

Management theorist Drew Carton has led several research efforts that build on this insight.[8] He finds that corporate visions that use *image-*

based rhetoric such as "a computer in every home" (from Microsoft) versus abstract rhetoric "aiming for excellence" (from any company anywhere) create quite different reactions. In experiments, Carton and his colleagues discovered more subtle differences. For example, when participants were asked to build high-quality toys, the best results (as rated by a sample of seven- to twelve-year-olds) were achieved when the builders were given the vision for their work: "We build toys, all of them crafted flawlessly," that "will make wide-eyed kids laugh and proud parents smile." The less effective vision was also clear on the company's main value (quality) but was less evocative in its language: "all of them made to perfection" and "will be enjoyed by all of our customers."

Vivid imagery and language can play a similar role when we craft aspiration flex goals for ourselves. For example, for Raman Mehta, the chief information officer at Visteon, a global automotive electronics supplier, goals are based on real-life role models whom he gets to know personally. When setting growth goals for himself, he looks for "people who I believe in. Who I find are just incredibly authentic people. To watch them. See how they're living their life. See how they're leading their teams. See how they're managing their organizations. Watch them and try to learn from them. Grab ideas and time to talk with them and use them as a mentor to say, 'I wouldn't mind being something like that person. I wouldn't mind being a leader like that person. I think if I was that kind of leader, I would be happy with my life.'" The picture of a future self that he is able to develop for himself by doing this is motivating.

Similarly, Josh Shaw, the founder and CEO of Mission Athletecare, a company that designs products to enhance athletes' performance and recovery, formulated his future vision of himself as an effective leader by watching his current CEO take a company "from five of us to five hundred employees, from $4 million to $200 million, and then take it public." "Witnessing those things," Shaw says, "instills in me a lot of goal setting that came from making sure I approach things with discipline, I approach things with a wide lens. It certainly inspired me that anything was possible if you put your mind to it."

The way Mehta and Shaw derive aspirational goals from watching others is a common practice. Individuals infer the goals underlying others' actions and adopt them for themselves. I see someone who is a great influencer or listener, and I think, "I would love that for myself." Scientists call this process *goal contagion*, and it is one good way to approach the challenge of defining a flex goal.[9]

It's not always necessary to have an external role model to emulate. Laura Morgan Roberts at Georgetown and my colleagues at the University of Michigan have created and researched an exercise that uncovers what they call your "reflected best self."[10] In the Reflected Best Self Exercise, you solicit stories from others describing you at your best (thus, the "reflected" best self). By revealing your more important current strengths, the exercise helps you identify resources you can build on as you chart a plan for future growth. It both creates a trigger for aspirational growth and gives direction for that growth—all based on qualities you already possess, rather than abilities you observe in others.

These visions of the future are one source of higher-order goals to be pursued while you flex. The task, then, is to translate them into more specific, immediate goals for an upcoming experience or set of experiences. But before that translation, there's one more input to goal setting for you to consider.

AVERSIVE GOALS AND THE POWER OF PRESENT PAIN

If aspirational goals grow out of our fantasies about the future, aversive goals derive from the pain we experience in the present. A parent discovers that her daughter is so severely depressed that she has been cutting herself to relieve her distress; in response, the parent adopts the goal of learning to be more present and to listen better. A manager participating in his company's first-ever 360° feedback process learns that his team thinks he micromanages them. Surprised and embarrassed, he adopts the goal of giving his subordinates greater freedom to control their own work. Through a long-delayed angry confrontation with a coworker, an office manager realized that her habit of avoiding difficult conversations is backfiring; she adopts the goal of being braver and more honest.

Sometimes the pain that triggers a goal is not just emotional but physical. Chris Marcell Murchison is the former vice president for staff development and culture at HopeLab, a California-based social innovation organization focused on designing science-based technologies to improve the health and well-being of teens and young adults. Chris always had a tendency toward perfectionism. He thought of it as a double-edged sword: on good days it led to innovation and creativity, but on bad days it made him obsess over small details and insist on excessively high standards for himself and others. When his dentist recommended a mouth guard to reduce the painful grinding of his teeth at night, Chris realized that his perfectionism had become a real problem. He set himself the goal of becoming more tolerant of merely good work rather than demanding perfection in every case.[11]

These goals all stem from pain. We want to change in order to reduce the pain felt by others or by ourselves as a result of our failure to live and act in accordance with our highest values. This kind of pain can be a powerful stimulus for growth when you draw upon it to set specific goals you want to tackle in your upcoming experiences.

COMBINING BOTH DRIVES IN A SINGLE GOAL

Sometimes we find ourselves drawn toward flex goals that are driven by both aspiration and aversion—goals that reflect fantasies about a better future as well as a desire to escape the pain of today. Studies show that goals of this hybrid type have the power to generate especially intense and sustained effort. People who are in touch with negative aspects of their present situation and who also have a positive fantasy about their future tend to be strongly committed to their goals for change. However, that commitment translates into goal-directed action only if they create a plan for moving forward toward their goal, something we will take up in chapter 4, on experiments.[12]

Lindred (Lindy) Greer is an accomplished business school faculty member who took on a new leadership position. She exhibited the kind of twin-drive goal I just described. She envisioned a "future Lindy" who could emulate the inspiring example of a mentor, a high-powered woman at a former workplace. Lindy described how this mentor would sit listening in silence during a high-level meeting, bide her time, and then quietly offer a single remark that transformed the entire conversation. "It's a life goal of mine to be able to communicate like that," Lindy said. "No emotion, no bluster, no talking too much, no saying the wrong words."

Lindy's goal was also driven by the pain she was feeling in the present. She had received feedback from colleagues saying that she "showed too much emotion," which had the effect of making her look "weak" or "scary," depending on circumstances. As a new leader, Lindy was determined to overcome this problem. She set herself the goal of becoming more intentional about which emotions she displays and shares, whether verbally or through body language, in order to be the best leader she might be. These twin drives—aspiration and aversion—made Lindy's goal an especially compelling one for her. A year into her new assignment, Lindy's leadership center showed great momentum and Lindy described her relationship to her team as "amazing."

Marc Ingram was also helped by the power of hybrid drives. Marc was a finance specialist working for a large public school system who felt stuck in his career. He had been told by his boss, the system's chief financial officer, that he was seen as a "doer," not a leader. To grow, he needed to change this image. He was aided in the effort both by having his boss as a role model and by being able to attend a series of short courses in leadership development. These courses helped Marc to create a vision of himself as a leader as well as to understand more fully the negative impact that his current lack of leadership skills was causing. The combination of aspiration and aversion proved to be an effective learning motivation. Marc ended up taking his newly developed leadership skills to a different organization where he could start afresh.

FLEX GOALS FROM THE SIMPLE TO THE COMPLEX

Sometimes the flex goals people adopt are simple and relatively straightforward—not necessarily easy to achieve, but at least easy to understand. Simon Biel's goal of being more approachable and Chris Murchison's goal of reducing his perfectionism are both examples.

Some goals can be quite specific. Remember Jane Dutton from chapter 2? She shifted her mindset regarding the need to master online teaching during the coronavirus pandemic from resenting and fearing the change to accepting it as a growth opportunity. Jane has also set herself a flex goal based on a specific personal quality that she has discovered causes her problems in interpersonal settings—namely, the intensity with which she experiences and expresses emotions. When she's enthusiastic, she's super-enthusiastic; when she's negative, she's powerfully negative. Over the years she has learned that the intensity of her feelings tends to intimidate people and sometimes to silence them. Taking into account both the "pain of the present" (i.e., seeing that she was causing people around her to hold their tongues, afraid to share their points of view) and her vision for the future (of the person she most wanted to become), she set a specific flex goal: "to temper my emotional displays so that they don't overwhelm people."

Some flex goals are more complex and nuanced. Marc Ingram's goal of wanting to be seen as a leader is one example. Defining what it takes to be regarded as a leader is complex. Marc had to spend time carefully examining his organization to identify the specific traits and behaviors that marked those viewed as leaders in that context. As he began to learn what it meant to be a leader, he set the flex goal of letting go of control over details and focusing more on the big picture in his interactions with his team.

Anders Jones might not seem to have much in common with Lindy Greer. Greer is a university professor with teaching and research responsibilities, while Jones is a CEO in the financial technology (fintech) industry. But both are young, highly successful professionals who face similar dilemmas. Greer is taking on a new role at a new university that involves leading a staff for the first time. Anders is leading a start-up company staffed by people far older and more experienced than he. Both wonder how to balance having and exercising power with creating openness for others to express themselves.

Anders describes the challenge this way: "As a thirty-two-year-old who's never done any of those jobs, how on earth could I possibly manage those people?" His flex goal is "to be humble and also understanding that everyone wants to be led and wants to be mostly managed, no matter what level they are." He wants to be direct and decisive while still being open to the ideas of others, believing this balanced approach will enable him to get the most out of his experienced employees.

Lindy frames her challenge differently. She previously worked in the Netherlands, where, she says, "you always have to make yourself little, to lilt your voice, and to act like you are not successful in order to be liked." Now, in an American university, she needed to define a new balance. Recognizing the power distance between leader and followers, she feels an urge to manage this distance by "making herself little"—for example, through self-deprecating comments. But she also knows that she needs to exert authority.

Both Lindy and Anders have flex goals that require complex balancing acts: learning to define the ideal blend of varying traits in order to lead effectively in the short term and to improve their personal skills for the long term.

EXAMPLES OF POPULAR FLEX GOALS

Over the years, we've talked with many leaders about their flex goals and led workshops in which many individuals have defined flex goals for themselves. I advise people who are wondering how to choose their own flex goals that the first thing that comes to mind is probably the goal that you should work on. Most of us know where we need to improve; it usually relates to an issue that has shown up in our lives before and that we've seen highlighted in the comments, feedback, or unspoken reactions we get from those around us.

To illustrate the kinds of flex goals people typically set, here are the results from a single semester's work with two sections of a weekend MBA course on leadership with students working full-time in addition to pursuing their MBAs. After learning about the Power of Flexing, more than a hundred students were asked to choose an upcoming important experience and to identify a personal development goal they could work on during that experience.

The experiences chosen by the students varied widely. They included managing a student project that was going awry, assuming leadership of a new team, and handling a tough interpersonal situation with someone at work. The personal development goals that students defined also varied widely. They identified eighty-five goals that fell into a small number of categories. Table 1 lists the most popular among the goals named. The list gives us a glimpse into the leading concerns of young business professionals seeking to become more effective organizational leaders.

While the goals named by the students vary widely, they fall into a few broad categories. One group of goals deals with learning how to influence people over whom we have no direct authority. In combination,

Table 1: Popular Student Flex Goals and the Percentage of Students Naming Them

Enhancing presentation skills	14
Managing relationships	13
Getting better at delegating and empowering subordinates	9
Becoming more influential	9
Developing better skills in managing tasks (e.g., finishing work projects before getting distracted)	8
Becoming more assertive	7
Staying open to other people and new perspectives	7
Learning to deal with difficult people	6
Getting better at managing emotions (e.g., being less self-critical or more optimistic)	6
Communicating better	5
Reacting non-defensively to feedback and challenges from others	5
Becoming more approachable	3.5
Establishing oneself in a new role	3.5
Listening better	3.5

the goals that fall into this category account for 28 percent of the goals chosen by the students. Another group of goals deals with presentation and communication skills. In combination, the goals that fall into this category account for 23 percent of the goals chosen. Other popular categories of goals deal with issues such as building empowering relationships with direct reports; handling difficult relationships or challenging interpersonal problems; and managing tasks better. All of these are worthy goals and would likely serve the students selecting them well if they were to make progress on them.

Some students had trouble identifying a useful flex goal. Some seemed so caught up in the *content* of an upcoming experience that they were unable to take a step back and ask, "What kind of personal skill can I work on within this experience that will help me improve my future effectiveness?" For example, as you prepare for and manage the staff retreat that you've been tasked with running—an important content goal—what kind of personal effectiveness skill might you work on simultaneously? Distinguishing content goals from personal flex goals—and then learning how to tackle both kinds of goals at the same time—is a crucial element in the Power of Flexing.

Some students set *too many* goals. As you go into a challenging new experience, we recommend choosing one or at most two flex goals to focus on—no more. If you try to tackle a larger number of goals—such as the five goals a few of our students named—you will probably suffer from distraction and confusion, thereby wasting time and energy that could have been used productively.

Other students set goals that were *too vague* to be useful. For example, one student's goal was "to develop interpersonal skills with new people in new environments." This is fine as a general description of a worthwhile life objective, but it is very unclear as a definition of the specific skills the student seeks to master in a particular environment with a particular set of people. As a result, this goal statement is less useful than it might be. Reframing this goal as "working on listening better to the people in manufacturing as I pitch my marketing ideas" would give the student specificity regarding what interpersonal skill to focus on (listening) and when (while talking to the folks in manufacturing about marketing ideas). This specificity makes the goal much more useful.

By contrast, some students set goals that were *too specific*. These goal statements named tactics rather than broader skills that the student hoped to attain. For example, one student said that his goal was "to remember clearly the name of everyone I meet for the first time." I suspect that a better description of the student's real goal might be "to establish my credibility with new people," "to have more influence through authentic connections in the organization," or "to create closer interpersonal relationships with my peers at work." Remembering people's names is a worthy tactic, but just a tactic—not a goal.

A good gauge of whether your goal is specific enough is to ask yourself, "If I assigned this goal as stated now to someone else, would they know what to do?" To determine whether your goal is too specific—perhaps more of a tactic than a goal—ask yourself, "If I achieved this goal as stated now, would it give me the boost in effectiveness that I am really looking for?" If the answer to either of these questions is no, then some work on defining your goal is required.

FINE-TUNING YOUR GOAL

Once you define your flex goal, you need to do two more things. First, check out how you state the goal. Heidi Grant Halverson, a psychologist and author who studies the science of motivation and communication, recommends stating your goal using phrases that describe a process of improvement, like *improve on, get better at,* and *grow in.*[13] Simon wants to *become* more approachable; Chris wants to *reduce* his perfectionism; Lindy and Anders want to *learn* to balance assertiveness and restraint; and you might want to *get better at* listening. Goals stated this way are empowering. They also help to keep you in a growth mindset: you can always *get better at* something, and this is what flexing is all about.

By contrast, avoid stating your goal using language that describes a specific end state, such as *being great at* or *being the best at.* Phrases like these put you into a performance-prove mindset and encourage you to engage in comparisons with others rather than focusing on getting better than you were in the past. Both of these attitudes will hamper rather than enhance your ability to learn and grow.

Second, state your goals in terms of a journey rather than a destination. Recent research suggests that the more you see yourself as being on a path toward a goal, the more you will continue to strive toward it—including after you've made some initial progress along the way. This concept was tested with goals such as shedding a certain number of pounds in a weight loss program. The researchers found that the "journey" metaphor did not make a difference in how much individuals strove to meet the initial weight loss goal in the early stages of the quest, but it did increase the likelihood of continued goal-related behavior.[14] When they met the initial goal, those who thought the effort was a journey were more likely to continue with healthy behaviors. The journey metaphor encouraged them to think more about the learning process as a whole, including the ups and downs along the way, leading to a satisfying feeling of overall growth.

COMMITMENT IS CRITICAL

Commitment means a strong sense of determination to achieve your goal, the willingness to invest effort in it, and impatient striving toward the goal's implementation. Research shows that commitment is the single most important element in the flex goal process.[15] The familiar saying has it that "experience is the best teacher." But experience also offers a lot of distractions, such as the inevitable complications that arise in getting the task done, the need to respond to new demands from the context, and the interpersonal conflicts that emerge within the task team—all things that can draw your attention away from your personal development goal. Bringing to experience a learning goal to which you are committed helps to keep your focus.

You can enhance your commitment to your goal in several ways. (You might want to write down your answers to the following prompts to make them more tangible and memorable to you. Also, journaling gives you a physical artifact to refer back to, which can be helpful.) First, *remind yourself of why you care*. Think about the things that drove you to select your flex goal. Ponder the fantasy of a better "future you"; reflect on the present pain that the issue is causing you now; and imagine the benefits that will come to you and to your team, family, organization, or community when you achieve your goal. Considering these costs and benefits will help you deepen your commitment to your flex goal.

Mentally Juxtapose and Contrast the Goal and the Obstacles You Face

Research shows that thinking about both where you want to go and the obstacles that you face in getting there helps you grow your commitment to overcoming those obstacles. Say, for example, that you want to improve your physical fitness. If you think both about how you want to look and feel *and* the obstacles you might face, such as getting out of bed and heading to the gym on a cold January morning, you'll do better than if you ignore the obstacles altogether. Psychologists have found that people who engage in this kind of thinking do nearly twice as much physical exercise, eat healthier diets, and practice more physical mobility while combating chronic back pain.[16] This mental exercise sets you up to better face and overcome the obstacles when they inevitably arise.

Make Your Commitment Concrete

Even a step as simple as writing down your goal can enhance your commitment to it. Your goal is further enhanced when you share your intention with someone else. This is why, in my workshops with leaders, I set them up with a peer coach and have them share their flex goals with the coach. This step makes the commitment "more real" and increases the chance that you will pursue it avidly.

Make Your Goal Public

The power of this step has been shown in many research studies. In one study, homeowners who publicly agreed to reduce their energy consumption in fact reduced their consumption far more than homeowners who only committed privately.[17] In another experiment, kids persisted longer in working on a difficult task when they'd made public statements about their expectations for success.[18] In yet another a carefully controlled randomized experiment that tested various ways of increasing commitment to a goal, the strongest effect was associated with making the goal public.[19] Making a public commitment to your goal reduces the chance that you'll "forget about" the goal, make excuses for ignoring it, or claim you're "really achieving" it when in fact you're simply moving the goalposts. Merely seeing someone with whom you shared your goal has been shown to trigger goal-directed action; it's that powerful.

So commitment to your goal is key to the Power of Flexing process. Once you choose a flex goal, do everything you can to enhance your personal commitment to it. You may be surprised and delighted to see how much more quickly, easily, and thoroughly you can develop skills that you've previously struggled to master.

CEO ARI WEINZWEIG'S OBSERVATIONS about creating a corporate vision and transforming it into reality apply to the process of setting and implementing a flex goal. Weinzweig describes the importance of defining a clear vision of where you want to go that is emotionally engaging and to which you feel committed. "Then," he says, "you have to do the work. Those are the two pieces: the vision and the work."

In the next chapter we'll turn to the work you'll use to change your flex goal from fantasy into reality.

CHAPTER 4

UNLEASHING YOUR INNER SCIENTIST

Planning and Conducting Experiments

To learn and grow—to enjoy the potential benefits offered by a changing variety of work experiences—you need to flex; that is, to *try doing something different*. And the best way to maximize your learning is to *plan and carry out specific experiments*—flex behaviors that you think will increase your leadership and personal effectiveness. As the experience unfolds and you perform your planned experiments, you'll monitor the results, observing the degree to which they positively impact your work, your environment, and the people around you (or fail to do so). In this way you can learn which flex behaviors enhance your personal effectiveness or effectiveness as a leader and which do not.

PLANNING EXPERIMENTS: TRYING NEW BEHAVIORS IN PURSUIT OF YOUR LEARNING GOAL

Carrying out experiments related to your goals is important for several reasons. First, people are notoriously bad at following through on goals. Just check out the local gym in February, when the goal-driven January rush is over. You'll have no difficulty finding an unoccupied treadmill to use!

Follow-through is especially difficult when it needs to occur sometime after the initial plan was formulated, especially when that follow-through needs to happen in the midst of a challenging experience. Such experiences are exactly the ones that have the greatest learning potential. So it's doubly important to do whatever it takes to ensure that you extract all the valuable lessons you can from what may be a difficult, perhaps stressful activity. Preplanned, thoughtful experimentation is an effective way to make this happen.

The kind of experimentation that the Power of Flexing requires involves small, realistic changes in your behavior—any sort of activity that is different from what you've done in the past. The goal is to move out of your comfort zone by trying something new so you can determine whether it leads to improvement.

Moving out of your comfort zone may not sound like an immediately appealing prospect. Many of us feel that our lives and careers are already uncomfortable enough; why deliberately choose to take on even more discomfort?

But experts on learning and growth are unanimous in saying that some degree of discomfort is a natural side effect of doing anything that is unfamiliar and new—which means that discomfort is an essential accompaniment of growth. Here's how the renowned psychologist Abraham Maslow puts it in his book *The Psychology of Science: A Reconnaissance*: "One can choose to go back toward safety or forward toward growth. Growth must be chosen again and again; fear must be overcome again and again." Leadership guru John Maxwell echoes the same theme: "If we're growing, we're always going to be out of our comfort zone";[1] and bestselling author Bryant McGill observes, "Whatever makes you uncomfortable is your biggest opportunity for growth."

Our students and colleagues who have explored the Power of Flexing confirm the same point based on personal experience. David McCallum, the business school dean whose efforts to adopt and maintain a growth mindset we recounted in chapter 2, describes how leaning into discomfort became a conscious part of his growth program. "If I did find myself in the comfort zone," he says, "I would consciously push myself back out again and just trust that that's where the learning zone was—not when I was comfortable in a routine, doing the same old thing."

If you accept the proposition that learning and growth require a willingness to stretch yourself beyond your comfort zone, the natural next question is: Exactly how do you do this?

To answer this, let's return to the concept of goal setting. Gabriele Oettingen is one of the researchers whose work undergirds the notion of using fantasies about a better future as a source of personal goals. (You'll recall this idea from chapter 3.) She and her partners have described the challenge this presents in the following words: "A person who holds fantasies about a desired future can also be understood as somebody who is confronted with a problem: he wants something and does not know immediately what series of actions he can perform to get it."[2] In other words, setting a goal is not enough. You also need to answer the question "How do I get there from here?"

Imagining one or more experiments you might try is a way to solve the problem Oettingen describes. To harness the power of your goal, it needs to be connected with specific actions you will take to achieve it. And since the actions needed to reach a complex, challenging goal are often unclear, experimentation is a necessary connecting step. You need to think of one or more small, specific behavior changes you can try in a particular situation in the near future. The observed results will tell you whether those changes have moved you in the right direction. If so, congratulations! You can continue to practice the new behaviors, perhaps extending and intensifying them to make even greater progress. If not, that's fine: you've now learned something that does *not* work for you. Now think of another, different experiment you can try. Say you've set the goal of being more influential in meetings with your peers. You might start out by trying experiments with where you sit at the table (e.g., at the corners rather than along the side) to see if that might give your comments more weight in the discussion. If that doesn't seem to make much difference, you might try speaking first or last to see if your comments will hold more sway. You might experiment with shortening the arguments that support your ideas.

Repeated experiments like these will eventually enable you to zero in on the action steps that will bring you to your goal.

Based on what I've said so far, you may recognize that the experimentation we recommend as part of the Power of Flexing is a version of what scientists call *the experimental method*. It's the method of developing insights that has been responsible for most of the major scientific breakthroughs of the past three centuries. Scientific experimentation is a process of trial and error. The idea is that every trial generates new insights into a problem, and that even errors generate useful information. Some scholars describe the process this way: "Imagine trying to unlock the door with a set of unfamiliar keys. Putting one key into the lock to see if the lock will turn is experimentation; even if the experiment fails, new knowledge is created that narrows the scope of subsequent trials."[3]

An open-minded willingness to try things without knowing whether or not they will work is an essential ingredient in experimentation. The legendary inventor Thomas Edison put it this way when a reporter asked him about how it felt to conduct a thousand unsuccessful experiments in search of the right material to use for the filament in his electric lightbulb: "I didn't fail a thousand times. The lightbulb was an invention with one thousand steps."[4] The more you can reframe your views of failure along these same lines, the better off you will be. While obviously you don't want to seek out major failures, your ability to rebound from inevitable small failures will depend largely on the way you frame them. If failure is framed as the end of the world (or treated as if it were emotionally), then you likely won't rebound. Considering it as a mistake from which you can learn—or a step in the process, as Edison did—gives you a better chance to rebound afterward.

Of course, experimentation in science is serious business. It involves articulating hypotheses (that is, theoretical descriptions of possible cause-and-effect relationships to be tested), selecting methods and measurement techniques that have been validated in past experiments, conducting the experiments with precision and transparency, and then submitting the results to review and analysis by an audience of one's peers. Only then will other scientists accept your experiment as making a valid contribution to knowledge.

The Power of Flexing applies this same method in your everyday work life, though with fewer test tubes and beakers! First, the experiments we recommend will be less formal and rigorous, more playful and open-ended. The idea is to try some new ways of behaving (e.g., where you sit or when you speak in peer meetings), to decide whether those new behaviors bring you closer to your learning goal, and to repeat the process over and over again, picking up new insights from each iteration.

You may also choose to bend some of the rules that scientists generally follow when planning and conducting experiments. For example, rather than rigorously separating individual experiments so as to avoid "contaminating" one set of results with another, you may decide to conduct two or three experiments simultaneously (such as speaking last and shortening your arguments). This is okay; after all, you're not working on the development of a new medicine whose efficacy must be tested with scientific precision. You're simply looking for life strategies that will work for you. So if you try two or three behavior changes at once and find that, in combination, they help bring you closer to your goal, then that's great.

Second, the kinds of experiments we recommend are completely *personal*. You can entertain any "hypothesis" you want without worrying about formulating a theory that your fellow scientists would deem plausible, and you'll judge the results of your experiments subjectively based on how they make you feel and the effects that you observe. Do you like the reactions you get from colleagues when you try a new way of running a meeting or leading a seminar? Does your new system for organizing a project seem to produce better results? If you like the outcome of your experiment, chalk it up as a win. It's as simple as that.

Often, getting to the fun in experimenting is just a matter of "right-sizing" the endeavor. Lois, a wonderful artist who paints fairly realistic interpretations of natural scenes, offers the perfect metaphor for this "right-sizing." She has long wanted to be "looser" in her painting style. During the COVID-19 quarantine, with time on her hands, she started painting flowers on eight-inch-by-eight-inch boards instead of her usual twenty-inch-by-twenty-inch paintings. And there was something about the small size of eight-inch-by-eight-inch space that made a huge difference. It was small enough that she could just experiment and let things flow, and if they didn't work, no problem, it was only an eight-by-eight! After many weeks, she actually developed some affinity for painting in the freer style she had long desired and felt more confident about using a more expressive style in her larger pieces as well—all from making the experiments small enough so that she had a more playful attitude toward them.

Experimentation in the Power of Flexing puts you in charge of your own learning and growth. You don't need to wait for someone to acknowledge your potential, send you to a course or a training program, or assign you a mentor. Instead, you can set yourself on a path to growth simply by trying out different behaviors and assessing their impact. You can make it fun for yourself as you make experimentation a hopeful, positive process—one that holds out the promise of continual growth, learning, and improvement, all as a natural outgrowth of activities that you can freely incorporate into your daily routine.

HOW DO YOU PLAN YOUR EXPERIMENT?

Planning an experiment as part of your flexing program is simple. First you need to come up with an idea about something you might be able to do to improve your leadership skills and your personal effectiveness. The next step is to imagine how you can test your idea by identifying specific flexes in your behavior that you might try in an upcoming experience. The final step for planning your experiment is to define success—that is, to decide in advance what evidence you will look for to determine whether or not your idea was correct.

Suppose you have a flex goal of becoming more influential in meetings; in other words, you want to become better at shaping the attitudes and opinions of the others attending meetings so that the group makes more decisions that you support. You might decide to pursue this goal by changing your behavior during your work team's weekly meetings. Then you come up with an idea to test: that holding back and speaking last in your team meetings might increase the degree of influence you have over the decisions made.

Now you need a concrete plan to test this idea. For example, you might plan to deliberately refrain from speaking until every other team member has spoken during every weekly team meeting for the next two months. Then you can determine whether your experiment is working by keeping track of the decisions made in the meetings and comparing your rate of success in shaping those decisions with the same rate from past meetings. Suppose, for instance, that during the previous eight team meetings (two months' worth) the major decisions made by the group went "your way" three times. Your experiment could be considered a success if you achieve a "win rate" of five or six during the next eight team meetings.

These few simple ideas make up your experimental plan. You can start to carry it out, and to learn from it, as soon as your next team meeting is held.

As you recall from chapter 3, Simon Biel received feedback telling him that his behavior in meetings made him appear "formidable"—stern, cold, even a bit frightening—which caused his colleagues to avoid working with him. Simon wanted to change this image. When he was asked to lead a new cross-departmental committee, he decided to use the opportunity to test some ideas about how to produce this change. He planned three small simultaneous experiments to perform over the committee's life span.

First, he decided to arrive early at each committee meeting so that he could greet the committee members as they arrived. This was in contrast to his usual pattern of overloading his schedule so he arrived just on time for meetings—or even a bit late, arriving flustered and jumping right into the task at hand.

Second, in an effort to reduce the power distance between him and the committee members, he decided to flex his seating behavior. Rather than sitting at the head of the table, he would sit on one side, among the other members.

Simon's third experiment was a simple one but perhaps the most powerful. He noticed that while he was thinking warm thoughts and caring about others, his face didn't show it. Hypothesizing that his facial expressions contributed to his formidable image, he decided to flex by smiling more. Taken together, he hoped that these three actions would begin to change his colleagues' perception of him from "formidable" to "approachable, open, and friendly."

Simon performed his experiment by incorporating all three behavior shifts into meetings over the lifetime of the committee. He tested the effectiveness of these changes by closely observing the behavior of the other committee members. Did they seem more comfortable and willing to participate in the committee through behaviors like showing up on time (or even early), remaining through the meeting, and joining freely in the discussion? Did they appear comfortable expressing their ideas and opinions openly, even when these differed from Simon's own? Did they respond to his smiles with grins of their own? These and other forms of implicit feedback would help Simon determine whether or not he was becoming more approachable.

Of course, he also listened closely to any direct feedback. A comment like "It's been a pleasure working on this committee with you, Simon!" went a long way toward confirming the effectiveness of his experimental plan.

Karin Stawarky, the executive coach we've met before, employed a series of experiments in her efforts to discover a way to transform the impression she left with clients from stiffly professorial to warm, caring, and generous. In each case she brainstormed a new behavior that she hypothesized might positively impact her relationship with clients, tested the behavior in one or more business engagements, and monitored the results.

In one experiment, Karin would find a quiet space prior to a client-group engagement and devote time to mentally centering herself for the meeting. She often used specific mental imagery as a tool for this purpose—for example, picturing herself preparing a meal and serving it to her clients. "I could see myself extending my hands, almost like wings, to offer a tray of food," she recalls. This symbolic gesture conjured up the spirit of service and hospitality that she hoped to embody. In a second experiment, Karin used breathing exercises before an engagement to control her stress level. And in a third, she prepared for a presentation by reciting a series of affirmations—positive statements that grounded her in who she was and what she knew to be true about herself.

College life offers a lot of potential leadership experiences and therefore a lot of room for experiments: chances to try things, make mistakes that are usually not too costly, and then recover and grow from them. That certainly was the experience of an ambitious young associate at a major consulting firm eager to lay the foundation for a highly successful career in business leadership whom I will call Nadia.

Nadia held a significant leadership role during college and began to notice some negative reactions from other people. As she put it when looking back on the experience later in life, "I think my personality comes across as a bit more controlling than other people's." This tendency was exacerbated by having run for student body president on a reform platform. She'd assumed her electoral victory had given her a mandate to push her fellow officers around, right down to the timeline for implementing the changes she'd proposed. Those around her began to get increasingly frustrated, which Nadia finally recognized.

In response, she adopted a goal of letting go a little bit—not all at once, but slowly, testing a variety of strategies over time. This was a classic Power of Flexing move: trying different things, putting out feelers, and deciding on one's next steps based on the feedback and results achieved.

Nadia's first experiment was simply to back off a bit on dictating *how* things got done while still setting parameters for *what* should get done. The first time she tried this, the results were astounding. A fellow student government officer "came up with this amazing idea, then just went and made it so much better than anything than I could have imagined!"

Nadia's second experiment involved a new way of enforcing project schedules. Her old approach would have been to scold a teammate who failed to meet a deadline. Now she tried modifying that method. On the day a project was due, she would send an email to the tardy partner with a message like "Hey, I see that this is still pending. Let me know if you need any help finishing it up, because I want to make sure that you can still deliver on your really exciting project." Once again the results were gratifying. Her colleagues responded by feeling empowered rather than controlled, and generally finished their work quickly after receiving Nadia's message.

Nadia's successful experiments helped her establish a path for improving her leadership style. Not that they instantly transformed her ingrained personality traits—Nadia says she still has a tendency to be controlling; however, she says, "I gradually learned how I can be controlling but in a way that isn't too harsh for other people." During her subsequent years as an MBA student and a club leader, she developed an even more empowering style, one whose core message is "Tell me what your goals are and I'll help you to achieve them." This perspective should set her up well for success as she starts her career as a consultant at McKinsey.

As these stories suggest, practically every experience you have can be an opportunity for experimentation and learning. The ideas for experiments can come from many sources and take many forms. Some experiments, like Simon's with changing his style of leading meetings and Nadia's with project management techniques, focus on interpersonal dynamics. Others, like Karin's pre-engagement exercises, focus on intrapersonal forces: moods, mindsets, and expectations that influence her later behavior.

Sometimes experiments can focus on *not* acting rather than on acting. Nadia's husband recently made an observation that triggered a new experiment: "Sometimes you respond to people so fast that it puts them on the defensive!" Nadia recognizes the tendency: "I think I picked it up when I was on the debate team in high school." Now she is experimenting with a one-second pause before answering someone else's question or challenge. Based on the results this experiment elicits, the one-second pause may become a new tool in Nadia's communication arsenal.

Experiments don't always need to be conducted in the workplace. Fajar is an MBA graduate who recently became director of product development at an Asian technology company. His technical, managerial, and financial skills are all excellent, but he wonders whether he has the creativity to help make his company a leading innovative force in the world of technology. Fajar says, "My left brain is in great shape, but I'd love to bring my right brain to life."

In pursuit of this goal, Fajar has undertaken an unusual experiment:

he is practicing the ancient Chinese art of calligraphy. He was inspired by seeing a friend who had taken a calligraphy course practicing with brush and ink. Fajar signed up for a course of his own, and now he is finding that his mind is changing in some interesting ways:

> I'm learning to control my hand, my posture, and even my emotions, so that the flow of ink and the end result are more balanced and beautiful. In the process, I'm also noticing other changes. I'm becoming more appreciative of the beauty of works of art, for example, as well as more sensitive to my environment. I'm becoming more observant and more patient. I used to say, "I have no talent for art." Now I'm not worrying about that. I'm approaching this new challenge in the spirit of thinking and acting outside of the box, and it's opening me up in new ways.

Calligraphy is not directly related to Fajar's goal of becoming a high-tech innovator—although we might note that Steve Jobs spoke frequently about how a calligraphy course he took at Reed College in Portland, Oregon, helped inspire the fascination with design he brought to the creation of the earliest Apple computers. But Fajar's experiment is helping him develop new mental skills that have the potential to enhance his effectiveness in business and in life—and that's what the Power of Flexing is all about.

Sometimes you may design a personal one-off experiment whose success is measured primarily by your own sense of well-being. Hannah, the TFA teacher we met in chapter 2, designed an experiment to test a way of reclaiming her personal life while doing gig work as a tutor for high school students and as a contractor for a company providing captioning services. Both jobs required her to be online frequently, especially during the 2020 COVID-19 pandemic. Overwhelmed by the demands on her time as well as by the constant flow of news and information updates, Hannah said she felt at times as if "my days were happening to me instead of me taking charge of them."

To push back, Hannah decided to experiment with having a "No-Tech Weekend," which she hoped would give her some time and space to think about what she actually wanted and needed from life instead of having it just happen.

As the No-Tech Weekend approached, Hannah almost fell into a common trap: she began feeling pressure to make the weekend productive, perhaps by taking on a new project or deep-cleaning her bathroom. She resisted this urge. Instead, she decided to keep her time completely open. She even warned her friends in advance so she wouldn't feel guilty about ignoring their calls, texts, and social media posts. She spent her time doing yoga, cooking a more elaborate dinner than she normally would do, reading a book, and taking her dog on a longer walk and sitting in the park with him instead of rushing through it. It was nothing fancy—she just took the time to do things she wanted to do without feeling that she should be more productive and without being distracted by her phone or expectations from others.

Hannah really liked the results. She spent two entire days freed from the temptation to compare her weekend with those of her friends as highlighted on social media and she also ignored the constant stream of news on TV and online, which kept her from going down the rabbit hole of anxiety and anger that so many people find irresistible. Most important, she felt noticeably more refreshed on Monday—and far more energized for the week ahead.

If you're having trouble coming up with ideas for experiments, try talking with friends, colleagues, mentors, coaches, and classmates. In my Power of Flexing workshops, we crowdsource ideas for experiments. Participants describe the goals they want to work on and listen to strangers offering ideas about new things they can try. Some of the ideas will be half-baked, but others will be brilliant, and of course the participant seeking inspiration is free to try any suggestion they'd like.

DIALING DOWN THE PERFECTIONISM: ONE FLEXER'S TEN EXPERIMENTAL PRACTICES

To see the power of experimentation more fully, let's take a look at how one highly conscientious person tackled his personal growth challenge. Remember Chris from chapter 3? When his dentist warned him that he was spending his nights painfully and destructively grinding his teeth, Chris set himself the goal of becoming less of a perfectionist. But he didn't stop there. He went on to outline in a blog post all of the steps he planned to take to reduce his perfectionism. Some of these were intrapersonal explorations, but some of them were true experiments, which Chris planned to conduct both in his head and with others in his work setting. Here are the ten practices Chris laid out in his post:

- **Increasing self-awareness.** Understanding the source of my perfectionism has been essential. Where does this tendency come from? What is it serving? Seeking the help of workshops, books, counselors, coaches, friends, and family has been necessary to answer these questions.
- **Self-compassion.** Seeing and appreciating who I am, as I am. Being kind to myself as I let go of being perfect and let others see the real me.
- **Interrupt catastrophic thinking.** Asking myself what is the worst that could happen! Amplify that thought multifold until the outcome is clearly preposterous.
- **Reframing.** Accepting that my perception is not reality. Opening up to seeing the opposite of my version of reality and challenging my own mental models.

+ **Letting go.** Acknowledging the noise in my head when I am in the grip of perfectionism and letting it pass. Using mindfulness practices to help me get out of my head and into my body.
+ **Seeing life as an ongoing experiment.** Practicing vulnerability by taking small risks and recalibrating my self-image based on the results.
+ **Seeking feedback.** Seeking very specific feedback to prevent rumination over what I think went wrong.
+ **Improvisation.** Practicing planning less and being more open to the spontaneous moment. Learning to laugh at myself and take life less seriously! Taking part in improv workshops has been transformative for me.
+ **Trust.** Trusting that I am enough and that more hard work will not always be necessary nor helpful.
+ **Letting friends in.** Breaking the secrecy, letting others know of my perfectionist tendencies, and allowing them to help and support me . . . even laugh with me as I deal with it.
+ **This is a practice.**[5]

Most important, note how Chris ends his blog post: with the words "This is a practice." The tone of that statement fits beautifully with the Power of Flexing. It's about trying things out—testing ideas with action in the real world, observing the impact, and then trying something else. And once you find something that works, expect to practice it until it becomes habitual—part of a "new normal" that makes your daily life and work more effective and rewarding.

WHAT KINDS OF BARRIERS DETER EXPERIMENTATION?

People tend to have two concerns about experimentation. The first is a worry about consistency: "If I start acting differently starting tomorrow—

and especially if I drop one experimental change in my behavior and then try another—won't the people around me be bothered by my lack of consistency?"

The second common concern is about possible failure: "If I change my way of relating to people, managing projects, or leading teams, and then suffer an embarrassing failure, won't my reputation and image be seriously harmed in the eyes of my colleagues?"

Interestingly enough, these concerns are so common that there is research testing the validity of both of them. Researchers showed people descriptions of leaders following courses of action that were consistent or inconsistent over time, along with information as to whether these leaders failed or succeeded with the initiatives they led. Then they asked the study participants to rate the performance of the leaders described. The findings showed clearly that one of the two fears about experimentation—fear of inconsistency and fear of failure—is better grounded in reality than the other. Can you guess which one?

The research shows that fear of inconsistency has little basis in fact. However, fear of failure is supported by some evidence.

In these studies, leaders who followed a course of action that was inconsistent but successful fared quite well. It seems that most people are happy to support and praise a leader who changes her style and strategies from time to time, so long as the results are good. Thus, if you personally hesitate to engage in experimentation because you worry about appearing inconsistent, try to shed that concern. Inconsistency is not a problem for most leaders, provided you can generate good outcomes along the way.

By contrast, leaders who were consistent but failed received lower grades from the study participants. Apparently, in the eyes of most people, being consistent is not much of a virtue if your efforts don't produce successful outcomes.

Thus, the fear of failure taps a real risk. However, this risk can be managed. One way to minimize it is by keeping your initial experiment small. If you want to experiment with a new way of organizing team projects, start with a project that involves a small group of workers engaged in a task whose stakes are relatively minor. If this experiment is successful, you can then apply the same change with a bigger project whose visibility and importance are greater. This approach lets you enjoy the benefits of a successful experiment while reducing the risk of pain from a failure. This is comparable to the way pharmaceutical researchers test a new drug on a handful of patients to eliminate the possibility of using a formula with potential lethal effects. Only after a small-scale test demonstrates the drug's basic safety will the researchers move on to engage in large-scale studies of its efficacy.

Still, the issue of risk is a real one. In particular, taking risks through experiments will always be difficult for people who hold a performance-prove mindset. By contrast, the learning mindset that we described beginning in chapter 2 makes sensible risk taking easier. The learning mindset, in effect, gives you permission to try new things, even when failure is a possibility.

Lisa Shalett, the financial services professional from chapter 2 who was challenged by life in Japan during her student days, describes the importance of the learning mindset this way:

I think that putting yourself in situations outside your comfort zone is incredibly important. Making a conscious effort to do so opens your mind and enables you to have experiences you might not otherwise have. It's unfortunate that a lot of people orient themselves only toward achieving a specialization. They say, "I want to be the best at this; I want to be an expert at that." Then they find themselves living narrowly in that zone.

It doesn't mean you need to drop yourself off in Japan. It's about putting yourself in a situation where you have no choice but to learn.

Flex experiments are a great way to put yourself in that kind of "unavoidable learning" situation. They give you a chance to grow and develop, all at a cost that you can manage through thoughtful risk-containment efforts.

Nadia exemplifies the spirit of experimentation beautifully. As she describes the challenges she is working to overcome and the new behaviors she is testing, she repeatedly uses phrases like "I'm trying hard to do this," "I'm not perfect at that," and "I'm still a work in progress." Language like this reflects her openness to change and growth, as well as her willingness to accept a modest level of risk in exchange for the broader horizons that experimentation opens. Adopting this attitude is the best way to overcome the mental barriers that discourage too many people from engaging in experimentation.

IMPLEMENTATION INTENTIONS: PLANNING TO FLEX WHEN EXPERIMENTS GO AWRY

There's one more thing that you can do to make a successful experiment more likely. As you approach a particularly important experience with a significant flex goal in mind, spend some time developing what goal researchers call *implementation intentions*. These are plans concerning things that might happen to interfere with your experiments along with effective ways you could respond. In other words, implementation intentions are about preparing if-then contingencies to use if events don't go according to plan.

Here's a simple example of how Simon Biel used this technique. You'll recall that Simon's experimental efforts aimed at increasing his approachability included arriving early at committee meetings. As he planned this experiment, Simon reflected on the fact that controlling his work schedule was often complicated by last-minute interruptions and emergencies—

urgent, unplanned tasks that tended to make him late to meetings rather than early.

To prevent these sorts of events from thwarting his experiment, Simon developed the following implementation intention: He would set his computer to give him a visual and aural reminder of an upcoming committee meeting fifteen minutes in advance of the scheduled start time. Then, as soon as the reminder appeared on his screen, he would leave for the meeting immediately rather than following his usual habit of trying to squeeze in one more small task—an invitation to being interrupted and sidetracked.

Here's another example. John's goal is to become more open to input from his team. He plans an experiment to be carried out during team meetings: when another participant offers an idea, John will start his response by summarizing what he's heard. The idea is for John to force himself to listen carefully and fully "take on board" his team member's insight before offering his personal reaction. It's a good idea that might well help him move closer to his goal.

But in planning the experiment, John pauses to consider ways his plan could get sidetracked. One possibility immediately springs to mind. John knows that he has a particularly hard time listening to people who speak in what he considers a "whiny" tone of voice. There's a team member, Marty, who tends to use that tone pretty often. When that happens, John's teeth are set on edge, he stops listening, and an impatient reaction quickly gets written all over his face. Any effort by John to be more open goes by the board.

To prevent this from happening, John thinks through an implementation intention particularly for the whiny-voice contingency: "If someone on the team raises an issue in a whiny tone of voice, I will be hypervigilant about listening with care and then paraphrasing back what I heard."

Will simply formulating this intention in advance help John stick to his experimental plan? Actually, yes. A substantial amount of research supports the finding that when people think through occurrences that could distract them from their goals and plan what they will do when that occurs, their ability to stay focused and effective is greatly enhanced. In social science terms, developing an implementation intention helps to ensure that the obstacles you encounter will be salient (that is, obvious and recognizable), the choices you'll consider will be circumscribed (based on your preplanning), and your behavior is more likely to be automatic, goal directed, and successful.

ANY ONE EXPERIMENT, OF course, can only teach you so much. The Power of Flexing involves making experimentation a routine part of your working life. It turns growth into a kind of game that you play every day, competing against yourself to see how much smarter, stronger, and more effective you can become. Over time, the small results that each experiment generates will mount up, leading to big changes that can produce remarkable levels of achievement.

CHAPTER 5

IT TAKES A VILLAGE
TO GROW

Seeking Feedback to
Amp Up Your Learning

When it comes to personal effectiveness, it's not enough to decide on your own whether or not you're effective. You really need to understand how others view you.

If you're like most people, you have important stakeholders in your life whose opinions about you matter greatly. In the workplace, these people include your boss, your peers, your clients or customers, and your subordinates. At home and in the community, they include family members, friends, neighbors, and other associates. All these people can play crucial roles in your growth, which means it's important to know how they view you. And figuring that out often takes feedback seeking. In the eyes of others, are your experiments working? Are you getting better at the skills you decided to work on? To answer these questions, you need to attend closely to others' reactions and sometimes directly ask for their feedback.

Feedback seeking can be accomplished in a variety of ways. Take Nadia, whom you'll recall we met in chapter 4. Eager to learn and grow, she knows that she does not always see her own weaknesses clearly. Luckily, she has

THE POWER OF FLEXING

an ally: her husband. "Duncan" will sometimes nudge her when they are in public, sending a quiet signal that only Nadia understands: "Oops, you probably shouldn't have said that." After an important event—a meeting or presentation—Nadia and Duncan will often stay up late talking about what went well and what didn't. Duncan is like an extra set of eyes and ears, noticing little things that Nadia could have done better and that she can work on in advance of her next event.

When we interviewed Nadia, we asked her, "Is it hard to listen to a critique from Duncan?"

"Not really," she replied, "because I always ask for his feedback. And anyway, I know he is trying to help me. Although I admit that once or twice I've gotten a little teary and responded defensively to something he's told me. It's not always easy to think about your mistakes!"

We can all relate to Nadia's feelings. Feedback can be difficult to absorb, but we all know how important it is. Because others' subjective views matter, without feedback you won't learn much from an experience regarding your personal effectiveness, how your experiments are faring with this particular group, and how you're doing on your specific goal.

Other people know a lot about you. They see how you look and notice how you come across; they interpret your actions and pay attention to and interpret even small things, such as your voice inflection; and they get a holistic sense of how you show up—whether you are trustworthy, authentic, and approachable, for example. They often know a lot about you that you don't know yourself. The "It takes a village" reference in the chapter title is about the importance of this information. One of our interviewees used that exact expression to describe the value that he had come to see in getting feedback from others.

When you're doing something on your own, solely for yourself, you can decide what goals you want to shoot for and how you want to go about it, and you can evaluate your actions any way you wish. You can affirm your efforts and the results and go on with your life. Many of us do this daily as we sing in the shower—laughing at how good we sound and affirming our vocal skills. But if you're doing something more complex and doing it in a world where others are inherently involved in what you're doing (as opposed to being alone in the shower)—and if their subjective evaluations of your performance matter—it helps to have some signposts to ensure things are going as planned.

In short, to grow, you need feedback. Much of what professionals do in organizations and all of us do in life is subjectively evaluated; it is how others view you that matters. This reality makes understanding how you are seen by others critical. You may think you come across as warm or charismatic, but if you aren't seen that way, your effectiveness is impaired. You may think you've just articulated a very clear and inspiring direction for your team, but if you've confused the message or your actual presentation was lackluster, it won't have the effect you want. You may think you are a "tough love" leader, but if those around you see only the toughness or only the love, you will be less effective than you want to be. The only way you can know if any of these things are true is by seeking feedback: finding out from others around you how you are coming across.

Eric Marks, partner and director of human resources at Marks Paneth & Shron LLP (now retired), cites this as an important lesson learned over the years. He says: "When you're interacting with people, in a business setting or even in a personal environment, the value of what you bring to them is based on their perception, and you don't always know what they are taking from what you're doing. You don't know how they are evaluating what you're doing. Sometimes even the simplest thing that seems not to be important is extremely important."

His comment echoes the old axiom that we judge ourselves based on our intentions, while others judge us based on our actions.

To truly understand your impact on others, you need feedback. You need feedback for your long-term development and in the moment. Long term, you need to know where you are strong, where you have learning to do, and what that learning might be. Then you get there in steps as you learn from your experiences.

WHY FEEDBACK IS HARD TO GET

Feedback, then, is essential to your professional and personal growth. But it's not always easy to get it.

Some professionals get useful feedback from their annual performance reviews, but this is often problematic. Managers have come to dislike the review process for the burdens it lays on them each year and the modest effect it seems to have on employees' performance. Many organizations have come to find annual performance reviews so ineffective that a growing trend over the last decade has been to abandon them altogether.

Even in places where annual reviews continue to be used, their content is often of dubious value. Sometimes bosses and others are reluctant to give anything approaching negative feedback because doing so makes them feel uncomfortable. Some fear that criticism will make matters worse rather than better. Researchers have documented that the tendency to avoid giving negative feedback, even when it is accurate, is especially pronounced when the subordinate is female or a member of a minority group, often leading such employees to discount the validity of the good messages they receive.[1]

For example, one of our interviewees who is African American commented, "A lot of times what I find is that people expect a whole lot less of me as a woman and as an African American woman than I expect of myself. If I use their feedback as the 'manager,' it would often be less than what I'm capable of . . . The feedback will be 'Great! You did wonderful, you did wonderful,' because they expect so little." If this woman were to rely only on the feedback she gets from the annual performance review, she would not be pushed, and she would not learn what people actually thought of her work. To get that information, she needs to seek it out actively.

You also cannot rely on the annual performance review when what you need is more immediate feedback. For example, in specific situations in real time, you may need to know how your comments are landing, whether you are perceived as warm and/or competent, whether people think you are authentic or fake, whether you do some strange thing when you are anxious that undermines your effectiveness, and so on. And while you can often interpret feedback from observing your task success—you won the new account, the spreadsheet was completed on time, you received the promotion you sought—the more personal feedback you need most in order to learn and grow often doesn't come to you as easily. There also is no such thing as an annual performance review for many people whose most important growth is occurring outside of your company— for example, in their personal relationships, in professional or civic organizations, or in charitable or community work.

Across these situations, in companies or outside, politeness norms often prevent people from spontaneously giving you feedback. They may notice something about your behavior or a particular performance that might help you, but they worry about hurting your feelings, speaking inappropriately, or damaging their relationship with you, so they often won't tell you.

A final problem—perhaps the trickiest of all to address—is that we often don't realize when we need feedback . . . which means the times when we need it most may be the times when we fail to seek it.

University of Michigan social psychologist David Dunning documents this behavior in his description of what has come to be called the Dunning-Kruger effect: the tendency for people with below-average skills to overestimate their abilities. They think they are doing better at a wide variety of tasks than the objective data would indicate. In contrast, people with above-average skills tend to (slightly) underestimate their abilities—perhaps due to modesty, the desire to avoid complacency, or other factors.[2] David Dunning notes that "while other people might tell you small things such as that your fly is open or that you have a spot on your face, they won't tell you the big things and so you don't know what you don't know. So the jerk in the office doesn't get invited to the parties but doesn't know that he is not invited and doesn't know that he's turning people off—so he doesn't get a chance to improve."

In particular, Dunning and colleagues have found that people are better at self-measuring well-defined traits such as punctuality but poor at judging more complex traits of personal effectiveness such as leadership skill or sophistication.[3] And because we are unaware of the fact that we are misgauging our own skill levels, the problem is one of "unknown unknowns" that are almost impossible to solve without external help. After all, when you don't know what you don't know, you can't even determine what questions you ought to ask.

The Dunning-Kruger effect makes it hard for us to use feedback to flex. After all, if we don't even recognize that we have a problem, we won't attend to feedback cues or seek feedback from others about how to remedy the problem. We don't know what we don't know . . . and so we can't flex, because we don't even realize that flexing is desirable or necessary.

Failing to ask for feedback can have important consequences for people who want to improve their effectiveness over time. Seksom Suriyapa, the vice president of strategy and corporate development at Twitter, counts this as one of his most important lessons. As he puts it, "It wasn't until later in my career that I got the hang of the fact that to really be successful with any kind of work, you always have to be conscious of who your stakeholders are and to be constantly asking them: Are you being effective with them? Are you being effective with respect to what you're doing?" He concluded early on that asking for feedback was important, because "if you don't ask, you just don't get it."

TWO STRATEGIES FOR FEEDBACK SEEKING

As we've seen, useful feedback probably won't come to you spontaneously. Fortunately, there are strategies you can employ that will enable you to overcome the inherent difficulties in seeking feedback. The flex system proposes two ways of seeking feedback. One way is through the process known as *inquiry*: asking people for feedback formally, informally, directly, and sometimes indirectly—for example, by raising the topic of interest and hoping that the person you are talking to conveys something that you might use as feedback.

Inquiry is attractive because it seems so straightforward. Ed Koch, the iconic mayor of New York City, used to do this all the time. He would stand up before large crowds and bellow, "How'm I doin'?" To which the crowd would usually roar back, "You're doing great!" Koch would use the same question when encountering individual citizens on the street, in the subway, or at a town meeting, and would sometimes receive a less flattering response. In both cases this simple question-and-answer technique helped the mayor stay in touch with the pulse of public opinion regarding his policies.

While Mayor Koch may not have been seeking accurate feedback from the crowd—or receiving it, for that matter—his actions do suggest a straightforward way to get feedback: by simply asking for it. You can ask your boss how your speech went, your subordinates if you were clear in a particular meeting, or your peers whether your contribution to an interdependent project was effective.

Alternatively, you can simply pay more attention to the verbal or nonverbal actions and reactions of those around you. *Implicit feedback* is available to us all the time. We can monitor facial expressions while we talk to other people and interpret messages from others' behaviors. For example, if I'm teaching a large group and toward the middle of the session individuals start getting up and walking out to the bathroom, I take it as feedback that I've gone on too long and they need to break. There is feedback in the reactions of others to our stories, the looks exchanged between subordinates, the blank faces when you're trying to explain something, the nods of affirmation.

Jane Dutton, my faculty colleague who worried that her enthusiasm was often too forceful for other people, started noticing when the room turned silent after she spoke. Pondering why this happened, she often concluded, "Oh, man, I just overdid it again!" Monitoring these sorts of cues can often give you enough information to guide your behavior and make changes to be more effective.

In some cases, implicit feedback requires noticing things that *don't* happen—a bit like the famous clue of "the dog that didn't bark during the night," which the fictional detective Sherlock Holmes used to help unravel a mystery. (The fact that the watchdog didn't bark during the night when a valuable racehorse was stolen from the stable revealed that the criminal was not a stranger but someone well known to the dog. It turned out that the horse's trainer was the culprit.) If your flex goal is to improve your listening skills, implicit feedback might include the increased willingness of your colleagues to speak with you about problems, concerns, or disagreements they may have—or, more subtly, their continued reluctance to do so.

Executive coach Karin Stawarky, whom you met in an earlier chapter, has engaged in both of these strategies in her attempt to become a more present and impactful organizational consultant. When working with a roomful of employees as part of her client services, she would sometimes invite a colleague to attend and offer feedback. "One person in particular has known me for some time," Karin says, "so he has kind of seen the longitudinal view of me, which I value."

Karin also monitored for implicit feedback, paying particular attention to people's emotional reactions and the kind of engagement they seemed to be experiencing. She would look at whether people were "leaning into the conversation, or if they'd kind of checked out," and she would "viscerally sense what the energy feel is like and how it's shifting." She also noticed the extent to which workshop participants would repeat things she said, describing it as "the highest form of flattery, where they take something and repeat or redo it in new ways." She describes the elation she felt when this would happen: "Oh, they were really in that moment with me, and they've taken that and made that their own!"

This combination of feedback through inquiry and implicit feedback through monitoring helped Karin determine whether she was on track and what she needed to do differently to meet her goals.

David McCallum, the business school dean we introduced in chapter 2, uses a very explicit system for seeking feedback whenever he communicates with close friends and associates. It's a system called "the four parts of speech" that David has borrowed from the writings of William R. Torbert, author of the book *Action Inquiry: The Secret of Timely and Transforming Leadership*.[4] (Torbert happens to be a friend of David's.) Here's how David describes it:

> I use the four parts of speech in every communication that I engage in, by email or in a meeting or presentation. The four steps start with framing, which explains where I'm coming from and what I think we need to accomplish. The second step is advocating, which is saying what I'm thinking, feeling, suggesting, or planning. The third step is illustrating, in which I provide my rationale using an example or specific case. And in the fourth step, inquiry, I ask people for feedback. I ask, "Am I missing something? What's your perspective on this? If you were to do this differently, how would you do it?" That practice of inquiry, which

I've learned over the years, is incredibly valuable to me. When I ask for feedback in this way, I'm offering an invitation to my friends and colleagues to help me to learn and grow. Generally speaking, people are pretty responsive to it, and the results are beneficial to all of us.

THE FEEDBACK FALLACY AND OTHER BARRIERS TO FEEDBACK SEEKING

So while on the surface it may sound easy to simply ask for feedback more often, it is the receiving after you have asked that can be difficult. Although feedback is essential, it can also be painful. Consider a young professional named Ashlyee, who told me that she deliberately refrains from asking for feedback when she knows she's struggling with a particular task. "I don't want anyone else to know that I know I'm having trouble," she says. "That way, I figure I can buy some time to fix the problem. Or maybe I can make up for it by being phenomenal at something else." And even the brash Ed Koch stopped using his signature "How'm I doin'?" call when his popularity numbers began slipping in the polls.

Many people feel and behave like Ashlyee and Ed Koch. We avoid feedback because we want to protect our fragile egos. We avoid it in hopes of preserving the illusion that we are the only ones aware of our imperfections. And sometimes we avoid it because we fear that asking for feedback may make us appear weak, insecure, and unsure of ourselves. In the words of one young manager, "I worry about damaging the image of being an authority figure by asking for feedback." Many seasoned executives feel the same way.

Yet this last concern—that asking for feedback may damage your reputation—turns out to be largely unfounded. Call it the *feedback fallacy*. In a large-scale study of managers, those who sought feedback were actually seen as more effective managers by everyone surveyed: their bosses, their subordinates, and their peers. The positive effect was especially strong when managers showed themselves to be open to *negative* feedback. And in another study, bosses rated newcomers who sought feedback during their first three months on the job as better performers than their peers who did not.

So while seeking feedback may cause some temporary pain, it's better than the alternative—because getting feedback and learning from it will help you to be a better leader and colleague, and it will help you to be perceived that way, too.

Still, feedback seeking has its challenges. In fact, each form of feedback also comes with problems that must be overcome. The biggest problem with the implicit feedback gathered through monitoring is *misinterpretation*. Unspoken messages sent through body language and other subtle signals are easy to misunderstand. A favorite cartoon of mine shows a boss and his subordinates sitting around a conference table. The boss has a somber look on his face, and the thought bubbles of his staff members reflect their varying interpretations of his expression: one thinks, "He hates my idea," a second worries, "What did I do wrong?" while a third despairs, "I'm too old for this job!"

Meanwhile, a glance at the boss's thought bubble shows what he is really thinking: "Hmm, it looks as if we're running low on pencils."

I suspect that these kinds of misinterpretations are all too common. When we feel anxious about a presentation, we notice and respond to behaviors and expressions that we think reflect negative judgments about it. Conversely, when we feel great about a speech, we notice only the affirming cues from our audience.

One consultant acquaintance of mine recounted a time when he was doing a full-day workshop. Midmorning he happened to notice his main client looking at his watch. Inferring that he was being boring or too slow, the consultant began to amplify his gestures and talk faster.

Later, the client expressed puzzlement over the consultant's sudden change in behavior. "I did it because you looked at your watch!" the consultant responded.

"Oh, I was just checking to see if I still had time to eat a bagel without ruining my lunch," the client explained.

So using your observations to gain feedback clearly carries some risk of misinterpretation. However, directly asking for feedback through inquiry can involve the same risk, since the feedback given in response to a request is not always honest or complete. The problem is especially acute when hierarchy is involved. Subordinates often believe they need to tell their bosses what they think their bosses want to hear. Church members are likely to be reluctant to tell the pastor—a powerful authority figure—what they really think about the Sunday sermons. And bosses may hold back on giving honest negative feedback for fear of damaging a subordinate's motivation or self-confidence.

Finally, even when we're willing to accept feedback and the feedback we need is offered openly and honestly, the message doesn't always get through. Human nature is such that people often refuse to accept the feedback they receive, especially when it's largely negative.

One research study illustrates this point vividly. Subjects were asked to take a test that measured their level of emotional intelligence. Those who scored relatively low typically reacted in one of two ways: by saying either "This test is not accurate" or "Emotional intelligence isn't important anyway!" And here's the kicker: the participants were all offered a chance to buy a highly recommended self-help book on how to increase one's emotional intelligence. Of those who scored high, 65 percent bought the book. Of those who scored low—the ones presumably most in need of the book's advice—just 25 percent did so.

Clearly it takes more than just being exposed to feedback to achieve real growth.

OVERCOMING BARRIERS TO EFFECTIVE FEEDBACK SEEKING

Thankfully, there are ways you can adjust your approach to get around the various problems most people have with feedback. Let's start with some strategies you can use to make monitoring for implicit feedback more effective.

One thing you might do is to simply recognize that your own issues, anxieties, and preconceptions color your views. If you are worried about how things might be going, you will be especially attuned to negative reactions. If you think you "have this nailed," you might miss those reactions altogether. Simply recognizing this bias can help you to interpret what you are seeing more accurately.

You might also consider combining the monitoring strategy with the inquiry strategy. When you gather feedback through your own observations of people's responses, try following up by directly asking people for their views, thereby checking what you think you've seen and what you concluded from it. Research suggests that both strategies are necessary to clarify what you need to do and what you might do better. Using your own observations without asking for feedback can lead to inferential errors (you read things wrong), but relying on inquiry alone can also be problematic if others give you only the information they think you want to hear. Using both together provides a more complete picture.[5]

It is also smart to look for patterns. For example, when I'm teaching, if one person looks like he or she is falling asleep, it's probably that person. If many people look that way, it's probably me not doing a great job on that particular lesson. That's an example of observing a pattern.

Finally, you might ask someone else to observe along with you. If you worry that you have become somewhat of a long talker and have lost your effectiveness in leading meetings, have someone come and observe with that issue in mind.

There are also ways you can make gathering feedback through inquiry more effective. For example, if you make a conscious effort to help the person you are speaking with feel more comfortable giving you feedback, you will probably receive more useful and accurate information. One of the leaders we interviewed described how an executive at YouTube added a line to his email signature that read: "How's my driving?" When an email recipient clicked on it, a little poll popped up inviting anonymous feedback. You could type in anything you liked—for example, "I think you are doing a great job at explaining company strategy, but I think you suck at persuading me that it matters." The email signature device was a clever one, but, more important, it told all of his correspondents in no certain terms that the executive who'd sent the email really wanted feedback—good or bad.

Always be thoughtful about how and when you ask for feedback. A strategy that is difficult to pull off is asking a group in a public meeting (and having them feel comfortable answering you honestly) versus asking a single individual in a private conversation. The latter setting will likely provide you with a very different and probably more accurate reaction.

Also consider finding a way to solicit feedback anonymously, as the YouTube executive did. A growing number of companies are providing supports for soliciting anonymous feedback. Software firms such as Kaizen (https://kaizen.app) are creating tools that allow people to own their feedback seeking and work it into the flow of their day. Kaizen was founded on a belief that is central to the Power of Flexing: that individuals, not just organizations, can own their professional growth. It created an app that you control, linked to your calendar, allowing you to automatically send an email seeking feedback immediately after meetings, product shipments, or project milestones. The app can be set up to measure how well you're practicing the company's values and share the results with the human resources department. Alternatively, you can identify personalized growth areas and seek feedback strictly for your own use.[6]

The way you couch your feedback inquiry can also make a significant difference. If you ask for feedback in person, you may want to begin with a self-deprecating remark or an expression of vulnerability, phrased in a way that fits your personality and style. (For some people, humor may fit better; for others, a more serious approach feels more comfortable and comes across as more authentic.) This kind of opening will communicate your openness to honest feedback, whether positive or negative.

You might also try framing your request by asking for what executive coach Marshall Goldsmith calls *feedforward*: advice about how you can do something better in the future rather than an evaluation of how well you've done in the past. For example, you could tell a colleague about something you are working to improve—being a better listener, eliciting varied opinions, answering questions succinctly—and ask, "What would you suggest I try that could help me achieve this goal?" The future framing reduces the judgmental edge from the conversation and may help make it more comfortable for both parties.

Marc Ingram, the financial analyst for the big-city public school system who was introduced earlier, likes to seek feedback by asking people, "If you were in my shoes, what would you do differently?" He feels this wording allows people to give him feedback in a less direct way, which makes them more willing to provide it. Another manager decided to make feedback seeking into a routine part of her team's schedule. During every Monday morning staff meeting, she requested feedback on her behavior during the previous week. Over time, people became desensitized to the practice of giving feedback through sheer familiarity, which made it easier for them to be open and honest.

Perhaps most important, remember to maintain your learning mindset as you gather feedback. Executive coach Karin Stawarky has noticed how much more effective her own feedback seeking has become now that a learning mindset has become habitual for her. "My focus before was internal," she says. "I put a lot of pressure on myself, asking, 'What am I

going to say next? What am I supposed to do? What was on my script?'
Now I'm able to direct my energy externally, which means I can observe
and respond to what other people are doing and saying rather than focusing inwardly."

Bing Chen, a venture capital executive who helped architect the
multibillion-dollar YouTube creator ecosystem, stays positive about feedback by remembering what his mom taught him: "If people give you constructive feedback, it means they respect you so much that they want
you to get better. When they stop giving you feedback, that's when you
have to worry, because it often means they no longer care about you."

The more you can maintain the kind of learning mindset that Karin
and Bing exemplify, the more open and attentive you can be to other
people's insights. Brené Brown describes this as a move from "proving
and perfecting" to "stretching and learning." The more you can make and
maintain this shift, the more you can benefit and learn.[7]

PROMPTING A FEEDBACK-SEEKING CULTURE

Feedback seeking is a social activity. It involves interactions among two or
more people, and therefore it inevitably reflects the organizational culture in which it takes place: communication patterns, power relationships, and other norms. If you work in an organization where feedback
seeking is rare or even discouraged, it will be harder for you to engage
others to give and receive feedback comfortably.

By contrast, an organization where feedback is facilitated, encouraged, and rewarded is one where learning and growth are habitual. One
executive describes the atmosphere in this kind of organization this way:

> Of course, you do lots of 360 reviews, getting comments on your
> performance from people you work with at all levels. And those
> are helpful. But they're nowhere near as helpful as building a

culture where your peers, your board members, and your boss all feel completely comfortable giving you feedback in real time. So when you're running a meeting that is going off the rails, they don't even wait for the meeting to end. They immediately shoot you the look that says, "Hey, you are screwing this up!" And that gives you a chance to fix the problem immediately.

Maggie Bayless, the leader in the story I introduced at the very start of this book, is fortunate. The company she cofounded and now leads is one whose culture is richly supportive of the feedback process. Maggie and her team members are comfortable speaking openly about what happens on the job, offering one another advice, support, and, when necessary, constructive criticism.

In the months after Maggie took over the management reins of the company, she took full advantage of this existing culture to jump-start the growth she needed. She arranged feedback sessions with a wide range of people who knew her work style and could evaluate her strengths and weaknesses, including the other members of the partners' group and the staff members who reported to her. In some cases she asked open-ended questions seeking any and all sorts of feedback about how she could enhance her personal effectiveness and her leadership skills—for example, "Is there anything I could be doing to help your job go better?" In other cases she focused her questions on specific flex goals or challenges—for example, "In yesterday's meeting, something I said seemed to shut down the discussion. What could I have said differently that would have made you feel more comfortable and made it easier for us to continue our conversation?"

Notice the nature of Maggie's question here. She didn't ask, "Did I make you uncomfortable?"—a question that could be answered with a simple yes or no. Instead, she used an open-ended question—"What could I have said differently?"—which invited the person to think a bit more deeply and share more of their impressions.

Maggie's willingness to ask questions like these—and the fact that her team members see feedback as a natural part of business life—greatly enhanced the spirit of open communication needed to accelerate her learning.

If you, like Maggie Bayless, are part of an organization with a traditional culture of feedback seeking, you're lucky. Unfortunately, many of us aren't. It's possible, however, for well-meaning people to change the culture of a group to enable more feedback exchange. For example, in an organization, top-level managers can encourage the creation of a feedback culture by emulating Ed Koch and asking those around them with some sincerity how they are doing. Michael Dell, founder and CEO of Dell Technologies, is one such manager. He regularly seeks feedback from customers and employees and is known for doing so. His company has also instituted a "Tell Dell" survey that asks employees to give feedback on their bosses every six months. When the head of the company, the head minister in a church, or the director of a nonprofit models feedback seeking as Michael Dell has done, it has an impact on those down the line. As the feedback-seeking behavior of the organization's top executives begins to influence mid-level managers, a sense of psychological safety begins to pervade the organization—the shared, tacit, belief that interpersonal risk taking is permitted and will be rewarded. This leads to more feedback seeking by employees at all levels.

Companies can also encourage feedback seeking by amping up the provision of training and education to employees. Feedback seeking is a rich-get-richer phenomenon: research shows that people who believe they have all the ability they need to do their jobs well are more likely to seek feedback from others, while those who doubt their ability—and therefore probably need feedback the most—are much more reluctant to seek feedback.[8] Thus, the more skills managers give their employees and the greater the sense of belief they convey about their employees' ability,

the more comfortable those employees will be with seeking feedback and the more they're likely to grow in the future.

In addition to enhancing the general skill level of employees, managers often need to train them explicitly on feedback giving and receiving itself. Chris Murchison, the former vice president of strategy and culture at HopeLab, whom we met in an earlier chapter, certainly found this to be true. He thought employees in his small, mission-oriented nonprofit with its strong organizational culture would have no problem delivering and receiving feedback. But he was wrong. Instead, he discovered that their feeling of being part of an organizational family heightened the fear and anxiety associated with feedback. In a sense, they were way too nice to be honest with one another!

To remedy this problem, Chris tried out a variety of experiments to improve the ability of HopeLab's people to have candid conversations with one another. First he offered the staff multiple group opportunities to reflect honestly on their personal experiences with feedback giving and receiving, including times when it had gone well and not so well. He then went on to create optional informal study gatherings where staff could learn more about various perspectives and practices regarding feedback from a variety of guest speakers, including me discussing the Power of Flexing. He encouraged each employee to write a learning plan reflecting on personal strengths and areas of growth. The plan included a process for seeking feedback from managers and others to identify the employee's most important growth goals.

In addition to these steps, Chris worked to enhance the quality of meetings between supervisors and their direct reports, as well as offering employees the opportunity for skip-level meetings in which their boss's boss could participate in the employee's learning.

As a final step, Chris brought in associates of Douglas Stone and Sheila Heen, two Harvard Law School professors who authored the book *Thanks for the Feedback: The Science and Art of Receiving Feedback Well,* for an all-staff learning retreat to further enhance the staff's feedback skills.[9]

You may not choose to go as far as Chris Murchison did in his efforts to create a feedback culture. But the variety of tactics Chris tried offer some great ideas for anyone who wants to push their organizational culture in this direction. And if you are not the CEO of your organization but rather a mid-level manager with a limited sphere of influence, you can use some of the same techniques on a smaller scale. You may be able to gradually turn your department into a model of feedback-seeking culture that may even begin to influence other parts of the organization.

Once you've made feedback seeking a natural part of your organizational life, employees at every level will begin to benefit from it.

Lisa Dawe was an up-and-coming manager in DaVita, a health care company that delivers dialysis services to patients with renal disease and chronic kidney failure. Lisa and several other managers at her level were invited to a retreat with executives from the top levels of the firm. To her surprise, after dinner on the first night, the high-potential junior managers were divided into teams and asked to prepare a case for presentation to the top management group the next day. When Lisa and her team made their presentation, it was harshly criticized by one of the senior executives. Lisa pushed back, defending their work.

Later that evening another senior executive blindsided Lisa with the feedback that she had acted inappropriately. According to this executive, Lisa should have listened, accepted the feedback, and refrained from defending her team.

Lisa was taken aback. Had she done something seriously wrong? Had she failed an unexpected test? Did she even have what it takes to play in the "big leagues"?

Lisa might have been tempted to shut down during the rest of the retreat, licking her wounds. Instead she decided to seek feedback from others about her actions. During the next couple of days she found occasions to engage several executives in conversation. She described her thoughts about what had happened and asked them for their perceptions of her behavior and suggestions for what she should do differently. She received a range of feedback and also got understanding from others along the lines of "You know . . . there're bumps in the road," "Don't worry about it," and "Here's one thing you might want to think about for the next time . . ." A painful and embarrassing incident had been transformed into a learning experience.

A year later—much earlier than she'd expected—Lisa received a promotion. When congratulating her, several executives mentioned the retreat and her handling of the controversy. She'd demonstrated the ability to learn the skills needed to handle adversity at the highest level of corporate life.[10]

Feedback seeking isn't important only for aspiring managers. It can be just as valuable for leaders who have already reached the top of the corporate ladder.

I recently invited a widely respected CEO to speak to 450 new MBA students at the Ross School of Business. He did a great job. But then he did something that no other speaker I've invited has ever done, before or since: he emailed me to request feedback on his performance.

I gave the CEO a few general reactions to his speech, mostly very positive. But I did offer a couple of negatives, including pointing out that most MBA students starting their study at a top B-school aren't particularly pleased to hear a rival program referenced so explicitly and so frequently in an opening speech. (The CEO had referred to the Harvard Business School a number of times in his address.)

The CEO wrote back immediately, thanking me for my feedback and admitting that mentioning Harvard repeatedly had been a mistake. He then surprised me with this conclusion: "I have copied other company execs, who will help me make sure I make these changes in the future! As well as my kids, so they will know I added some value, but have lots of room for improvement."

I mean, seriously, what CEO does that: shares the feedback he receives with his fellow executives *and* with his kids?!

But the last and biggest surprise of all was yet to come. The CEO ended up addressing students from several other MBA programs that year. At the end of the year he wrote me to say his speeches had improved based on my feedback—and to assure me that he'd never mentioned Harvard Business School even once!

By now you may be wondering about the identity of this CEO who takes the power of feedback so seriously. His name is Kent Thiry, and at the time he was the CEO of DaVita, the kidney care company where Lisa Dawe was promoted, in part because of her readiness to learn and grow through the benefit of feedback.

It seems clear that Kent created a company culture of feedback seeking at DaVita—thanks in part to enthusiastic support and encouragement from the top down.

NO MATTER WHAT KIND of work you do or what kind of organization you belong to, you have a number of stakeholders whose support is important to you. Feedback seeking is one of the best ways to manage stakeholders effectively and to get the information from them that you need. Getting feedback can be tricky and sometimes painful, but the payoff it provides is very clear. As you apply the Power of Flexing to your work and life experiences, feedback from others will help you discern which experiments are working, which ones are not, where to invest your efforts in the future, and how you can best continue to grow and learn.

CHAPTER 6

WRINGING MEANING FROM EXPERIENCE

Systematic Reflection for Long-Term Gain

When I served as the senior associate dean at the Ross School of Business, I occasionally fielded requests to review programs for other schools as part of their effort to obtain or renew their accreditation by our official industry group, the Association to Advance Collegiate Schools of Business (AACSB).

I passed one such request off to the chair of our accounting department and an accounting faculty member. Aware of how busy these individuals are, I accompanied the request with an email saying, "Please review this department at University X. Don't take any time on it, it's not that important, I just need a few comments."

The powerful chair of our accounting department sent an email in reply that was terse, resentful—and eye-opening: "Sue, it's very demotivating when someone asks you to do something and then tells you it's not important! Plus, given all the accounting scandals going on right now, asking an accountant to certify something and telling them not to spend any time on it is offensive."

I was taken aback. It's certainly not typical for a faculty member to explode in anger in response to a request from a dean. Deeply shaken, I stopped and reflected on what had happened, what role I'd played in it, and what lesson I should take from it.

This was an unusual step for me to take, because my days, like the days of most managers, were crowded with professional demands, while my nights and weekends were devoted to three kids and a husband who all needed my attention. I told myself I had no time for reflection. But reflection is a crucial process for anyone who really wants to learn from their experiences.

Our experiences give us a lot to think about. Some of our most important takeaways about who we are, what we are good at, and what we value come from gigantic crises in our lives—major transitions, spectacular failures, or preoccupying disasters. Other times, big lessons come from momentary or passing events like mine. But in both cases they only come through thoughtful consideration of what happened and its meaning for you. That's why *systematic reflection* is the sixth step in the Power of Flexing.

Through systematic reflection, would-be learners examine their experiences and synthesize takeaways for the future. When you engage in reflection, you need to look back on what has happened and consider questions such as: *"Did I make progress toward my current flex goal? Why or why not?" "What feedback did I receive or observe? What should I make of that feedback?" "Do I need to continue to work on that goal for my next experience—perhaps engaging in new and different experiments—or do I need to set a new goal to capture what they most need to learn next?"* It's systematic in that questions like these have you examining many different aspects of your situation and your behavior in it.

Such questions can lead to new insights and learning. Yet, despite its value, reflection does not come naturally or automatically to most of us, as my own example makes all too clear. And without systematic reflection, experiences simply pass by, resulting in little or no learning. I'll return to my experience with the accounting department chair later in this chapter. But first, let's consider why so many people—like me—find it challenging to engage in systematic reflection.

OUR REFLECTION RELUCTANCE

Unfortunately, most people shy away from systematic reflection. They tend to put it off or to give it short shrift when they do engage in reflection. In fact, research shows that people tend to dislike reflection and even fear it. Most people seem to find it uncomfortable to spend time alone with their thoughts and feelings. In fact, some argue that the busyness many people complain about is, in part, an unconscious strategy used to avoid spending time in reflection.

This tendency is so prevalent that John W. Gardner, the well-known leadership scholar and founder of Common Cause, says, "Human beings have always employed an enormous number of clever devices for running away from themselves."[1] Gardner goes on to list many of the distractions people use to avoid probing what he calls "the fearful and wonderful world within" and concludes that, "by middle life, most of us are accomplished fugitives from ourselves."

Gardner is right. While we might say, echoing the famous dictum of Socrates, that the unexamined life is not worth living, modern humans seem to prefer action to reflection. We rush around from one thing to another, having convinced ourselves that the world requires us to do just that. Studies describing managers as maintaining a frenetic pace of problem solving, firefighting, and crisis management show this pattern. They think of reflection as something that, regrettably, there is just no time to do. In the words of poet and organizational thinker David Whyte, "Speed has become our core competency, our core identity." As a result, Whyte says, we "stay well away from our pains and vulnerabilities"—the same pains and vulnerabilities that could be a major source of growth.[2]

Jerry Colonna, an executive coach and author of the leadership book *Reboot: Leadership and the Art of Growing Up,* has observed the same phenomenon. Rushing around has become so habitual for many of us that it is deeply ingrained in our self-image. As Colonna puts it, "Success and money—and even more important, the busyness needed to create those—become proof of my worth as a human."[3]

Science confirms the widespread reluctance to reflect. One study asked a group of participants: Would you rather spend fifteen minutes alone with your thoughts and feelings . . . or receive an electric shock from a nine-volt battery? Fully 67 percent of men and 54 percent of women chose to zap themselves rather than be alone with their thoughts. On average, people chose to receive three shocks over the study period. And one man jolted himself 190 times! This is a man who *really* doesn't like being alone with his thoughts and feelings!

In another recent study, participants were asked to undertake a task that required some strategy and would involve several rounds of activity. After round one, participants were given a choice: either to spend some discretionary time practicing the task or to reflect on what they'd done, examining what had worked and what hadn't. The results were clear: participants were more than four times as likely to choose practice over reflection. Somehow, redoubling their work efforts appeared more appealing and useful than pausing to think things through.

A number of the thoughtful people and business leaders we've interviewed have observed the same pattern in themselves and their colleagues. Ari Weinzweig, founder and CEO of the iconic Ann Arbor food company Zingerman's and whom we met in chapter 3, comments, "No one in business would say, 'We never think about what we've done; we just keep going.' But that's what we do. We're simply not trained to do reflection." Similarly, veteran entrepreneur Michelle Crumm told us, "Reflection takes time, and people are so used to charging ahead that they forget that reflection is just one of those things that you have to do to become better." Ari often quotes the twentieth-century philosopher Rollo May, who perhaps said it best: "It is an ironic habit of human beings to run faster when they have lost their way."[4]

Jane Dutton, the award-winning academic we met earlier, noted this same tendency throughout her career. Avoidance kept her anxiety about being an inadequate mom to her two daughters at bay. As she put it, "I kept so busy, I didn't want the pain of it during the day. That's a lot of pain—just a realization that I feel deep regret, shame, sadness, and grief about not being there [with them]." It was only when she retired that Dutton really reflected on and confronted this pain and took steps to be more present and available to her daughters. Dutton views this new chapter in her life as a chance to "make peace with not growing [in the past]" and seek some sort of redemption.

Like Jane Dutton, many people put off reflecting until they reach a turning point in their lives. Researchers Adam Alter and Hal Hershfield found that people are more likely to examine their lives for meaning— and to engage in more meaning-seeking behaviors—in a year preceding the start of a new decade of life—for example, during the year before their fiftieth birthday. Striking evidence of this "fresh-start effect": among first-time marathon runners, those who had ages that ended in 9 were overrepresented by 48 percent![5]

Reflection is a powerful practice whenever you do it. My goal in this chapter is to persuade you to engage in it on a much more regular basis.

REFLECTION'S PAYOFF

Michelle Crumm is right: reflection is an essential component of learning. The study we mentioned above, in which participants were four times as likely to prefer additional practice rather than reflection, also found that participants who did choose to reflect outperformed those who chose more practice. Apparently, something occurs during reflection that enhances subsequent performance.

Reflection is particularly valuable when it comes to developing the complex, personal skills that are the focus of the flex system. It's a wonderful tool that is fully under your control; all you have to do is commit the time and energy to reflection, and you can begin to reap the benefits it offers.

Again, experimental research bears out this pattern. A team of experts investigated the use of six emotion-regulation strategies using an experience-sampling methodology. They found that reflection was one of the more powerful strategies, associated with increases in positive emotions, especially among women.[6]

In another study, an entering cohort of MBA students was required to go through a set of experiences over their first year designed to help them grow their leadership. They also got together in small groups to discuss those experiences. Half of these groups were instructed to reflect on their experiences systematically using a specific template for doing so, while the other half were told simply to chat about their year. At the end of the first year, trained observers rated individuals in the systematic reflection groups as showing greater leadership and having more leadership potential than those in the casual discussion groups. And when companies came to campus to recruit students for internships, the reflection students received 9 percent more offers and 10 percent higher starting salaries.[7] Apparently, reflection helped these students not only to lead more but also to tell a better story about their learning in the program.

We experienced similar positive results from reflection among the sample of MBA students at the Ross School of Business working full-time on group consulting projects that lasted seven weeks. One issue that is often contentious in groups like these is who will lead and who will follow, since there is no assigned boss and all the students are peers. To see if reflection enabled individuals to better emerge as leaders, we asked at about the midpoint of their seven-week consulting stints how much they had been reflecting on four topics: the goals the group was pursuing, the methods they were using, their individual relationships within the team, and how they themselves were impacting what was happening. When we checked in with our student consultants again at the project's end, we found that students who reported engaging in this kind of systematic reflection were more likely to be seen as leaders by their teammates. Reflection allowed them to assess what the group was doing, what might be needed, and how they might best offer it.

Novelist and essayist Aldous Huxley famously said, "Experience is not what happens to you; it's what you do with what happens to you."[8] Reflecting on your experience can make "what happens to you" into a source of learning and growth.

STRUCTURING TIME FOR REFLECTION

The U.S. military uses one of the most rigorously structured forms of reflection, the *after-action review*. After every operation, exercise, mission, or sortie, members of groups and units meet together to systematically discuss what worked and didn't work. Transparency and honesty are insisted upon, and high-ranking officers are expected to talk about whether the orders that they issued were ill conceived or poorly planned. Decades of experience in learning from after-action reviews is one of the main reasons American military leaders pride themselves on running one of the world's foremost learning organizations.

While most of us will never be quite this rigorous, we can all become more systematic in how we reflect on our daily experiences. There are many ways to engage in systematic reflection, and experienced leaders often make use of several of them, depending on how their lives and work are structured as well as the ways their minds happen to work.

Set aside regular time for thinking about and evaluating the successes and failures of your day.

One approach is to adopt the practice we encouraged the MBA students at the Ross School of Business to employ: following important or perplexing experiences in your work life and spending some time reflecting systematically on what occurred. This can enhance your own understanding of yourself and the challenges you face as well as your ability to communicate your understanding to others. For experiences that extend over a longer period—say, a troublesome relationship, a challenging work assignment, a special project, or a complex task—there is also value in reflecting during the event.

Building a brief, regular period for reflection into your daily schedule, just as you may try to set aside time for exercise, is an ideal way to make it a familiar habit. Diana Tremblay, who has nearly forty years of manufacturing experience and is the former vice president of global business services at General Motors, uses her hour-long daily commute to think about what she calls "the goods and bads of the day." Anders Jones, the fintech start-up CEO we met in chapter 3, reports that he reflects most often during his morning shower. The process often yields good insights, but he has learned not to say to folks, "I was thinking of you in the shower this morning!"

Executive coach Karin Stawarky works hard to create a space after specific experiences to think about what just happened. Her reflection practice often begins with a quick energy check as she leaves the room after a presentation: "I read my body and read my mind, asking questions like, 'How do I feel? Am I wound up? Am I really excited? Am I at ease? Am I at peace? How did today's session make me feel?'"

While not as systematic as the reflections tested in research, these post-experience questions have the advantage of being quick and very focused on her learning goal, which was to teach with greater energy than in the past. The immediate, active, and almost joyful character of her reflection is very consistent with the Power of Flexing. The process of trying something and then thinking about how it went before trying again or trying something new is the heart and the power of flexing. Your development lies in your hands: you can always try new things and see what you might take from them to improve some aspect of your behavior over time.

Also note that, in her daily reflections, Karin pays particular attention to her more extreme emotions. If she is feeling super-excited, it gives her a clue that something happened that she is particularly passionate about. She uses that emotion to stimulate further reflection, asking herself what happened there. "I need to chase that down to figure it out," Karin says, "because that, for me, is the kernel of an idea that's just popped up."

By contrast, if Karin is feeling tired walking out of the room, it means that something in the experience was hard or challenging for her. She then reflects on the causes and implications of that feeling: "Was it me in the conversation, or was it the room? Is there anything I could have done to shift or change the atmosphere?" Reflections like these often provide Karin with insights she can use to make her next presentation better.

Megan Furman, the IT professional at the Department of Defense, described having a long-standing process similar to Karin's. But as she learned about the Power of Flexing, she decided to change her process to be more focused on the learning goals she had set. In other words, she decided that she wanted to shift her reflection question from "How did that situation go?" to "How much progress did I make toward the goal I set for myself in that situation?" The specific questions you'll ask yourself will depend on the learning goals you're pursuing, the nature of the experiments you're conducting, and the insights you aim to develop. What matters is that you dedicate time and energy to look back at your experiences and to examine what they have to teach you.

Keep a journal, notebook, or diary in which you record the events of the day and your intellectual and emotional responses to them.

Many people find that the discipline of writing down their thoughts, feelings, and reactions to the experiences of the day is a particularly valuable way to reflect.

Shishir Mehrotra is a Silicon Valley entrepreneur on the fast track to success. Just thirty-nine years old, he has already parlayed his training in math and engineering into leadership stints at several of the biggest and most innovative digital powerhouses in the world. More recently, he used his knowledge, creativity, and connections to launch his own new software company, whose initial products are already generating significant buzz in the industry. Mehrotra is also an enthusiastic practitioner of systematic reflection, and he has developed a number of tools and techniques for reflection that he enjoys using. One method Mehrotra likes is writing in what he calls his *reflection journal*, which he uses to capture thoughts about a challenge or problem he is wrestling with.

"I often write in my journal while on vacation or when I'm taking a plane flight during a business trip," Mehrotra says. "I'll think of something that has been bothering me—for example, 'I keep leaving meetings with an uncomfortable feeling,' or 'I wake up every morning feeling stressed because I went to bed last night with my email box full of unanswered messages.' Once I've identified the problem, I just start jotting random reactions, thoughts, and observations about it. Very often, the germ of a solution starts to emerge this way—not usually the first day I write about it, but after a number of days or weeks. That's one reason I like to keep my reflection journal with me at all times—so I can return to it and learn from it whenever I have a few minutes to spare."

Ari Weinzweig, the Zingerman's CEO, has kept a journal for over thirty years. He spends twenty to thirty minutes every morning writing about whatever is on his mind and he finds that, if he skips his morning journaling, it throws him off for the day. "I'd rather get up a little earlier to have time to write," he says, "because it makes my day better. I don't meditate, but, for me, journaling is like that—just like doing yoga for your mind." Weinzweig also appreciates the simplicity of journaling: "The cost is very low, basically zero. You need just paper and pen—or your phone and your thumbs."

Laura Blake Jones, the dean of students at the University of Michigan, says that she reflects best "with a pen and paper, and thinking in writing," although she doesn't engage in daily journaling. Instead she keeps a written set of goals, mapping what she is trying to do in her life and work, and pulls it out whenever she has a long plane ride scheduled. She uses that quiet downtime, without phone calls or emails to respond to, to review her goals, reflecting on her progress and making notes to herself. This periodic practice of written reflection supplements Jones's regular Sunday evening habit of looking back at the previous week and asking "What are the areas that I didn't get to, and what is this next week bringing?"

"Scott Brown," who heads a think tank after both military and government service, keeps what he calls a "decision journal," which allows reflection over an even longer span of time. In this journal, Brown captures the choices that he makes and the reasons behind them. The journal allows him to go back in six months, look at his rationale, and reflect: "In hindsight, did I make the right choice? Were my assumptions correct? Was my decision-making process adequate?"

For these professionals, reflection is done best via some form of writing—brief or extended, formal or informal, frequent or sporadic. But writing isn't the only way to reflect.

Schedule regular, purposeful conversations about your flexing experiments with a friend, mentor, coach, or support group.

Some people feel drawn to processing experiences interpersonally rather than on their own. When asked how she learns from the experiences she's gone through, Jane Dutton's immediate answer is "Well, I do a lot of reflecting with friends." She speaks for many people who engage in what you might call *person-to-person reflection*—talking with others about the things they are learning or striving to master.

Involving a second person in the act of reflection energizes the process by creating a sense of accountability, forcing a deeper engagement. A young professional named Tommy Wydra ended up building in just this kind of accountability when he involved his entire cohort of financial professionals in the Power of Flexing. Wydra had explained the flexing concept to his colleagues in the finance development program at the University of Michigan's medical school, and they immediately sensed its potential value. They also quickly realized that they needed what they called "accountability partners" to make sure that they followed through on the process, particularly when it came to reflection. As Tommy puts it, "No matter how much I want to do it by myself, the hecticness of the workday can get in the way. So when I have that time on the calendar to debrief with a partner, I know that I really need to carve out some time to think about how my different experiments have been working and what I might want to do differently."

Marshall Goldsmith, an eminent executive coach, practices person-to-person reflection using a different technique. During a nightly phone call, he has a friend ask him a set of questions that Marshall previously wrote for himself. Then Marshall asks the friend a set of questions that his friend wrote for himself. This simple process keeps both parties focused on the life areas in which they want to grow. It also introduces some accountability for tackling those challenges.

If you find the idea of a nightly phone call a bit extreme, consider how you might adapt the idea to your own lifestyle. Maybe it's a weekly chat with a peer at work or a spouse at home. The Ross School of Business incorporated this idea into its executive MBA program, setting aside ten minutes at each monthly residency for students to meet up with a partner and ask each other their chosen reflection questions. The goal was to keep a focus on personal development while they also coped with the busyness of their MBA program (not to mention their family lives, executive positions, community activities, and other commitments).

Teach others about what you've learned.

The entrepreneur Shishir Mehrotra says, "Whenever anyone asks me to give a talk or take part in an interview, I always try to say yes, because I find that being forced to talk about what I am doing—and explain it—always teaches me something new. I also find that teaching a class about something I've learned is a great way to reflect on my knowledge, deepen my understanding, and develop new insights. That's why I've created a system at my company where our team members take turns teaching portions of the new employee orientation program. By having everyone serve as the instructor for the various parts of the program, I make sure that all of us have a crisp, accurate understanding of the details of how our company works. There's no better way to keep learning than to start teaching."

As you can see, there are a variety of ways to make reflection part of your life routine. Experiment with different approaches to reflection until you find one that works for you, and feel free to modify it as changes in your life require. Most important, if you really want to engage in reflection on an ongoing basis, then you need to set up a structure to enable and support it. For example, Scott Brown suggests that, when you schedule some important event—a major presentation or meeting, a difficult

REFLECTION BEST PRACTICES

TO UNDERSTAND PROGRESS ON YOUR LEARNING GOAL

Following an important experience, consider three sets of questions:

1. What happened and what was the outcome?
   a. What part of this would a video camera recording the scene have captured and what am I adding in based on my biases and anxiety?
   b. Did I try any of the experiments that I outlined for making progress on this goal?
      i. If not, why not?
      ii. What obstacles held me back? (Consider both situational obstacles and internal obstacles such as fear, anxiety, or ego.)
   c. Did I seek feedback in this situation as I intended—either by observing reactions or by directly asking others for feedback?
      i. If not, why not?
      ii. If yes, what did the feedback tell me about how I am doing on my goal?
   d. What positive and negative outcomes were created for me in this experience? What positive and negative outcomes were created for others?

2. Why did things go the way that they went?
   a. In what way did I contribute (positively or negatively) to what occurred?

3. What lessons do I distill from this experience?
   a. What are the most important takeaways about me?
   b. What do I take away about situations like this?
   c. What do I conclude about my learning goal?
      i. I still need to make progress. Should I keep it as a focus in future experiences?
      ii. I feel more settled about this goal. Should I perhaps adopt another?

conversation or a project kickoff—you should also schedule time to engage in reflection on the event. Habits like this will help you overcome the human tendency to avoid reflection and thereby fail to enjoy the benefits it can bring.

TOPICS FOR REFLECTION

As we've seen, reflection can be performed in a number of ways: through inner reflection, through private writing or journaling, through purposeful conversations, or through teaching others about the lessons you've learned. But sometimes the biggest challenge is not figuring out *how to reflect* but rather deciding *what to reflect on*. Here are some helpful suggestions from the business professionals we've interviewed. Again, we urge you to experiment with each of these approaches to discover which work best for you.

Analyze the Details of a Specific Experience

One good guide for reflection after an event involves three steps: getting clear on what actually happened; considering causes; and distilling the lessons learned. This process can be useful when you've experienced something important, for either good or ill—for instance, a troubling setback at work, an unexpected opportunity, or a confusing misunderstanding.

The first step challenges you to separate what actually occurred (for example, as a video camera might have recorded it) from your personal perceptions, which may be biased because of anxieties, desires, or a distorted mindset. In the context of flexing, you may want to ask yourself such questions as "Did I try any of the experiments that I've outlined for making progress on a personal goal? If not, why not? Did I seek feedback from others? If not, why not? If I did, what did the feedback tell me? And what outcomes, positive and negative, were created for me and for others?"

The second step involves examining cause and effect by asking questions like "Why did things unfold as they did? What role did you play in the event? What other factors influenced what occurred? For example, what role was played by the social or business context? By the actions of other people? By the availability or lack of resources?"

The final step calls for you to think about the takeaways from the experience. What lessons have you learned about yourself or about situations like this one? This step should also involve a consideration of the event in the context of your current learning goal. What progress have you made? Should you retain this goal for upcoming experiences, or is it time to move on to a new learning goal? Is a new learning goal suggested by what happened in this experience?[9]

This three-step reflection process can help you make the most of the potential growth that may be hiding within a particular experience.

Reflect on the Positive Things in Your Life

Eric Marks, whom we met in the last chapter, has more than twenty years of executive management experience. He uses his morning drive time to reflect with a very specific focus—namely, to think about and name the blessings in his life. The goal is to put his current work situations in perspective, allowing him to see that, no matter how challenging the changes he is going through may be, there is a lot of good that has come from the conditions he is coping with. Keeping a conscious focus on the positive elements of a situation and experience can build optimism and efficacy for taking subsequent action.

One serial entrepreneur-engineer, "Gavin Nielsen," also starts the day with a focus on what he's especially grateful for. It might be a moment of connection or success, a time when his creativity was particularly expressed, or one when he experienced joy in his work. He then moves on to reflecting on what didn't go so well, on times when he felt regret, on moments when he wishes he'd done something different, and times when he got in his own way. Nielsen ends his reflection by looking at the hours left in the day and setting an intention regarding how he wants to act differently moving forward. Nielsen's reflection takes him just fifteen minutes a day, but he covers a lot of ground!

Lindy Greer, the new head of the Sanger Leadership Institute at the University of Michigan, also covers ground in her systematic reflection exercise. It's easy to remember, as it's based on the six vowels in the alphabet: *A, E, I, O, U,* and *Y.* Each letter represents something important about your day. *A* is what did you Abstain from?—particularly something numbing or unhealthy, like mindless TV, social media, or excessive alcohol. *E* is Exercise. *I* is yourself: Did you do something for yourself today? *O* is Others: Did you do something for others? *U* is the Unexpressed emotions you may be feeling: Did you name any of these today? And *Y* is Yes: what you're excited about.[10]

One study focused on the potential impact of a focused practice of reflection that involved asking leaders to reflect each day on "three things"—for example, "Name three things you are good at that make you a good leader," or "Name three personal achievements that you are proud of that make you good at your job." The study found that leaders who engaged in this daily reflection experienced greater energy, enjoyed an enhanced impact on others, and had more clout at work.[11]

This kind of broad, set-format reflection can help you make sure you get a full picture of your day, even in a brief, easy exercise that may take only a few minutes to complete.

Step Outside Yourself

Beyond expressing gratitude, Eric Marks also engages in a process sometimes called *metacognition.* This involves stepping outside yourself, looking at your situation, and reflecting on the circumstances as if the person involved is not yourself but someone else. Marks explains that this technique can be helpful when he wrestles with a tricky decision: "Sometimes if I have two competing thoughts, I'll play two different roles within myself. I'll let these two sides of myself talk with one another, as if I'm having a negotiation with myself about the situation."

The technique of metacognition recalls research by psychologist Ethan Kross on what he calls *psychological distancing*. Kross observes that people often fail to reflect effectively on negative situations because they get too emotionally caught up in their own experiences to be able to reason objectively. Kross has tested the effectiveness of a simple technique that shifts an individual's vantage point: namely, thinking about oneself in the third person when one reflects—for example, by asking, "What should *Sue* take away from this situation?" rather than "What should *I* take away from this situation?" Kross finds that this distancing technique helps people reframe negative situations in ways that reduce distress and negative feelings. It can also help you learn more and be more resilient.[12]

Jeff Parks, whom we met way back in chapter 1, has found a different way to achieve a similar kind of psychological distancing: running. When thinking through a tough issue while running, he is able to get outside of his current emotions and look at his situation from a broader, less subjective, and more creative outside-in perspective.

Grapple with Painful Moments

It can sometimes be a challenge to reflect without falling into negative rumination. That's natural; after all, the experiences that most often prompt reflection and for which reflection may have the biggest payoff are ones that raise anxiety and other negative emotions. Rob Herman, director of lab operations for NSF International, refers to these as "cringe-worthy moments": memories that generate a complicated, painful mix of emotions, making them difficult to examine. The experience I described at the start of this chapter, when the chair of the accounting department rebuked me for the way I requested his help, was an example of such a moment.

It's easy to get stuck reliving the pain of such situations to the point where learning and growth end and self-flagellation takes over. Ethan Kross's psychological distancing technique of talking about yourself in the third person can help you to avoid such unproductive rumination.

MINDSET MATTERS

In chapter 2, we explored the importance and value of a learning mindset. The same mindset can help you engage in more effective and powerful reflection. For example, studies show that people with a learning mindset experience enhanced neural activity in the part of the brain associated with learning, which predicts how much they benefit from feedback.

The mindset you bring to any experience that could be considered a failure is especially important. One research study found that people who had recently been denied a promotion at work tended to react in two different ways. Some got mired in feelings of envy and perceptions of unfairness. In general, these were people whose thinking was confined to the present version of who they are; in other words, they embraced a fixed mindset, focused on "This is who I am." Researchers found that this way of thinking promoted pessimism and defensiveness, which in turn makes it unlikely that they will grow. As the researchers put it, "If people only blame external causes that are out of their control, then there's really nothing they can do and learn."

By contrast, others who'd been denied promotions reflected on the experience in ways that yielded long-term benefits. The key was constructing a *growth-based story* about how they learned something new about themselves that could help them to thrive in their future careers. In the researchers' words, "If they say to themselves, 'I had some role in this,' or

'I could have done something differently,' then they're setting themselves up to learn."[13] A learning mindset here helps them to shift from being obsessed with ability (Did I demonstrate enough? Did I demonstrate more than the other guy?) to focusing on how to get better and enables them to see more levers for doing so (e.g., the possibility of seeking out a mentor, asking for more time, finding ways to get help from others, and so forth).[14]

The lesson from this study is that when an experience goes bad, the results are devastating, and you feel as if an important relationship or your career is on the line, be open to what you can learn from it—and particularly to explore your own role in what happened. It's painful, but that's where the most important learning is. If you blame others or find yourself concluding that it occurred due to factors out of your control, then there's really nothing left to do, nothing to learn.

A successful broadcast journalist whom I will call "John Peters" has used reflection on painful life moments to help him develop and build on his learning mindset. He recalls going on an audition as a fledgling TV reporter and being thrown a curveball during a mock news report—a sudden announcement in his earpiece of a breaking story from halfway around the globe (a plane shot down over Iran). Unprepared to cope, Peters froze for several agonizing seconds. That reaction was enough for the producers to conclude that he wasn't ready for an on-air job. He left the audition feeling deflated and doubting whether he would ever succeed in TV news.

With time, however, Peters turned his own cringe-worthy moment into a springboard for growth. "I've kept it, I've remembered it, and I've made sure that I learned something from it," he says. The biggest lesson? "I used to believe that you've got one shot, and that one shot can make or break you. But if you cut yourself some slack, process it, and go on, then you can move forward in a positive direction." Today Peters is a reporter-anchor for a major station in a large U.S. city and has won multiple awards for his work, including an Emmy for outstanding hard-news reporting.

WRINGING MEANING FROM EXPERIENCE

TAKING A DEEP DIVE INTO YOUR PAST

Reflection can often become deeply personal, especially when you're seeking to develop complex personal effectiveness skills involving your emotional intelligence, your self-confidence and self-awareness, and the ways you relate with other people.

"Michael Witthuhn," a former U.S. foreign service professional, has found himself dedicating much of his reflection time to looking backward, trying to understand how his early childhood experiences helped to shape his identity and personality as an adult. Jones's goal is to get free from things that he experienced or didn't experience in his earliest years.

Like Michael Witthuhn, all of us have been affected by things that happened to us when we were young. We drew life lessons from these experiences, often before we were conscious that we were adopting lessons at all. We can think of these lessons as having been written directly to our "hard drives"—patterns of behavior and response that influence us in ways that are unseen and about which we are often unaware. Lessons we learn later in life—during college, for example, or during our working careers—can be thought of as forming our "software." They are also influential, but they are more consciously available to us and therefore more open to change. Spending some time understanding our "hardware" can make a big difference for our personal effectiveness by helping us to achieve greater control over our emotions, understanding the roots of our behaviors, and making it easier for us to deal with difficult situations with clarity, objectivity, and thoughtfulness.

The kind of reflection Michael Witthuhn is engaged in can be difficult. It's time-consuming and may sometimes be painful. If you find yourself taking this kind of "deep dive" into your early life, the advice and guidance of a professional counselor can be very helpful.

My painful interaction with the powerful chair of our accounting department drove me to engage in a bit of this kind of reflection. As I pondered why I had asked for his help in a way that was ineffectual and even alienating, I realized that my behavior had roots that could be traced back to my childhood. I come from a family of eight, and from my adult perspective I can see that my parents were completely overwhelmed by the enormous responsibilities they bore. I didn't fully realize that at the time, though, of course, but we six kids intuited early on that it was best not to bother our parents too much.

My reluctance to ask for help played itself out in ways that remain vivid to this day. For example, one time I was working on some small project out on my dad's workbench in the garage. He happened to come out and offered to help me. I remember feeling very anxious in this situation and trying to get the job done quickly and make it seem less important so that my dad wouldn't feel obligated to spend time on it. Clearly, I'd learned a powerful survival skill: Don't ask too much of others. But if you must ask, minimize the request.

Unconsciously, this lesson had remained in my personal hard drive ever since childhood. Now, in adulthood, it was hurting my ability to lead. If I asked people to do things while also telling them that what I was asking them to do is unimportant, I would never be a great motivator! This example also suggests that sometimes the smallest of experiences can yield the biggest insights. A long-ago interaction with my dad that lasted perhaps twenty minutes gave me real insight into my behavior and its impact all these many years later.

Reflection can help you to become aware of and then to exorcise these "ghosts from the past." I still occasionally catch myself minimizing the requests I make to others, but now I usually see it when I do it, and I can amend the requests immediately.

THERE'S AN OLD OBSERVATION about learning generally attributed to the Chinese philosopher Confucius: "By three methods we may learn wisdom: first, by reflection, which is noblest; second, by imitation, which is easiest; and third, by experience, which is the bitterest."[15] As we've seen, reflection on your own experiences can be a powerful way to take the potentially "bitter" fruit of daily life and transform it into the "noble" insight that can help you be a more effective professional and leader in the years to come.

But systematic reflection can be emotionally challenging. As suggested by John Gardner's observation about how we fill our lives with diversions, reflection exposes us to new ways of thinking and to levels of self-awareness that may sometimes be difficult to embrace. If you make regular reflection a part of your routine, in time you'll come to recognize the slight sense of discomfort that accompanies an unfamiliar perception as a sign that learning and growth are happening—and you'll ultimately begin to welcome it.

POWERFUL REFLECTIONS

In addition to helping you to achieve your learning goal as part of the Power of Flexing, reflection can also help with well-being generally. Here are two additional, research-based reflection practices that you might consider.

TO AMP UP YOUR ENERGY IN YOUR JOB

At the end of the day or at a particularly low point in your work life, choose one of the following five prompts and take a moment to picture and focus on it in your head:

1. three things you like about yourself (they can be anything) that make you a good XXX

2. three valuable skills that you have that make you a good XXX

3. three useful traits that you possess that make you a good XXX

4. three personal achievements that you are proud of that make you a good XXX

5. three things that you are good at (they can be anything) that make you a good XXX

In the research study, the XXX prompt for the questions was being a leader . . . for you, XXX is whatever role you are filling now, whether it be accountant, mother, doctor, sibling, activist, or friend. Pick one and then write three sentences that describe what these "three good things" are, why you like them, and why they make you better at your job. Research has suggested that people who engage in this daily expressive writing exercise enjoy more energy on the job, higher engagement, and higher clout when rated by others.[16]

TO ENHANCE YOUR WELL-BEING

Write for five to ten minutes about three things that went really well in your day and why they went well. These can be small things ("I got to have my favorite ice cream for dessert today") or big things ("The grant came through today"). They can be good things that happened at work, in your family, with friends, or in your community.

Next to each positive event in your list, answer the question, "Why did this good thing happen?" Any answer is acceptable. For example, someone might write that they got to have their favorite ice cream "because a colleague was thoughtful and brought it to me" or "because I was brave enough to ask for what I really wanted in the group." Why did the grant come through? You might believe that "God was looking out for me" or "I worked hard and did well on my job." Writing about *why* the positive events in your life happened helps you to see more fully the good in your life.

Research has linked engagement in this exercise over a series of evenings to reduced stress and better health and well-being indicators.[17]

CHAPTER 7

MANAGING YOUR EMOTIONS TO ENHANCE YOUR LEARNING

"Jason Hartman" is a senior leader in a well-known consumer packaged-goods company—an executive with major responsibilities for the productivity and profitability of a corporate large division. He works long hours continually juggling multiple initiatives and dealing with business pressures that often push him and his team in opposing directions simultaneously.

Perhaps this explains why he developed the habit of drumming his pen on the table during business meetings.

Jason himself never realized he had this habit until it was pointed out to him by the executive coach his company asked him to meet with. It seems that some of the members of Hartman's team had specifically mentioned his pen drumming as one of the warning signs they'd learned to notice. When a meeting wasn't going the way Hartman wanted—when others at the table would disagree with him, ignore his comments, or choose a path he disapproved of—he would become increasingly frustrated and upset. The pen drumming was the first telltale sign. If the meeting continued to deteriorate, Hartman's pen drumming might give way to sarcastic outbursts and even fists pounding on the table—at which point the meeting would effectively dissolve.

In team meetings, Jason's tightly wound emotions were making him an ineffective leader—even, at times, a destructive one.

Jason was genuinely surprised when his coach pointed out how he was undermining the usefulness of the meetings he attended. He and his coach dedicated some sessions to unraveling the problem. Little by little, Hartman began to develop the habit of paying attention to his emotional responses and the physical expressions of those responses. When a meeting became upsetting to him, he learned to notice his own outward signs: "Oh, I'm drumming my pen. I must be feeling frustrated." The recognition enabled him to take steps to flex his response to the frustration by choosing to behave in a way that would facilitate learning and growth for Hartman rather than blockading them.

Jason's challenge was not unusual. Maggie Bayless also sometimes was at the mercy of her emotions. Like many thoughtful professionals, Maggie set goals for how she wanted to be at work—how she wanted to interact with others. But often these goals would go out the window when she was dealing with strong emotions: she would find herself lashing out or her irritation would leak out in ways that were noticeable to all around her. People started shying away from sharing their true opinions if they thought it might set her off, so she often did not get the information she needed to do her work. She would also feel guilty about how she was acting around her important colleagues. She knew something had to change: she had to find a way to get some control in certain situations that triggered strong emotions.

Like Maggie, we all like to believe we're solely driven by reason and logic. But the truth is that we're deeply emotional, sometimes irrational creatures, and at times our strong emotions can wreak havoc with our plans to learn and grow. But the same emotions also can be an important signal that learning is necessary as well as a source of joy and sustenance.

EMOTIONS AS DERAILERS

Learning from experience is not for the faint of heart. Many of the experiences that have the greatest potential to teach you involve high-stakes challenges, personal visibility, and the need to make difficult personal and professional changes. Under the circumstances, it's almost inevitable that strong emotions will accompany such learning. Risk, uncertainty, vulnerability, conflict—all of these conditions are likely to arise, provoking emotions like anxiety, self-doubt, defensiveness, and fear. And when your efforts to solve the problems that arise go off track, more intense emotions like frustration and anger are apt to follow.

As a result, when you are learning from experience and using the Power of Flexing to move boldly outside your comfort zone, emotions are likely to be the biggest derailer of your personal learning. There will be times when your body tenses, your head pounds, your mouth goes dry, your hands sweat, your breathing accelerates, and you feel flushed with adrenaline—all signs that a disruptive emotion is at work. Other times you may feel "down," "blah," disconnected, despondent, or "just not into it" as you drag yourself through the day. Though less dramatic, these reactions can also be signs of a disruptive emotion as well. When this happens, it can be very hard to stay focused on learning from your experiments. However, these kinds of emotions are also informative and worth investigating. Emotions aren't just "problems" to be dealt with or suppressed. They also signal that "there is something to be learned here." Understanding why you are feeling the way you are feeling can be an important stimulus for making change if you can prepare yourself to read the signs.

Many people never realize these benefits, however, because they cope with negative emotions using *emotion suppression*: an effort to fight or ignore the feeling. Unfortunately, this strategy for dealing with unwanted emotions has a number of negative side effects. Emotion suppression can leave you feeling stuck, working hard to keep your feelings under control rather than accepting or reinterpreting them. Suppression also rarely works without the emotions leaking out. The people who worked with Jason and Maggie were aware when they were upset without their ever needing to say a word. Jason's colleagues knew that when the pen started tapping, they should duck and cover! When painful emotions persist, suppression negatively affects your work performance. Unmanaged emotions can also leave a path of misunderstandings and damaged relationships in their wake, further weakening your ability to grow your effectiveness at work, at home, or in the community.

If left unexamined, emotions can derail our efforts to learn in other ways. There may be times when you feel reluctant even to formulate an intention to improve in a certain area because you have anxiety about your ability to get better at it. At times like that, ignoring the issue may feel emotionally safer—although, of course, that strategy makes learning almost impossible. Thus, emotions can make it hard for you even to begin practicing the Power of Flexing.

Emotions can also block your efforts to learn from reflection. Remember that reflection involves three kinds of thinking: understanding the situation as a video recorder might have captured it; understanding your assumptions about the situation and the stories you tell about it; and considering counterfactuals that might have changed the situation. This is a complex mental activity that requires a clear head. The more you are derailed by your emotions, the harder such thinking becomes, and the less you can engage in effective reflection along these lines.

Strong emotions may also be sparked by the feedback we receive during our experiments. We may get conflicting feedback or feedback that we don't understand, triggering confusion and frustration, or we may get negative feedback that produces distress, pain, and anger. Strong feelings like these can dominate our minds so thoroughly that it becomes very difficult to derive any useful lessons from the feedback. As we've seen with Jason and his colleagues, they can also take a toll on our relationships if unmanaged.

For some people, keeping emotions in check is not very difficult. Diana Trembley, the longtime General Motors executive, notes that she scores much higher on "thinking" than on "feeling" in personality inventories like the Myers-Briggs Type Indicator assessment. As a result, emotions don't often get in her way in dealing with situations and experiences. Similarly, Steven Aldrich, the former chief product officer at GoDaddy, describes himself as stoic. He credits the emotional discipline he learned as an athlete as the source of his ability to resist getting too excited or too upset, no matter what happens around him. "I've learned to approach good news and bad news with basically similar emotional responses," he says.

Trembley and Aldrich are more the exception than the rule. Most people are more like Maggie and Jason: prone from time to time to strong feelings that can throw them off stride if they're not handled effectively.

The problem is that once we feel a strong emotion, whether it is anger, guilt, hurt, fear, or outrage, the thinking part of our brain—that part that sets us apart from other mammals—is taken over by a more primitive fight/flight/freeze reaction. We want to push back; we feel an urgency to show the other person how they had misunderstood us or how they erred in their interpretation; we try to exit the situation; or we stay but we freeze—we shut down emotionally and stop communicating interpersonally. If unaddressed, the problem often gets worse from there. We now feel anxiety about interacting with that person or entering that situation. We cope with that anxiety by avoiding, postponing, or undertaking other strategies to avoid experiencing the strong emotions again. The other person, perhaps knowing none of this, feels confused and often hurt by our emotion-tinged response.[1]

Through every step of your growth program, it's important not to ignore or minimize awareness of the emotions that arise within you. These emotions, negative or positive, may be sending you valuable messages about issues you need to address. For example, feelings of anxiety, insecurity, or fear may reflect the fact that you are confronting one or more of the genuine risks of change and growth such as exposure to criticism or taking responsibility for negative results. Thinking honestly about these risks, making a plan to reduce them, and determining your readiness to accept the risks that can't be eliminated is a necessary step in workplace growth—one you will probably have to take more than once. As the renowned psychologist Abraham Maslow put it: "One can choose to go back toward safety or forward toward growth. Growth must be chosen again and again; fear must be overcome again and again."

Thus, emotions are a two-edged sword. While recognizing your emotions and dealing with them honestly helps performance, intense emotional reactions can also get in the way of learning. This ambiguity makes managing your emotions a tricky problem that requires some deep analysis.

MANAGING YOUR EMOTIONS *BEFORE* THEY TAKE OVER

People who want to learn more from experience while flexing need to learn the techniques of *emotion management*. Managing your emotions allows you to stay open to what's really occurring in the situation and to draw important, accurate lessons from it.

Emotion management means both regulating specific emotions—raising or lowering the volume of anger, excitement, dread, anxiety, or any other feeling that is getting in the way of your ability to learn and grow—and getting a handle on what psychologists call *nonspecific emotions*. These are very much like what normal people call moods or stress levels. An excessive level of emotion, whether it's a very negative mood, a more specific anger, or even too much of a positive emotion, such as excitement, can get in the way of the lessons that a particular experience has to teach us. The more you can regulate these emotions, the more you can maximize takeaways.

Psychologists have been studying this issue intensively. They've helped to define a variety of strategies you can use to influence the emotions you have, when you have them, how you experience them, and how you express them. Let's begin by considering some strategies you can use to manage your emotions *before* they take control of an experience.

Situation Selection: "Not Going There."

In this strategy, you choose to stay away from situations that induce specific strong emotions that you want to avoid, such as anger or anxiety. By carefully selecting the situations to which you expose yourself, you regulate the emotions you experience throughout the day, week, or month.

There is a big drawback to using situation selection in conjunction with the Power of Flexing. Since the kinds of experiences at work that have the most to teach us about our own personal effectiveness or leadership tend to be ones that involve strong emotions, then it is not wise to avoid these situations and experiences; that's where the learning is!

In addition, many of these experiences are unavoidable even if you might want to opt out of them. Sometimes stress- or emotion-inducing activities are inherent parts of your job. And in life you often have ongoing commitments and issues you need to address that are unavoidable.

However, you can still use situation selection while practicing the Power of Flexing. Suppose you want to improve a specific personal skill that unavoidably involves coping with intense emotions—for example, the ability to speak up forcefully and bravely when you have a disagreement with a colleague. Knowing that emotions like fear and anxiety are hard for you to manage, you may want to devise a plan for experimentation that deliberately limits the number of situations in which you will practice your new skill. You might choose *not* to test your ability to confront a colleague in most work situations, such as in meetings where routine and relatively unimportant matters are discussed. Instead, you'll limit your experiments to one or two situations in which the new skill is vitally needed—perhaps in a committee dealing with crucial issues like workplace ethics and norms.

In this way, you can avoid throwing yourself into emotion-inducing situations throughout your workweek, instead limiting those moments to a small handful of selected occasions for which you can prepare yourself mentally in advance.

Situation Modification: "Changing the Script."

This second strategy involves making changes in a situation you face so as to avoid the onset of particular emotions. I practiced situation modification in my role as a university dean. I had one direct report—I'll call him Harvey—who frustrated me no end. He didn't listen, he was whiny, and he always seemed to focus on the dark side of things. I would come out of meetings with Harvey feeling frustrated, drained, and even a bit depressed—and I'm sure I showed it. This was not the way I wanted to feel when I was around a member of my team.

I decided to use situation modification to forestall those emotions by telling my assistant to avoid scheduling my meetings with Harvey on Mondays. Somehow, on that day, Harvey's style was particularly prone to amplifying my negative emotional reactions. This simple modification of the terms of our relationship allowed me to cope with Harvey better and made my workweeks noticeably more pleasant as well.

There are many ways you can use situation modification to make emotionally fraught activities less difficult. For example, suppose you are facing a particularly important meeting with others in your company, church, or community, or need to have a difficult conversation with one of your kids. You might want to avoid spending the hour prior to that meeting with someone who tends to be negative, demanding, or subtly dismissive. By modifying the emotional context surrounding your crucial experience, you'll be better prepared to maintain the learning mindset so critical to flexing, allowing you to stay open to any feedback the situation might offer and to reflect more systematically.

Seksom Suriyapa, the Twitter executive we met previously, uses situation modification to manage the emotions associated with his stressful role. "I do not schedule myself back-to-back all day long," Suriyapa says. "Instead, I try to make sure that I block out times of the day that are unstructured, which gives me a kind of release valve."

Situation modification is enhanced when you have a strong awareness of the kinds of circumstances that tend to "push your buttons" and, conversely, those in which you find it easy to remain calm and rational. Let's say you've been asked to give your colleagues a final report on the outcome of an important project—a task you find rather stressful even to contemplate. If you are a good public speaker, you can offer to present the report verbally and in person. But if that's not your strong suit, you can ask to present it in writing, limiting your in-person exposure to answering specific questions from your colleagues.

Attention Redeployment: "Looking on the Bright Side."

Sometimes you don't have the ability to change a situation so as to avoid intense emotions. Fortunately, there's one thing you do have control over: your attention. You can use this power to help control the impact that emotions have on you.

For example, if you have a colleague whom you've found to be negative or even mean-spirited, you can use attention redeployment to lessen his effect on you. During meetings, focus your attention on him only very briefly while paying much more attention to others in the room who are more positive. In addition, when your unpleasant colleague does something particularly irritating, rather than dwelling on it mentally, shift your focus to other things he does that don't elicit negative emotions. "Yes, I hate it when Tim acts like he has to prove that he's the smartest guy in the room," you might say to yourself. "But at least he always remembers to bring donuts to our committee meetings—and they're delicious!" By refocusing your attention, you control your emotion.

This strategy explains how many parents survive their kids' teen years: by focusing their attention not on the snarky, oppositional things their teen engages in but on the facets of their teens' behavior that they find admirable or lovable.

Several of the leaders we talked to use attention deployment in a broader way by making an effort to focus on the positive things in their lives—the things they are grateful for. Kathleen Craig, founder and CEO of HT Mobile Apps, an innovative fintech company serving banks around the country, has experienced sleepless nights worrying about her ever-increasing number of direct reports, plagued by the feeling that their lives and livelihoods were dependent on her. To deal with such nights, Craig says, "I always go back to positives. I always circle back to gratitude and to my positive vision for the future." Craig's practice has been confirmed by several psychological studies showing the power of gratitude reflection.[2]

Jane Dutton describes using a strategy that combines situation modification with attention redeployment to cope with her anxiety about an important online presentation. On the day of the presentation, she modifies her situation in several small ways that help her maintain a positive attitude—for example, by wearing her "special" earrings and a turtleneck in "my mom's favorite shade of blue," she says, and by putting pictures of her grandkids next to her laptop, she can see them as she talks. "I surround myself with things that evoke positive emotions," Jane explains. "And they really help me: they make me happy, even when I have a job to do that is very stressful."

Attention deployment can be a powerful tool for managing emotions.

But there's one situation in which you should *not* practice attention deployment. After experiencing a significant failure, you may be tempted to ignore the negative feelings it produces and focus your attention elsewhere. However, research suggests that this is a mistake. Experimental economists have shown that study participants who were instructed to focus on their negative emotions following a task failure invested 25 percent more effort in the following task, thereby improving their future performance. Note, however, that this result only held when the tasks were somewhat similar. Thus, if you fail at a specific job that you know you'll confront again, pay attention to the pain you feel. As the authors put it, "If you focus on how bad you feel, you'll probably work harder to ensure you don't make the same mistake again."[3] Of course, if your focus on the negative edges into rumination, then these positive effects evaporate and other, more negative effects occur.[4] The goal is to examine and understand your failure, but in a way that leaves you with a sense of efficacy for doing better in the future.

Cognitive Reappraisal: Managing Emotions *After* They Arrive

The strategies we've considered thus far can help you forestall and control an emotional reaction before it takes hold. But what about when you've already been hit by a wave of powerful emotion?

One consistent research finding is that emotion regulation strategies are likely to be both easier and more successful if applied earlier in the process rather than later. In other words, dealing with difficult emotions before they hit you is much more effective than coping with them after the fact.

Still, sometimes we have no choice but to manage emotions after they've overwhelmed us. The most effective response for doing that is something that psychologists call *cognitive reappraisal*. This strategy capitalizes on the human ability to "story" what something means. We all are meaning makers. We all story all the time: we add to reality as a video recorder would record it. For example, a video recorder might capture a boss saying to her subordinates, "You don't need to attend the meeting tomorrow." Some subordinates might think, "Great, I can get other work done," while others will be thinking, "She doesn't value my ideas," or "She is power-hungry and wants to keep me sidelined." These added "stories" drive us to one emotion or another. Also, whenever we experience strong emotions, we have an innate need to make sense of the situation and its impact on us. The meaning we assign in the stories we choose to tell can be correct—an accurate representation of what's actually happening—or incorrect, but it is the stories that govern our emotions and reactions.

Fortunately, we have another ability we can deploy. We can also engage in cognitive reappraisal, which might also be called *re-storying*. This strategy enables us to change the meaning of an experience if we need to.

In my various administrative roles, I've had the opportunity to serve under three different deans. One of them did not believe in thank-yous. His view was: "Why should I thank someone for doing their job?" He also was fairly introverted and did not comment much on the work of the people who reported to him. This combination of behaviors used to drive his associate deans nuts.

Knowing this, when I became one of those associate deans, I made a conscious decision regarding how I would interpret his lack of comments about what I was doing. I would view the dean's behavior not as criticism or indifference but as a sign that he had utter confidence in me. Was this true? I don't really know. But I do know that this revised story served me very well. Presuming he had confidence in me helped me to stay proactive and leader-like in my role. It left me feeling far less stressed and more empowered than my colleagues.

Here's another example: Suppose you believe that a colleague is attacking your ideas through constant questions and occasional interruptions during meetings. With this take on the situation, you respond by shutting down. You are no longer open to this person and any feedback he might have for you, thereby limiting your ability to flex. But there is a better alternative. You can see those same actions and respond quite differently if you change the story. For example, if you could think about your colleague's questions and comments as "playing with your ideas" instead of attacking them. When you choose the meaning, your interpretation of the actions you observe changes, and so do the emotions you feel in response.

You can also re-story your own feelings. For example, prior to a stressful performance, you can reinterpret your sense of anxiety or panic as excitement or passion. Even as simple a mechanism as saying out loud "I am excited!" can help make this happen—and with it, an improvement in your performance. Research suggests that those who are able to reinterpret the rush of emotion that they feel in this kind of situation are able to alter not just their performance but also their physiology—their cardiovascular functioning.[5] A calmer, more centered you is also likely to be better at flexing: able to focus on self-development as well as on the tasks at hand, to feel confident about trying the experiment you've committed to, and to be more open to feedback.

Of course, this kind of reinterpretation might be dysfunctional if you practiced it in a truly dangerous situation—let's say, being caught alone in the wilderness at night with wild animals around. Times of real danger are what adrenaline was made for! But cognitive reappraisal is highly functional in most ordinary business and interpersonal situations where we need to learn something about ourselves. Seeing your anxiety as being "psyched up" or "passionate" can help you move through a situation in a way that leaves you open to learning and not fall prey to your emotions.

Doug Evans, whom we met as a producer in chapter 2 and who now serves as the executive director of the YMA Fashion Scholarship Fund, recalls using this technique explicitly both with himself and with his coworkers. At two of the companies he ran, when the team hit a very stressful patch, he would calm himself by saying, "This isn't the Pentagon. This isn't the Pentagon. We're not at war." In other cases he would say to his people, "Gang, this is the arts. This is the fashion industry. This is Broadway. Nobody is going to die if the show does not go on." His general advice when emotions are extreme: "Step back and say, 'Not the Pentagon. It's not the Pentagon.'"

CONVERTING A NEGATIVE STORY TO A POSITIVE ONE

Sometimes the stories you tell yourself may create needless pain and prevent growth. To move forward, two steps are needed. First, you have to recognize that you are telling yourself a story that isn't helping you. Then you can begin to work with the story to change it, both in the moment when you find yourself repeating it and more substantially over time.

We all "story" our experiences in our head. Sometimes those stories help us to keep going and other times they can create pain and prevent growth. Here are some examples of the many kinds of stories that can get in the way of your growth:

+ "I can't do it!"
+ "They won't like what I have to offer!"
+ "There is no point in even trying anything around here!'"
+ "I have nothing to learn from someone in that department."
+ "I have nothing to learn from a person like that."
+ "They're out to get me!"
+ "I failed at this when I tried it before. I guess I probably am going to fail again."

We have all on occasion thought, "I can't do it," where the "it" might be holding a difficult conversation, offering an inspiring vision of where your group should go, or giving a persuasive speech at a community event. When we tell ourselves this story, it hurts our progress and growth. We don't try things, so we don't ever find out whether our story is true.

To escape the power of such negative stories, psychologists recommend trying to question the underlying belief. See whether you can convert it to a positive belief that you can buy into, laying the foundation for a story that will change your future attitudes and behavior. This practice of "re-storying" is the basis of *cognitive behavioral therapy*, which has benefited millions of patients over the years. The same concept has been popularized by coaches and self-help authors like Byron Katie and Brooke Castillo, who suggest a number of specific ways to shift your stories:[6]

+ By mentally asking yourself whether the opposite might be true. For example, if you are stuck in the story "I have nothing to learn from someone in that department," try saying, "I wonder whether there might be something useful I could learn from someone in that department." This question opens up a space in your mind that allows you to be more open to input.

+ By thinking about what life would be like if you abandoned a particular story. For instance, if you habitually say to yourself, "They will not like what I have to offer," ask yourself, "How would I behave differently if I knew they would like what I have to offer?" The answer to this question may open up the possibility of behaving in a new, more constructive way.

+ By stating the opposite of the negative story with the addition of a moderating phrase—for example, "It is possible that I can do it," or "I am open to the idea that I may be able to succeed next time." The moderating phrase may make it easier for you to begin to shift your thinking away from a negative story that has become habitual.

The more you explicitly identify thoughts that are causing you pain or limiting your growth and interrogate them, the more you create a space of openness in which you can reconsider reality and find a new path forward.

RESPONSE MODULATION: SHAPING HOW YOU FEEL AND WHAT YOU FEEL

Another useful tool for managing emotions is *response modulation.* When you are feeling a particular emotion, you take steps to modulate (change) the physiological, experiential, or behavioral expression of that emotion. For example, you can ease or reduce emotion using deep breathing or progressive muscle relaxation, which involves tightening and releasing each muscle throughout the body in a specified sequence. These kinds of interventions can affect the intensity of the emotion and your subsequent responses to the situation.

Applying response modulation works best if you develop the capacity to spot an oncoming emotion early, as it begins to manifest physiologically. Before you can do anything about an emotion, you need to figure out that you are having one and what it is.

I had trouble with this challenge for years. Many times I realized that I'd been experiencing an emotion like fear, anger, or anxiety only hours after it happened. In real time I was reacting automatically, sensing that something was going off the rails and experiencing some of the symptoms of strong emotion, such as tightened muscles and a fast heartbeat, but not really understanding what was going on. Only after years of study, learning, and reflection did I discover that these physical symptoms— together with an intense desire to speak up—were my personal early signs of anger.

Now when these reactions occur I can say to myself, "This is anger," and I can take steps to deal with the emotion productively. Maggie Bayless similarly describes emotion management as one of the lessons that, for her, came with age. She learned that whenever she was feeling an emotion that made her want to act urgently to get her message across, she should wait until she's responding less to the emotion and is able to be more thoughtful about the outcome that she really wants and the best way to get it. Sometimes emotion regulation requires tuning in to your body and its capacity to experience emotions.

Gavin Nielsen, whom we met in chapter 6, echoes this lesson. "You've just got to know what your own emotions are," he says. "And it's not as complicated as you might think. You are not going to experience forty or fifty emotions. You are not going to randomly get to spin that wheel and land on one. You are going to, most often, land on the same two, three, or four emotions. You have to treat it like a mini science experiment. 'Okay, I keep landing on this emotion. Why is that?'"

Coming to recognize your most common emotions will enable you to deal with them better—and continue to grow and learn from your experiences.

Another strategy for response modulation recommended by many of the strong leaders we interviewed is to practice in-advance behaviors that prepare you to deal more effectively with the physical manifestations of emotion—behaviors like exercising, eating right, and getting enough sleep. As Royster Harper, the University of Michigan vice president, puts it, "One of the things I learned was how important it is to rest—that when you are dealing with a really tough issue that involves a lot of people, you have to take care of yourself physically and psychologically, because you don't do your best work when you're tired."

Michael Witthuhn recounted that, during his work as an ambassador, he dealt with stress through conscientious preparation, including vast amounts of background reading. He found that the reading "brought down my stress . . . put me in a position where I thought I was confident that I had something to contribute in almost every setting." He also mentioned that he slept a lot whenever he could—a crucial replenishing of his physical stamina, especially important considering he traveled almost 400,000 miles during his time as ambassador.

A second preparatory strategy prominent in our interviews involves starting the day with an exercise designed to facilitate emotional frame setting—for example, reading something inspirational. For people of faith, inspiration is often found in scripture reading or prayer.

Puput Hidayat, the head of product development at Tokopedia, a large Indonesian technology company, finds she can improve her mood by going back to a particular chapter in the book *Petir* (the Indonesian word for lightning) by the writer Dee Lestari. In the chapter, the heroine feels confused about a problem until she finally decides that it doesn't matter—that she will go on living even if the problem cannot be solved positively. Hidayat has read that book chapter repeatedly, and each time it has helped her put a troubling problem into a broader perspective.

Richard Sheridan is cofounder and CEO of Menlo Innovations, a software company based in Ann Arbor, and author of the book *Joy, Inc.: How We Built a Workplace People Love.* Sheridan manages his emotions using a dual strategy. First, he is careful about avoiding things he doesn't want to be exposed to. For example, he stopped listening to the local news twenty years ago: "It was like the murder, fire, and crime report. I just don't want to listen to that every night." Second, he spends a dozen or so hours a week doing inspirational reading that sustains him in his work.

Finally, many people find that a crucial element in their emotional management system is social support, whether in the form of a spouse, a circle of friends, family members, a formal support group, or any other kind of interpersonal network.

Puput Hidayat describes how social support works for her:

When you deal with negativity by yourself, it's amplified, because it's stuck in your head and you keep embellishing it with a lot of thought. Over time, one negative thought becomes two negative thoughts, to the point that it paralyzes you and prevents you from doing anything. Basically, for me, there is no way you can break from negativity by yourself.

So every time I have a doubt, every time I'm not confident

in myself, I will search for someone I can confide in, whether it's a mentor, my immediate supervisor, my friends, or a colleague. I suppose everyone has someone they can turn to. A friend can give me a fresh perspective on things.

Anyone who saw Tom Hanks in *A Beautiful Day in the Neighborhood*, the 2019 film about children's television star Fred Rogers, came away impressed by Rogers's dedication to his young viewers and the mission of consistently expressing acceptance, love, and support for them. Maintaining this emotional steadiness took its toll on the real-life Mr. Rogers. In the movie, Hanks effectively captured some of the life strategies Rogers used to stay on an even keel, including daily laps in the pool and regular engagement with prayer.

MANAGING POSITIVE EMOTIONS: AN OPPORTUNITY TO SEIZE

Controlling negative emotions is an important challenge for those who want to consistently learn and grow. In fact, negative emotions are what most comes to mind when people think about emotion regulation. For example, when we asked the people we interviewed for this book—ranging from celebrated leaders and people working in communities to young people on the rise—about how they managed emotions, they universally described how they worked to contain, reappraise, suppress, or manage negative emotions in their work and interactions with others. But positive emotions deserve some discussion.

A former University of Michigan colleague of mine, Barbara Fredrickson, developed a "broaden and build" theory that helps to explain the importance of positive emotions.[7] As Fredrickson explains, positive emotions are not just "nice to have" but also help to build important resources that support longer-term resilience and growth.

This works in several ways. First, positive emotions provide motivation for personal growth that may cause you to use the Power of Flexing more often. For example, recalling and savoring the positive emotions you experienced when you took a risk—the feelings of pride, excitement, and adventure—may make taking the next risk less daunting.

Second, positive emotions help people to expand their sense of possibilities. Laboratory studies show that people induced to feel positive emotions list more, and more varied, potential actions that they believe are worth doing compared to others without those emotions. Positive emotions also may help with setting goals for learning and growth. For example, experiencing the positive emotion of pride may stimulate fantasizing about even bigger accomplishments, leaving you feeling confident and self-assured about how you might grow. The positive feeling of inspiration caused by witnessing someone else achieving great things may create the urge to pursue your own lofty ambitions. The positive emotions you feel as you go through an experience may give you the courage to seek feedback from others. There is also evidence that positive emotions may stimulate reflection, based on explicitly identifying and considering the positive emotions produced by an experience.[8]

What's more, the evidence suggests that the impact of positive emotions tends to increase over time, creating a positive spiral.[9] When you feel more positive emotions, you see more positive elements in your life, circumstances, and relationships, and thereby feel more positive emotions once again. As Fredrickson puts it, "Positive emotions appear to both characterize optimal functioning and promote it."[10] Positive emotions help you build resources like self-confidence and self-insight that you can draw on to excel in the future. Research has even documented positive effects on heart rate variability that are influenced by positive emotions.[11]

How, then, can you make the most of the potential benefits that positive emotions provide?

One basic strategy is to allow yourself to enjoy positive feelings even when you are facing stressful, painful, or difficult times. Simply allowing yourself to laugh in the face of a setback can be enormously helpful. Studies of students in the immediate aftermath of the 9/11 terrorist attacks and survivors of dramatic events like the 2002 El Salvador earthquake have documented the beneficial impact of positive emotions.[12] Findings such as these dispute the idea that positive emotions are frivolous. If people in these more dire situations benefit from feeling and amplifying their positive emotions, *we* probably can as well. Amplifying your positive emotions should help you feel more confident in trying flexing experiments, more open to learning from them, and more able to confront all the aspects of a situation in your reflections.

Another strategy for managing positive emotions is *savoring*. This involves trying to prolong or increase the positive emotional experience. One way to do this is to express the positive emotions you feel nonverbally—for example, by smiling more. Of course, we smile when we feel happy, but studies show that the reverse is also true: when we smile more, we feel happier. Savoring can also be promoted by focusing your attention on positive elements of your experience. This can involve thinking about things that make you happy; it can also involve talking about them with others, celebrating them, and reminiscing about them later. So when your activities associated with the Power of Flexing go particularly well—when you make progress toward your goal or when others react positively to one of your efforts—savor the positive emotions you feel. Studies suggest that the ability to savor is correlated with subjective well-being, including feelings of optimism and control about the future, life satisfaction, and self-esteem.[13] That optimism and sense of control should feed your ability to set goals and pursue them through the Power of Flexing with increased confidence.

A third strategy for managing positive emotions involves gravitating toward positive stories about your life rather than negative ones. This means being conscious of the stories you tell yourself and making deliberate decisions to favor those that are positive. For example, when you earn an A on an exam, do you say, "Oh, that test was really easy!"? This is a negative explanation that discounts your own hard work. Instead, opt for a story that emphasizes the positive side of the event: "It's great how the effort I made to reduce my procrastination and improve my study habits has paid off!" Given the documented value of positive emotions for well-being, self-esteem, and life satisfaction, taking simple steps to alter your explanation (over and over again until you actually start believing them) seems like an excellent strategy for managing emotions in the Power of Flexing.

Some practitioners of the Power of Flexing adopt a deliberate discipline that encourages them to focus attention on the positive sides of their experience. Research shows the value of this kind of habit. In one study, researchers asked people to write three positive things about themselves, five days a week for five weeks—things like three valuable skills, three useful traits, three personal achievements, three things they are good at, and three things that made them a good leader. This simple intervention enhanced the subjects' work engagement, reduced their sense of "depletion" at work, and helped them have more impact on those around them.[14] That is a pretty strong payoff for five minutes of positive reflection per day!

One last idea, which some corporate managers might find "soft" but which has been shown to be valuable for people ranging from teenage students to basketball players and police officers: engaging in *self-compassion*. My colleagues and I have found that adopting a supportive, caring, and nonjudgmental mindset toward oneself helps people in leadership positions—particularly those facing tough challenges—to maintain more of a sense of themselves as leaders. It also helps them to be seen as more effective by others.[15]

Given that life throws most of us challenges on a regular basis, I suspect that self-compassion may emerge as one more potent way to manage emotions effectively.

AS THIS CHAPTER HAS illustrated, many of the challenges we face in life, from ordinary daily unhappiness to the barriers that make it difficult for us to learn and grow, originate within our own minds and hearts—not in the events in our lives but in how we *react* to the events in our lives. Perhaps the Dalai Lama, in a discussion with Archbishop Desmond Tutu, said it best: "Mental immunity is just learning to avoid the destructive emotions and to develop the positive ones."[16] The same wisdom can help us escape the traps that prevent us from learning and growing through our life experiences.

CHAPTER 8

THE POWER OF FLEXING
IN A VARIETY OF
CIRCUMSTANCES

The beauty of the flexing system is that you can apply it to virtually any upcoming experience. Suppose you have been assigned to take on a tricky task: to run a committee, plan a retreat, or negotiate an important contract. Or suppose you are facing a problem at work: you need to hold a difficult conversation with someone, are starting a tough new job, are working with a new boss, or have begun a new cross-departmental collaboration. Any of these experiences can be a great candidate for applying the Power of Flexing.

Experiences that are keeping you up at night or ones that you find yourself ruminating about are particularly likely candidates. Something is occurring in these experiences that offers the potential for skill development and learning. Flexing is particularly appropriate and useful when a change in your career circumstances is in the offing, but it can also be used anytime you have a goal that you want to achieve or a problem you want to solve. Similarly, in chapter 1, we talked about the kinds of experiences that have the most to teach emerging leaders; these, too, give us good clues about experiences that can help all of us to learn and grow.

The same kind of thinking applies to challenges in personal life as well. For many family members, simply going home for a holiday offers chances to flex—for example, to see if you can make progress at being more patient or listening better.

This chapter brings to life several places where you might especially look to apply the Power of Flexing. The hope is that, with these in mind, you can be more intentional when one is occurring in your life and look for ways to flex more often.

FLEXING IN TIMES OF TRANSITION

People transition all the time within organizations. They take on a new job in a different area, or they move to the same job in a different division with new colleagues, procedures, and norms. Perhaps most difficult of all, they make the transition to a leadership role for the first time.

Transitions are great opportunities for flexing. During transitions, you are already more "awake" in your work life, because your routines have been disrupted, you are clearly facing something new, and the transition often increases your visibility to others in the organization, further sharpening your self-focus.[1] As a result, your motivation to succeed is typically high. Research confirms that people also tend to be most open to learning and feedback during these times, because during transitions things are often confusing. The actions required for success become less clear, and your identity or sense of self becomes more fluid and changeable.[2]

At these times, people often develop intense curiosity about how they "should be" and how they "want to be." In the words of one executive coach, when you enter a transition, "the world is changed. Suddenly I have a whole new set of muscles that I have never used before, and I have got to make them work." Transitioners have the opportunity to try new behaviors. They encounter new stakeholders—colleagues, bosses, customers, suppliers, clients—who may think differently than they do and may perceive them differently than did past stakeholders.

Herminia Ibarra, an expert on organizational behavior, suggests that career transitions are ideal contexts for people to try on what she calls "provisional selves." Ibarra recommends an explorative and playful process akin to flexing in which people experiment with various professional identities and judge whether to retain or amend them based on their own perceptions and external feedback.[3] With colleague Roxanne Barbulescu, Ibarra further describes major transitions as a chance to develop an integrated narrative of who one is, suggesting that a further outcome of the Power of Flexing may be the development of a new and more complex identity. As people identify a flex goal, try various experiments, and seek feedback on them, their reflections on the process allow them to begin to internalize a narrative of themselves as, for example, the leader that they most want to be.[4]

In addition, transitions offer an opportunity for flexing because they are often expected, predictable, and somewhat regular. In many organizations, job rotations occur on a predetermined schedule, promotions follow schedules that are widely understood, and departmental reorganizations that create positional shifts for individuals are carried out only after extensive planning and discussion. These realities mean that people often have time to prepare for a transition as well as the opportunity to observe others going through similar transitions before them. These factors make transitions a natural time to perform useful experiments.

When we interviewed people about how they've used flexing in their lives and careers, transitions were frequently mentioned, including transitions into the leader's role and transitions from one kind of leadership to another. Some of the stories we heard were inspiring.

For example, Anson Dorrance, a renowned men's soccer coach at the University of North Carolina, discovered that he had to modify his approach when he was asked to expand his duties to lead a women's team for the first time. He developed an appreciation for the female players' collegial style, and adjusted his teaching methods to take advantage of the "family feeling" the women favored. At the same time, he encouraged the women to develop a competitive edge that most of the male players he'd formerly worked with had adopted as a matter of course. In the words of one of Dorrance's players, the legendary Mia Hamm, "I grew up always good at sports, but being a girl, I was never allowed to feel as good about it as guys were. My toughness wasn't celebrated. But then I got to the University of North Carolina, and it was O.K. to want to be the best."[5]

Lisa Shalett, a former Goldman Sachs partner, was appointed chief operating officer of global compliance and dropped into a division filled with experts; she successfully experimented with taking advantage of her outsider status, asking questions to learn from the people around her, who all knew more about the subject.

Scott Brown, having been installed as president and CEO of the Truman Center, applied his combat leadership experiences in Iraq and Afghanistan to motivate, inspire, and unify his new team while also striking a balance between their shared mission and the team's well-being.

Ralph Simone used flexing to spur his own growth when launching his coaching and leadership development company. He discovered that he'd become accustomed to operating on a model that was "constantly go, go, go," responding to every challenge by "hitting the ground running." Ralph realized that model was unsustainable over the long haul. In response, he experimented with ways to create more space for himself to do less work while also being more impactful.

"Deepesh Kumar" found that his success as an entrepreneur and business leader was greatly supported by a lesson he learned from a previous career transition. Being promoted to partner at a major law firm exposed Kumar to new responsibilities and new challenges. "When you're a partner," Kumar explains, "it's not enough to simply do high-quality work on the cases that are given to you. You also have to bring in cases somehow, or team up with people who can bring in cases. Otherwise you won't keep your partnership."

Of course, this realization forced Kumar to work on developing the new skills involved in attracting cases to the firm. But on a deeper and more personal level, he also discovered that he needed to learn to recognize stress and to handle it; otherwise you "just have it all around you like a temperature that you cannot perceive." Kumar's career transition helped him grow his ability to handle stress, which set him up well for creating a business that could prosper.

As stories like these illustrate, the transitions you undertake in work and life can be ideal times to create or renew a sense of focus on your personal growth as well as on the tasks of the transition itself.

FLEXING IN RESPONSE TO NEW CHALLENGES

A second set of opportunities for flexing arises when you do not necessarily move to a new role but the world changes around you in ways that create new demands, problems, and opportunities. Examples might include a significant shift in the market for your company's products, the departure of a key leader in a community organization you work with, or the emergence of a new technology that transforms an industry you're involved in. Such changes in your environment require adaptive changes, and the best way to discover the changes that will work is often through experimentation—which means flexing.

For Lucy, the longtime owner of a small inn in the California wine country, the new challenge that called upon her adaptive skills was the COVID-19 crisis of 2020. As states began to shut down and individuals began to self-quarantine in March, her inn's occupancy rate fell from above average to zero. Lucy was confronted with a host of unfamiliar problems: new health and environmental regulations, complex rules about employee layoffs and unemployment benefits, and confusing procedures regarding taxes and small business loans, all against a backdrop of mounting debt.

Lucy is one of the most positive people I know, but this new array of challenges threatened even her sunny disposition. It took time for her to master the feelings of anxiety, anger, and grief that momentarily overwhelmed her. Gradually, the practices of self-reflection and experimentation involved in the Power of Flexing began to help. Lucy recognized that one aspect of her habitual approach to business problems was holding her back. Every time she faced a challenge demanding an unfamiliar response—for example, conducting virtual meetings using Zoom or getting guidance from a local government official—she would freeze, feeling stymied. Rather than tackling the task, she would place it on a to-do list and carry on with other tasks she felt comfortable with. "I'll get to that one later," she would say—but "later" never seemed to come.

Lucy recognized that the COVID-19 crisis meant she needed to overcome this personal weakness. She set herself the flex goal of finding a way to keep going even when stymied. As an experiment, she tried the strategy of tackling just one unfamiliar problem a day. If her effort to master the new job initially failed, she would take a break, revisit the "why" behind her commitment in an effort to bolster her flagging motivation, and return to the problem until it was solved.

Lucy found this new approach worked—not with every unfamiliar challenge, but with enough of them so that she began to feel a real and growing sense of accomplishment, progress, and empowerment. Each small triumph gave her increased confidence about tackling the next challenge, and she became more comfortable about asking for help, seeking resources, and generally moving her business forward.

New challenges aren't encountered only in business. For many parents, raising a child can feel like an unending succession of new challenges, each requiring learning and growth as well.

A young mom whom I'll call Greta is a great example. A happily married mom, Greta is a person who relishes feeling in control, at work and in life, but experienced two profound parenting challenges within a couple of years. Her first challenge came during her pregnancy with her second child and led her to set a flex goal of learning to let go. Greta experienced pregnancy as "getting on a train that you can't get off and that is heading for an unknown destination—the most extreme surrender you can think of." And for her this pregnancy involved a life-threatening premature delivery; in fact, one of her doctors later said, "I've never seen somebody have such low blood pressure and come back out of it." Surviving and recovering from this medical challenge taught her that, sometimes, surrendering control is both unavoidable and essential. Her second challenge came a year later. Just as her older son was starting school—simultaneously with the cancellation of classes due to the COVID-19 crisis—he developed a significant stutter. Greta found her need to control reemerging. She obsessively read everything she could on the Internet about her son's condition, as if more and more knowledge would eventually enable her to vanquish the stuttering.

Eventually, Greta's therapist offered a piece of helpful advice: "Greta, you need to stop paddling and just ride the river for a second." Greta switched her approach to flexing. She looked for what she could do and where the opportunities lay. Here she set herself the new flex goal of being thoughtful about how she interacts with her son about his stuttering so that he ends up with a positive self-identity. She has engaged in a variety of experiments in her quest to achieve this, including reflecting (fretting) with friends and working to balance her tendency to catastrophize (fantasizing about worst-case scenarios) with the need to sometimes just "let things be." Facing this new parenting challenge has become a source of creativity and growth for Greta.

The first key to flexing when you face new challenges is to recognize them as opportunities. Greta truly took what could have been an overwhelming situation (her life-threatening pregnancy and long recovery) and viewed it as an opportunity to reorient her life, letting go of small issues that used to vex her, being more present with her kids. Research

THE POWER OF FLEXING

shows that people—and organizations as well—react to environmental changes in two differing ways. Some see changes as threats: "Something has changed. This is scary. I need to do something new. Can I do it? What if I fail? What kinds of bad things may happen?" When you see change as a threat, a range of predictable responses are likely to follow: you become more rigid, you seek less information, you consider a small set of possible responses, you seek to conserve your resources, and you engage in as much controlling behavior as you can. (As Greta would say, you start paddling.)

Others see changes as opportunities: "Something has changed. This is amazing. I need to do something new. How can I learn to do it? What if I succeed? What kinds of great things may happen?"[6] This view encourages greater expansiveness and a spirit of exploration—including exploration of the important ways that you need to grow in order to respond effectively and an openness to trying new things. When you face something truly negative, remembering that your viewpoint on what is happening to you has these important effects can help you to monitor your mindset and shift it—to begin to look for and focus on the opportunities present and enjoy the benefits of doing so.

FLEXING IN RESPONSE TO FEEDBACK

Many of the people we interviewed cited feedback as an impetus for their personal growth journeys. For many, it was negative feedback—a comment suggesting a deficiency or a need to change something—that had the crucial impact.

"Greg Holmes" is an East Coast senior executive in the financial services industry whose embrace of flexing began shortly after he was passed over for promotion. Failing to gain a position he'd hoped for was bad enough, but even more painful was having the new manager rate him as "Needs improvement" after observing his work performance for ninety days. This one-two punch might lead some people to become angry or embittered, but Greg decided to turn it into a learning experience. Determined to achieve more in his *next* ninety days on the job, he chose to work on improving his time management skills, and he launched several experiments to find ways to make it happen. The most important one—and one that he uses to this day—was to ask himself, "What is the most important project or task?" and then put all his resources on that most important project and get it accomplished.

Stephen Wroblewski, now a senior manager at a global consulting firm, put himself on a growth path after a manager described him as a "99 percent person," meaning someone who was great at *almost* finishing jobs but not quite. Stephen engaged in a series of experiments to find a better way of managing his and his team's projects. In the process he discovered the power of reflecting at the end of the day, at the end of the week, and at the conclusion of each project to examine whether he and his colleagues were bringing their tasks to successful closure.

Sometimes even casual, offhand feedback can send you on a growth journey. One night Ben Tawdowski was working late at the office. On his way out the door, another manager caught a glimpse of Ben. Chuckling, the manager remarked, "If you're working this late, either you're working too hard or you're no good at getting things done."

"Rod Pearson" chairs an important department within a major university medical system. He received similar one-off feedback when he was a resident. Facing an unfamiliar problem, he visited the chief of the service to ask for advice. "Why didn't you come up with any solutions?" the chief asked.

Rod made note of the comment. The next time he was confronted with a problem, he called on the chief, described the problem, and then suggested a few possible solutions. "Why didn't you put any of those ideas into action?" the chief asked.

It took these two separate layers of feedback, but Rod learned a valuable lesson: that he didn't need permission from on high to get things done. When problems arose, he began trying things out on his own with an orientation toward learning as he went, seeking feedback only after implementing solutions that he'd created himself.

Getting negative feedback is never any fun. As some wise person—or maybe it was a wise guy!—astutely observed, "People say they want constructive criticism, but what they really want is praise." Unfortunately, almost no one gets a steady diet of praise. When criticism comes your way, you can at least make it a force for good by using it as an opportunity to flex your way to improvement.

FLEXING TO BECOME A BETTER YOU

The trigger for flexing is not always a stressful experience or a perceived weakness. Sometimes it is simply a desire to build on and enhance an existing strength.

Dan Scheinman was a basketball player with big dreams as a kid—hoping that someday he might play for one of the top college teams in the country and—who knew?—maybe even make it to the NBA after that. But when he was twelve, a coach at an elite basketball camp told him, "Look, at your level, you can't favor one hand. If you can't go to your left just as well as you go to your right, you're not going to be an elite player."

Dan took the coach's words to heart—too much so. He spent an entire year working on his left hand, to such an extent that he effectively became a left-handed basketball player rather than the versatile, two-handed star the coach was urging him to be.

Looking back on the experience, Dan now sums it up by saying, "I forgot my strength." He worried so much about the (relative) weakness of his left hand that he failed to maintain and to take advantage of his existing right-handed strength.

Dan's lesson applies to many of us. Lots of people have strengths they fail to develop, enhance, and deploy to their full potential. Sometimes they don't even realize these are strengths at all. For example, early in my career, I often received compliments about how well I ran activities, such as a faculty committee or a workshop group. The comments surprised me, because I didn't feel I was doing anything special; I was just organizing and managing the activity in a way that seemed natural, even obvious, to me.

Only through reflection in the years since then have I come to realize that that feeling of "But I didn't do anything special!" is often a good indication of an unrecognized strength. And such unrecognized strengths are potential opportunities for flexing. When you realize that you have an ability that you've developed without consciously working on it, you can seize the opportunity to experiment with ways to develop it further, perhaps turning it into a talent that is truly exceptional.

In my case, I can build on my innate ability to run groups well by saying to myself, "I'm good at organizing teams to get tasks done. But I could do even better if I improved my ability to make people feel valued, affirmed, and motivated." In this way a natural flex goal emerges. By bringing focus to it, my strength becomes stronger over time.

Positive growth agendas can also develop in response to our observations of other people. Countless individuals have set flex goals for themselves based on role models they'd like to emulate, whether these are people they know personally or figures from the world stage. In other cases, you may observe someone doing some specific action, even a small one that sparks an aspirational yearning. Merely noticing a friend or a colleague perform a particularly thoughtful act of compassion for someone else who is sick or hurting, for example, may trigger a desire to find ways to develop such generosity in oneself.

Remember Stephen Wroblewski, the person who never quite finished his projects? After hearing that feedback, he drew inspiration for improving his "closure skills" from an experience he remembered from high school. At the time, he'd been a pretty good competitive swimmer, but watching a practice session of the three-time Olympic medalist Tom Dolan practice was a revelation. He noticed that, even in practice, Dolan never took it easy, never wasted a single stroke. Stephen's takeaway was that he should strive to do the same—to "never waste a rep," treating even practice workouts as if they were as important as races. Years later, recalling that lesson, he began applying the same philosophy to his work life, looking for ways to ensure that he made the most of every ounce of energy he expended on the job—and never left a task unfinished.

In still other cases, an aspirational goal can be set based not on a role model you've observed or even your own most heartfelt values but rather on what it seems to take to fit effectively into an organization or a role. Remember Lindy Greer, the academic leader whose story we shared in chapter 3? Lindy set varying flex goals for herself over time. When she was working within a university department in the Netherlands, she realized she needed to make herself "small" in order to fit the expectations for organizational membership and leadership as dictated by that country's cultural norms. Later, when she filled a similar role at Stanford, she had to make herself "big" in order to be perceived as an influential leader in that particular university context.

Sometimes particular organizations have such strong, clearly defined cultures that aspiring leaders set flex goals based solely on the need to better fit into the local culture. For example, people who hope to rise to leadership roles within Google may find they need to develop new ways of communicating and connecting with others in order to better fit the Google prototype.[7] In other companies, the desired behaviors may be quite different. To flex across a variety of circumstances requires that you pay attention to what those circumstances demand and the ways in which you can learn within them; whether the challenge you face is a work issue, a parenting problem, a changing financial situation, or any other flexing trigger.

PRESENTING PROBLEMS PEOPLE BRING TO
EXECUTIVE COACHES[8]

Maybe you like the sound of *developing a better you* but are uncertain as to what sorts of skills you might need to work on. The following list of common challenges that aspiring business leaders bring to executive coaches may provide some thought-provoking ideas. How many of these represent skills you would like to be better at? Any or all could become the basis for a new flex goal and a series of experiments aimed at testing various paths to growth.

+ Develop strategic thinking
+ Improve communication skills
+ Executive presence
+ Developing/coaching others (listening, asking open-ended questions versus telling, curiosity, nonjudgmental, co-creating solution, agency for others)
+ Career exploration (purpose, strengths, values, impact/meaning)
+ Negotiating on your own behalf and on behalf of team
+ Collaboration/engaging diversity of thought
+ Leading effective meetings
+ Decision making
+ Managing up
+ Giving, receiving, seeking feedback
+ Managing difficult work relationships
+ Team dynamics
+ Developing team competencies (people, process, results)
+ How to demonstrate value at work
+ Networking internally and externally
+ Boosting confidence
+ Taking healthy risks

+ Self-compassion
+ Perfectionism
+ Job search
+ Managing strong emotions
+ Building trusted relationships

FLEXING IN RESPONSE TO TRAUMA

As the stories we've shared attest, flexing certainly can help you find effective responses for the challenges that arrive in most aspects of everyday life and work. But experience as well as scholarly research have shown that people can also learn and grow in response to life's most difficult, even traumatic experiences. In fact, this form of growth has even been given its own name: *post-traumatic growth* (in contrast to the more familiar expression, *post-traumatic stress*).

Post-traumatic growth often includes such elements as a stronger sense of self, deeper and higher-quality relationships with others, and a new philosophy of life, often reflecting radically altered priorities.[9]

Even at age ninety, Sam and Lois Bloom are among the most growth-oriented people I know. Deeply religious, they have often felt "nudged by God" to grow through their life experiences. Lois's father suffered from manic depression, but in those days most people minimized the problem, describing it just as "a drinking problem." On many nights young Sam and Lois would be called by a family member to pick Lois's father up at a club or a bar. In response to this challenging family context, they developed a strong ethic of service to others, devoting their free time to volunteer activities. They moved to California with their three kids and raised them in a beautiful setting. It seemed they'd found a happy refuge that would define the rest of their lives.

In 1982 that idyll came to an end. Their son Sammy, who had been troubled in college, was lured by the appeal of a cult. He joined the group and remained with it for about a month until he was rescued by Sam. But Sammy's underlying psychological and emotional struggles continued. A few months later, he drove his car off a cliff, ending his life. Sam and Lois had to deal with a son's suicide, perhaps the most awful experience any parent can imagine.

How do you respond to a trauma like that, especially if you are a person for whom learning and growth are core values of life? There's no simple answer. But Lois responded by making a list. Late one night, tossing and turning sleeplessly in her bed, she finally switched on the light, grabbed a pen and paper, and began to write. She made a list of all the things that were troubling her—all the questions whose answers she desperately needed. How does a cult come into existence? Why do cults exercise such a powerful attraction over some people? What leads an individual to contemplate suicide? How can those left behind after a suicide come to grips with the tragedy? How can a person who has suffered greatly cope with an intense sense of anger at God?

That night changed Sam and Lois's lives by changing the meaning of Sammy's suicide for them. Of course, it was still a terrible, heartbreaking loss. But it also became the starting point for a new path of growth, one that gave their lives a deeper meaning and purpose.

Leaning on one another even as they turned their efforts toward helping others, Sam and Lois became involved in a nascent suicide prevention effort at UCLA. They benefited from the wisdom of counselors, expert researchers, and other families that had been down the same path.

Much to her surprise, Lois became a writer. Asked to review someone else's article on coping with suicide, she frankly said, "It was terrible." The editor replied, "Maybe you can write a better one." Lois agreed to give it a try. The result was a booklet called *Mourning, After Suicide*. Thousands of readers have benefited from the advice Lois shares in its pages.

The Blooms also grew through helping others even more directly.

One day a work friend stopped by Lois's cubicle. "I just wanted to say goodbye," he said.

Lois sensed that something was off about him. She followed him into the parking lot, begging him to let her help him, telling him how important he was to her. Seemingly oblivious, he drove away. But Lois was still worried. She called him later and somehow convinced him to go out to dinner with her and Sam. That call interrupted their friend's planned suicide. The three talked late into the night.

Years later, Lois ran into her old friend at a Costco store. His life had changed: he'd gotten married, had twins, and was living a happy and productive life. Thanks to Lois and Sam, that life hadn't been cut short before its time as their son's had.

The response of the Blooms to the trauma of losing their son offers lessons from which we can all benefit. Notice how they leaned into their horrific experience rather than running from it. You grow by being open to what an experience has to teach you. In the case of the Blooms, their religious values provided a framing that enabled them to be open to what a terrible ordeal could offer. They were accustomed to recognizing "nudges from God" even in painful life experiences. But it isn't necessary to have conventional or formal religious beliefs to grow in response to trauma. What's crucial is to retain the growth orientation that people like the Blooms exhibit.[10] After experiencing a devastating loss, all of us can follow the steps that Sam and Lois took: we can seek to learn, rather than angrily demanding answers; we can turn to others who may be able to provide important starting points for our growth journey; and we can ultimately make our own experience useful to others in need.

Our second story of post-traumatic growth comes from someone much younger. As a student, Elyse was a high achiever. Early on in college, she was voted president of her sorority, and then later she became president of *all* the sororities on campus, all while also serving on the student council and in other leadership roles. After graduation, she got a plum job in consulting. She was living the lifestyle of a striving twenty-something, working long hours, traveling extensively for work, and spending her leisure time working out and going out with friends. She was having fun, accomplishing a lot, and felt happy to be proving her abilities to others and, more important, to herself.

But then, like the Blooms, Elyse had an unexpected experience that would change her life forever. While she was in a rideshare late one night, having just arrived in her client's city, the car was hit by another driver. Elyse suffered a significant brain injury that left her unable to continue her work as a consultant. Her life, defined by high achievement and constant activity, was no longer possible. To maintain her sanity, Elyse had to find a different way.

Looking back, Elyse describes how she moved slowly and inevitably into a learning mindset, which was a new attitude for her. It showed up in how she engaged with new endeavors. For example, she signed up for an art class at a local school and quickly realized that she was one of the least skilled students in the group. The old Elyse would probably have quit. After all, why bother with an activity if you can't be one of the best? But the new Elyse stuck with it. "I like working on art projects," she said to herself. "It gives me joy." And for the new Elyse, that was enough.

Later, she tried her hand at doing computer animation as part of her rehabilitation, and again she realized that many of those around her were much better at it than she was. But rather than quitting, Elyse kept trying. She spent whatever limited screen time her brain injury allowed her on evenings and weekends studying videos that offered tips and techniques for improving her animation work. Slowly she found herself gaining skill and confidence. She still wasn't meeting the standard of achievement that an expert might set, but she was meeting her own standard, and in the process she experienced a sense of growth, fulfillment, and accomplishment that gave her enormous pleasure and satisfaction.

Elyse's recalibration of her own definition of *success* is a process we can all benefit from, even if we haven't lived through a profound personal trauma. After all, practically everyone needs to work on personal effectiveness skills that do not lend themselves to absolute definitions of achievement. The skills involved in being effective group leaders, communicators, team builders, and motivators are ones we can spend a lifetime developing and learning to apply in an endless array of varied circumstances. For this reason we all need to learn the lesson Elyse learned: that the most important standard of achievement is the one we set for ourselves, not the one some outside expert or society might set for us.

Elyse and the Blooms aren't the only people I know who have benefited from post-traumatic growth. Several other people we interviewed for this book spoke about traumatic events that triggered significant learning and growth experiences for them, ranging from the death of a parent to an unexpected health crisis. For example, Doug Evans told us how the sudden death of a friend helped him recognize that his single-minded focus on career advancement led him to rethink his life priorities. He set a new flex goal for himself: to pay more attention to the people he cares about, even while continuing to focus on being successful at work. And research by other experts confirms that post-traumatic growth is a surprisingly common phenomenon. For example, in one study, mothers reported that the stress of parenting a high-risk infant had the positive effect of prompting closer family relationships, emotional growth, and a better perspective on life.[11]

Reflecting on the power of post-traumatic stress, I recall the "lifeline" exercise I use on the first day of the executive program I run for emerging leaders. As you'll remember from chapter 1, most business leaders asked to look back on their life stories agree that they have learned and grown the most from negative events, stressful times, failures, and setbacks— even as they spend most of their lives trying to avoid just such experiences!

I don't recommend you start seeking out trauma and failure. For most of us, that's not necessary: painful experience has a way of affecting almost everyone, even those with lives full of satisfaction and accomplishment. But the attitude you take toward trauma can be life changing. If you approach tough times with a learning orientation, you can derive lessons from the experience that can empower you to pursue renewed success, achievement, and fulfillment in the years to come.

THE POWER OF FLEXING: A SEVEN-STEP GUIDE

1. Identify an upcoming experience that presents you with a challenge. It may be an experience with the characteristics we identified in chapter 2 as a high-potential learning experience: one that is visible, high-stakes, and involves crossing boundaries or interacting with new kinds of people.

2. Adopt a learning mindset with respect to the upcoming experience. How can you go through it as a learner, recognizing that, in addition to performing well, you want to be open to learning all that this experience may have to teach you?

3. Identify a goal. Beyond what you want to achieve in the experience, what is a personal skill that you can work on about yourself? The goal may come from some pain in your present (a place where you need improvement) or from some aspiration you have about the future (a better way you can be that you would like to begin working toward).

4. Plan some experiments: What might you try in the upcoming experience that would allow you to experiment your way toward your goal? What small first steps could you take? What bigger and bolder steps might you consider trying? Write down your experimental plan. If possible, share it with a friend or confidant. Become committed to it.

5. Set up some way to remind yourself in the thick of the action to keep trying your experiment(s).

6. While the experience is happening, be sure to stay open to the feedback around you. This may include things you notice as well as the responses people provide when you ask them, "How am I doing on X?" (where X is your goal).

7. Find time to reflect. What did this experience teach you about yourself with respect to this goal? Did your experiment work or fail? What new experiment should you try? Do you want to keep working on the same goal in your next challenging experience or move to a new goal?

CHAPTER 9

COACHING TEAM MEMBERS IN THE POWER OF FLEXING

The Power of Flexing allows individuals to build their personal effectiveness and leadership skills without traditional interventions such as management training and mentorship. It is an approach based not on filling heads with new knowledge about work skills but rather one that involves people in their own development—in experimenting with new practices that are useful for them, their communities, and their organizations.

To this point we've been focused on explaining what individuals can do to facilitate their own growth. This chapter focuses on how you can help others to grow as well. You may be a boss hoping to support team members who report to you as they strive to improve their skills, collaborate more effectively, and contribute more to the team you lead. You may be an HR manager charged with helping senior leaders to maximize the productivity and creativity of the people under their direction. You may be a leader, formal or informal, in a community organization or civic association seeking to help turn ordinary citizens into influential leaders who can bring positive change to a neighborhood or to the world at large. You may be a parent hoping to impart some of the benefits of flexing to your children as they begin to develop their own skills for success in work and in life.

In all these cases, even as you continue to use flexing to enhance your own personal effectiveness, you may want to use the insights from the Power of Flexing to encourage and stimulate the growth of others.

COACHES AS MIDWIVES OF GROWTH

Coaches are in the growth game. Coaches are helpers who work with functioning—often highly functioning—people who have run into a roadblock, face new challenges, or simply want to "up their game." Executive coaches and life and career coaches, much like sports coaches, provide valuable guidance and support to people ranging from young interns just beginning to understand the world of work to *Fortune* 500 CEOs tackling challenges that may affect giant corporations and the lives of millions.

Great coaches can teach us a lot about how to manage our own learning and growth and also how to help others around us to evolve as well.

As part of my effort to get deep into the world and mindset of effective coaches, I spent time with Karin Stawarky, the executive coach you've already met in this book. Karin was a successful partner and an eleven-year veteran at Monitor Deloitte with leadership experience as an interim executive in various organizations. She then left that world to found Spark Leadership Partners, where she works with a wide variety of executives around the world across many companies and industries, focusing on executive coaching and acting as a "thought partner" to senior leaders. In 2019 she was named one of the top 100 "leadership catalysts" for the world by Marshall Goldsmith, who is perhaps today's best-known and most distinguished executive coach.

I also interviewed Shahnaz Broucek, a professional coach certified through the International Coaching Federation. Shahnaz's approach to coaching has been shaped by her thirty years of experience in progressive leadership roles and small-business ownership. Broucek used her participation in the Ross Executive MBA program to rethink what she most wanted to do in life, and she made the decision to reinvent herself as an executive coach. Since that time, she has helped hundreds of executive leaders, teams, and organizations through her company, OptimizeU. She cofounded Care for Givers, which provides researched-based stress reduction interventions to frontline caregivers impacted by the pandemic.

The time I spent with Stawarky and Broucek taught me a number of valuable lessons about what great coaches do well for their clients. Remarkably, although these two coaches have never met each other and work with clients in different regions of the country, they offered many similar observations and suggestions, which suggests to me that there is a deep validity and strength to their approaches to coaching. Their ideas can serve you as a starter kit as you begin to work on helping people around you—your own "coachees"—to learn and grow. At the end of this chapter you'll also find a coach's guide that assembles in one place a number of powerful questions you can use at various stages of the process of helping others to learn to nurture their own growth.

CREATING A CONTEXT FOR GROWTH

An effective coach presumes that their client, or coachee, is the world's leading expert on themselves. The coach's job is to be an expert on the process of growth. Because you're reading this book, you're becoming an expert on the process of flexing. And when it comes to coaching another person in that process, the first step is setting up the conditions that allow one human being to work productively with another. This step is analogous to the work you did in chapter 2, where you examined and modified your mindset, seeking to reduce the ideas and assumptions that discourage growth in favor of different ideas and assumptions that enable growth.

For you as a coach, the goal is to create a *high-quality connection* with your coachee—a connection that is generative and open and allows for the expression of more and varied emotions, including those that are both positive and negative.[1] To create such a high-quality connection, you'll want to work to be fully present in your coaching relationship, to communicate understanding, and to truly listen, engaging your coachee in a curious and nonjudgmental manner. According to Shahnaz, "The key is helping the person being coached to feel seen, heard, respected and safe."

Here are some specific tips for creating the kind of context that will nurture your coachee's growth process.

Shape a Space and a Time for Growth

Start by making a safe place for the coachee to explore what's going on for them. That means a space—physical and psychological—where it feels safe to engage in interpersonal risk taking, safe for offering confidences, sharing stories that may be painful or embarrassing, confessing weaknesses, describing fears, and otherwise exposing one's vulnerabilities. Creating such a space is the crucial first step in being an effective coach. Many people have had few or no opportunities to enter such a space; they have no one in their lives with whom they feel comfortable revealing that they are troubled or in need of help. This issue of safety becomes increasingly important the higher up in an organization your coachee has risen. It is one thing to admit uncertainty or insecurity when you are a new hire, quite another when the person seeking your help is a long-tenured corporate vice president, an entrepreneurial CEO, or a university president. In such cases it may take time for you and your coachee to develop the necessary feeling of trust that's required to define a space in which growth can occur.

Karin Stawarky notes the importance of thinking about time. Inadequate time can stymie any effort to develop a sense of safety. Rather than trying to jam a coaching conversation into a spare ten minutes between other things you have to do, schedule a dedicated time for the process and block out possible interruptions: phone calls, text messages, and the like. Karin also recommends being expansive in your time allotment. If you expect the coaching conversation to last for twenty or thirty minutes, put a hold in your calendar for an hour. Your goal should be to communicate to your coachee, "This is important to me, and I have made the time available for it."

Be Ready to Dig Deep

Your coachee will probably start the conversation with what coaches call a *presenting problem*—an issue or concern that they are worried about and that they want help with tackling. This is an important launching point for your coaching relationship. But both Stawarky and Broucek note that, in many cases, the presenting problem is *not* the real problem the coachee needs to work on. So, as a coach, take the presenting problem with a grain of salt and be curious—prepared to engage in extended conversation to unearth the deeper problem that potentially may lurk beneath the surface issue.

For many coachees, the real underlying problem is a lack of self-confidence. Stawarky has been surprised at the number of high-level organizational leaders who struggle internally with questions like "Can I do this?" and "Am I good enough?"—questions they rarely ask explicitly but that hide "beneath what comes out in our conversations." Similarly, Broucek observes that no matter how successful we are, we all have an inner critic, "this voice inside their head that says, 'I don't know what I'm doing. I'm not sure whether this is the right approach. If I mess this up it's going to be a disaster.'" Even highly successful leaders with well-honed management instincts may have this kind of fear-based running monologue inside their heads that leads to rumination, overwork, and distress.

Because of the taboos many people sense about showing vulnerability, the fears associated with a lack of self-confidence are often expressed in disguised forms. Coachees may say, "I don't have time to try something new" when, deep inside, they are afraid to risk change. They may say, "My organization won't let me lead the way I really want to" when in fact it is fear that holds them back. For a coach, seeing the real issue means looking beyond the disguises to uncover what is driving the dysfunctional behavior or the lack of progress.

Set an Appropriate Goal

As you've seen, a key element of the Power of Flexing is setting a flex goal. As a coach, your job is to help your coachee identify a goal at the right level. For example, if your coachee is interested in creating better followership among their team members—the presenting issue offered by one of Stawarky's clients—your job is to work with the coachee to identify the steps to getting there. What is the missing ingredient in the coachee's current mode of behavior? Does the coachee need to learn how to listen more effectively? Do they need to work on developing patience or controlling their anger? Depending on the coachee, one of these adjustments, or some other similar change, might be an appropriate goal. If you can help your coachee identify the real challenge underlying the presenting issue, you can play an important role in helping them define the right goal.

Ask Questions That Can Generate Insights

One of the most important tools the coaches use is *inquiry*—asking questions to get coachees to go deeper into their thinking about the issues they face and the role of their experiences in nurturing their growth and development.

Sometimes even questions that seem basic or obvious may need to be asked. Stawarky had a client—I'll call her Rosa—who was being groomed for big things. She was seen as a future leader of the organization, which had made a serious investment in her development. Stawarky's job was to help Rosa take full advantage of this positioning as she prepared for a promising future. To launch the discussion, Stawarky asked Rosa, "What do you want?"

To Stawarky's surprise, Rosa simply stared at her silently. Finally she admitted, "I haven't thought about that."

Stawarky used inquiry to probe further. "As you look at your future career, what position do you aspire to? Do you want to be chief operations officer someday? Do you want to be the CEO?"

Again Rosa responded with silence. She had been so caught up in the tidal pull of daily events and the momentum of organizational decisions about her career that she had never really paused to ask herself, "What is the end game here? Do I want to be COO? Do I want to go on to be CEO? What would I really like to achieve in my career? What kind of role will make my life feel satisfying and fulfilling?"

In the conversations that followed, Stawarky and Rosa explored these questions in detail. Together they defined career goals that Rosa could personally embrace, thereby taking control of her future away from the organization and placing it squarely where it belonged: with Rosa herself. This was an important, empowering shift.

Inquiry can help to prompt *synthesis*—the drawing of connections among experiences and ideas. For example, suppose your coachee shares with you a story about an overwhelming experience they are having. You might respond with questions like "What can this experience teach you? Why did the experience happen the way it did? What might you try to do differently to produce a different outcome next time?" Questions such as these can help a coachee draw conclusions, create continuity between experiences, and generate ideas that can help to shape learning and growth for the future.

Trigger the Power of Imagination

Inquiry also prompts growth through inviting what innovation scholars call *ideation*—coming up with ideas.

One of Stawarky's favorite questions for new clients is "It's five years from now, and you and I are meeting for a cup of coffee in an airport. What do you want to tell me that's happened in your life?" The question invites Stawarky's clients to imagine the scene vividly—to briefly live in that future moment as they choose to envision it. The picture clients sketch is a first step toward thinking about what they need to begin doing in their current lives to turn that future vision into a reality. In addition to helping the client define what they need to do differently, what they need to learn, and what they may need to *stop* doing, the gift of imagination also helps the client recognize the cost of *failing* to change—in other words, the pain of the present, which change may help to relieve.

Challenge Assumptions

Part of a coach's job is to help a coachee break through assumptions—beliefs inherited from the coachee's upbringing, their education, their environment, or society at large. Unfounded assumptions, inaccurate perceptions, and stereotyped images are among the biggest obstacles to learning and growing.

Stawarky tells the story of a client who was being considered for an executive position in the organization for the first time. "Justin" was very smart and successful, but past experiences and feedback from a handful of people had led him to develop a very clear and very limiting self-image: "I'm not a strategy person; I'm a doer." If left unchallenged, this simplistic assumption had the potential to severely restrict his future career development.

Stawarky helped Justin break free of his limiting self-image by offering this challenge: "Turn off your analytical and practical self for a moment and just give space to what your intuition says. Now talk about the future direction of your organization." When Justin did this, he came up with some very powerful and impressive strategic ideas. Stawarky pointed this out, helping Justin to expand his sense of what it means to "be strategic" and discover how he might do that in his own style. As Justin began revising his self-image, it created greater opportunities for him to grow in unexpected new directions. By breaking through Justin's flawed assumptions, Karin helped him to step into his new job in a way that built on this strength and brought benefits to his company. He became more confident in asking simple but powerful questions and began following his strong, people-oriented instincts into conversations about culture and employee engagement, including his impressive knowledge of the tasks and his growing strategic intuitions.

One of Stawarky's favorite coaching mantras is "Shed the *shoulds*!" She urges clients to forget about who they think they *should* be and what they think they *should* be doing. Instead, she invites them to understand who they really are, what opportunities really exist, and what they really want to accomplish in the weeks, months, and years to come. Coaching interventions like these can help people get into a playful, can-do mindset that helps to empower them to take full advantage of the benefits of the Power of Flexing.

Promote Experimentation

Coaches are uniquely positioned to foster experimentation. As a coach, you can highlight concepts such as the learning mindset, feedback seeking, and reflection, showing your coachees how helpful these ideas can be in exploring solutions to their career and life challenges.

The executive coaches I studied help prompt ideas for experiments in a variety of other ways. Broucek likes to suggest that her clients look for a leader they admire to see if their most effective behaviors might be something they could try. Stawarky suggests that clients reflect on their own lives, looking for times when they engaged in experimentation, perhaps without fully realizing it: "When was there a moment when you tried something new? What happened? What did you learn from it? Is there something similar you could try today?" She also helps clients find actionable experimental ideas by urging them to break big ideas into smaller, "bite-sized" pieces they may find less daunting and easier to test. Ideas like these can help coachees develop the open-ended, playful attitude that is conducive to experimentation.

Great executive coaches also use their breadth of business experience and knowledge to assist clients in developing experimental ideas. If a client is feeling particularly stuck and there is an apparent knowledge gap, Broucek sometimes shares examples from other leaders in similar situations, suggesting ideas for strategies a client may want to experiment with. Stawarky draws upon her experience in varying functional domains. "I can meet executives where they are," she says. "If they're talking about marketing or manufacturing and supply chain, I can talk about that. If they're talking about organization, I can talk about organization. I've been in all those worlds, so there's a fluency." Her fluency helps her identify potential experiments, often introduced with her favorite suggestion: "Why not try this?"

You may not have the same specific range of business expertise as these executive coaches. But everyone has a set of unique personal experiences they can draw upon when helping another person to think about the challenges they face. Simply bringing another perspective to bear upon a problem that your coachee may have been wrestling with fruitlessly can play a useful role in breaking a mental impasse. In the spirit of open-minded discovery, don't hesitate to offer your own ideas and experiences as a way of helping a coachee develop a new way of thinking and, perhaps, a powerfully eye-opening experiment.

Help Build a Narrative Around Growth

Finally, inquiry is valuable because it can be used to reinforce a coachee's self-narrative or identity around growth. As a coach, look for opportunities to ask questions like "What have you been learning this week? What new skills are you working on? What new insights did you develop? How are you growing?" (And these questions are great ones to ask yourself, too, when you are flexing!)

Questions like these matter, and not just as helpful springboards to fruitful conversation. They also invite your coachee to see growth and progress as part of their identity—which in itself has been found to be an important element in personal development.[2] By helping coachees to see themselves as growing and reminding them of progress made, you help them to take on future challenges that will enable them to learn and grow.

HELPING OTHERS TO OVERCOME BARRIERS TO GROWTH

Like every truly worthwhile activity, the Power of Flexing often doesn't happen easily. As a coach for others learning this new skill, you'll want to be on the lookout for some of the barriers that can make it difficult. Here again our expert executive coaches have valuable insights to share to help mentees overcome some of the problems they face.

Get Beyond Perfectionism

Karin Stawarky points to perfectionism as one of the most common barriers to learning and growth. "People become very committed to the pursuit of perfectionism," she observes, "because it has served them well for so much of their lives in terms of achievement, recognition, and financial security." It's true that a determination to do everything right—to micromanage the details of a task in hopes of getting the work as close to perfect as possible, and to avoid taking on any job that you can't engage in the same aspirational spirit—can lead to stellar results when applied appropriately. But when a person tries to tackle *everything* in work or life in perfectionist mode, then open-ended learning, growth, and experimentation become almost impossible. After all, experimentation by definition means trying something new even when the results are uncertain and failure is a genuine possibility.

Overcoming a rigid adherence to perfectionism often involves some inner exploration. You may need to ask your coachee questions like "What makes trying something new difficult? What kinds of worries or anxieties does it provoke? What might happen if you try something new and fail? How might your self-image be affected if you achieve less-than-perfect results?" Simply talking about the emotional underpinnings of perfectionism can help coachees free themselves from the tyranny of such feelings.[3]

In other cases, you can help the coachee talk through current challenges in work or life in search of "safe zones" where moderating the perfectionist instinct involves little risk. Not every task we undertake is a matter of life or death. Most people can find opportunities to try new strategies and practice new skills in ways that pose no threat to their long-term success or reputation, and as a coach you can help them identify such opportunities.

Notice and Respond to the Negative Mind Chatter

During the coaching sessions they lead, both Stawarky and Broucek listen carefully to the mind chatter that emerges from their clients' descriptions of their goals and experiments. The things people say about their attempts to learn and grow often reveal a lot about how they think, which may be having a significant impact on their behavior.

Stawarky, for example, listens for remarks that reveal an underlying lack of self-confidence—comments like "I doubt I could do that" and "I wouldn't know where to begin." Broucek pays close attention to clues that expose the persistence of a fixed mindset rather than a learning mindset—for example, "I'll never be a good networker" or "There's no point in trying with her!"

You may be surprised by how pervasive and ingrained a fixed mindset can be. I once consulted with the head of a prominent independent high school that had implemented a leadership course for its seniors. In our discussions about the course, the headmaster astounded me by saying, "I'm careful about who I let into the course. I only want the *real* leaders." I was startled to hear him talk about seventeen-year-olds as if their leadership potential is fixed and can be accurately measured—beliefs that research has definitively shown to be false. Yet these beliefs remain widespread in corporate America and elsewhere.

Effective coaches use verbal and other clues to identify such negative beliefs and to work with their clients on possible mindset shifts. They ask their clients questions like "Is there another possibility here?" "How well is this mindset serving you, given the changes you would like to make?" and "Do you see any possibility of experimenting with a different mindset and observing its effects?"

Seek Opportunities for Small Wins

As a coach, you can encourage a coachee who may be hesitant about practicing the Power of Flexing because change seems hard or impossible in their setting by helping them to identify some early, easy wins to start with. My University of Michigan colleague Karl Weick calls this "the psychology of small wins."[4] A small win is a concrete outcome of moderate importance. By itself, it may be insignificant, but it can be important as it sets forces in motion that may favor the next small win—forces that may include gaining more knowledge or finding a valuable ally. In time, an accumulation of small wins can lead to bigger wins. Weick applies this philosophy to the pursuit of social change, but it can play a useful role in personal psychology as well.

Shahnaz Broucek likes to employ the small wins strategy with her clients. For example, she says, "If they wanted to improve their feedback seeking skills, I might suggest they start with someone that feels safer and ramp up to other relationships as they get more comfortable."

Karin Stawarky describes the same approach this way: "Some of my clients have big muscles to develop as they move into new roles or face significant new challenges. We've got to do them a little bit at a time, in small increments. This lets them get comfortable with growth and then build it over time."

Encourage Coachees to Use All the Information Available to Them

Sometimes a coachee may over-attend to certain feedback in experiences, giving short shrift to other input. For example, they may focus on negative feedback to the exclusion of positive feedback; or, conversely, they may over-attend to feedback that suggests success and ignore feedback that points to problems.

Shahnaz Broucek observes that people may tend to focus narrowly on feedback from only one stakeholder, typically their boss. Instead, she encourages them to consider *all* their various stakeholders (boss, subordinates, and peers) as they seek self-awareness about how they are perceived by others and set development goals. One helpful tool she often uses is a *360° feedback instrument* that collects quantitative input from a person's multiple stakeholders. Both coaches also supplement this kind of tool whenever possible with qualitative interviews that enable a deeper dive into a client's personal strengths and weaknesses and give them a better sense of how the people they are trying to help are experienced by others and allow the coaches to carefully observe what is being said and not said about their coachee. If you have access to tools like this when you are coaching someone, take advantage of the information they provide.

Also consider using the tool I mentioned in chapter 3, the Reflected Best Self Exercise.[5] Both of these coaches do. It is especially designed for identifying an individual's strengths. To use it, the coachee sends a brief email to twenty people they interact with: work colleagues or clients, community members, friends and relatives, and so on. The email asks a simple question: "Tell me about a time when you have seen me at my best." As a coach, you can help to identify specific themes, behavior tendencies, ways of showing up, styles of intervening, and other significant traits. The goal is to help the coachee set goals for growth by clearly identifying strengths they can build upon. Recent research suggests that this exercise can have a powerful effect at the team level as well. When people understand their strengths, they are less concerned about social acceptance and become more willing to share the information that teams need to excel.[6]

Work on Managing Difficult Emotions

Because fear, frustration, and anxiety are often at the root of a reluctance to experiment, part of the coaching relationship is helping people understand these difficult emotions and work with them.

Sometimes the solution begins simply with a different framing for the experiment, a different mindset. Stawarky prompts this by asking questions like "So why not?" and "What is the worst thing that could happen?" Questions like these appeal to the thinking self, which can sometimes override the emotional self.

In other cases, Stawarky has found that giving people permission to talk about and begin to deal with their difficult emotions is a useful step toward solving the problem. For example, she occasionally asks a CEO client wracked with guilt or anxiety to write out a note saying something like "I hereby give myself permission to take a day off," or "I give myself permission to answer 'I don't know' when I'm asked a question during a meeting." Physically writing a statement like this and then signing it can be surprisingly effective at reducing the guilt and anxiety associated with some kinds of personal experiments.

Make Growth a Habit

Broucek defines her ultimate goal as a coach as *new habit formation that aligns with her coachee's ideal self.* She wants to get her clients "experimenting with solutions and getting some repetition, so that they are building new neural pathways in the brain that become habitual over time."

Unfortunately, this can be surprisingly difficult to achieve. One powerful tool is engaging what Broucek calls an *accountability partner*—a person who provides feedback and encouragement on a regular basis. Your accountability partner might be, for example, a person who participates in the weekly meeting with you and whom you can approach afterward with questions like "How did the meeting go? What was your read on it? Help me to see something that I did not see." The best accountability partners are fully in your corner, supportive, and nonjudgmental. An accountability partner can help by believing in the person at times when they find it difficult to believe in themselves. Finding the right accountability partner(s) is key.

Stawarky points out two side benefits of engaging an accountability partner, a role she often plays with her clients. First: "It is one of the most powerful moves that you can make as a leader, because you are demonstrating a learning mindset: you are showing the vulnerability and the openness to learning and change that you hope others will also take up."

Second: "It is an awesome developmental opportunity for your accountability partner. They must actually pay attention to you and the dynamics in the room, observe the implications, and then give you feedback on them. These are important skills to develop for any manager and leader."

Structure also plays an important role in developing the growth habit. Coaching has a natural rhythm that works well with the Power of Flexing. When coach and coachee meet regularly—weekly, biweekly, or monthly—they can work together through the "do, evaluate, do, repeat" sequence, creating a natural space for reflection and consideration. The cadence builds in accountability. The structure also makes it easy to break down the needed behavioral changes into small chunks, using each meeting to set new goals, define new experiments, and adjust priorities as needed.

Assuming you're not an executive coach, you may or may not be able to set up a coaching relationship with this same regular structure. For instance, if you are a corporate boss coaching a subordinate, you likely will not have the bandwidth needed to commit to a weekly meeting. In that sort of situation, it's helpful if the organization can put in place a systematic approach supported by Human Resources and woven into the organization's larger culture. We'll take up those issues in the next two chapters.

Do Your Own Flexing

Karin Stawarky says, "I believe the best coaches are the ones who are always working on themselves." Asked to elaborate, she explains:

> You show up in every interaction that you have with a client. And you need to really understand when you're getting in the way of the conversation. You need to be aware of your unconscious

biases and how they are affecting where you are pushing your client. So a coach can only be truly helpful to a client by embracing their own inner evolution.

Stawarky's message applies not just to executive coaches but to anyone who wants to help others learn and develop. If you truly want to help others grow, be an active participant in and shaper of your own growth as well.

HELPING OTHERS TO FLEX: A COACH'S GUIDE[7]

Getting Started: Questions for the Coach

+ What steps have you taken to create a safe space for your coachee to explore their problem fully?
+ What can you do to create the potential for a high-quality connection?
+ During your coaching session, how can you enhance your ability to be fully present—not on your phone, answering emails, and so on?
+ What boundaries can you set so both you and your coachee know what to expect? For example, have you specified the amount of time you'll have together and the expected frequency of your sessions?
+ How have you been able to demonstrate your listening in ways that let your coachee know you are fully engaged—for example, by paraphrasing back what you're hearing?
+ In what ways have you offered your coachee assurances of safety—for example, a serious commitment to confidentiality?
+ What clues is your coachee sending about their mindset in their current experience? Are you detecting problems you may need to address?

ENGAGING THE PROCESS: QUESTIONS COACHES MIGHT ASK OF THEIR COACHEES

To Sharpen Their Focus

+ What is the most important issue for you to address in your effort to be the leader you most want to be?
+ What issue is most painful in the present for you?
+ Based on explicit and implicit feedback, how are people experiencing you currently?
+ What costs are there for you in the current situation—for example, costs to your relationships or an emotional toll?
+ Are there any perceived costs for others in your current situation?
+ What benefits are there for you in the current situation—for example, the benefit of minimizing the expression of anger?
+ How do you want other people to experience you? What would the leader that you want to become do in your current situation?
+ How would you define, in a few words, the most important goal you currently want to achieve?

To Prompt Experimentation

+ Now what? What actions might you possibly take to address the issues in your current situation and pursue your goal?
+ What are some "small wins" you might pursue on the path to your overall goal?
+ What experimental actions would you try if you weren't afraid?
+ How will you know whether your experiments are working? What metrics will show success?
+ How can you build accountability into your experimental plan? Is there an accountability partner you might enlist to give you feedback and help you stay on track?

To Assess and Solidify Progress

+ How does the situation you chose to work on feel now?
+ Have you received feedback that suggests improvement? Have you received feedback that reflects new or continuing challenges?
+ What new reactions to you have you noticed that are different than you saw previously?
+ Who could you ask for feedback—for example, using a question like "I've been working on X [e.g., my listening, being more open]. How's it going?"
+ How can you create a context in which it is safe for others to give you feedback?
+ How well are you receiving the feedback others offer? Do your verbal and nonverbal signals reflect openness?
+ What might you try next based on what has happened so far?
+ Is the current goal still relevant? Is anything new happening that might suggest a different goal? If so, what?

AUTO-FLEXING: A SELF-HELP COACH'S GUIDE

While this chapter's focus has been on helping others to learn and grow, the coaches' questions are also great for individuals to use when they don't have a coach and only have themselves for help. Many of the questions outlined above are great when applied to oneself; use the following questions as you begin to get in the right mindset for the exploration:

Getting Started

+ Is this the right time to engage in self-coaching?
+ Are you able to get yourself into a self-compassionate space so that you can explore your problem fully?

+ Are you able to be fully present—not on your phone, watching TV, answering emails, and so on?
+ Can you commit to being open to the full set of your thoughts and emotions and work through your issue?

ENGAGING THE PROCESS

Now that you're in the right headspace, please use the questions above to continue your self-coaching.

CHAPTER 10

FLEXING YOUR COMPANY

Building an Employee Development Program Around the Power of Flexing

Much of the beauty and value of the Power of Flexing comes from the fact that it is "employee-owned." You can decide to invest in your own growth and development, controlling all the elements that foster and support that growth as you synthesize and solidify the lessons learned— all without the direction or encouragement of others. It's great to enjoy this kind of autonomy, especially in today's world, where people move from organization to organization more frequently and millions work on their own as entrepreneurs, freelancers, and independent contractors.

But well-run organizations recognize the value of having team members who are continually learning, developing, and growing. Such organization can realize enormous benefits by adopting, supporting, and reinforcing the Power of Flexing as part of their employee development efforts. However, this requires a new way of thinking about how to encourage, spread, and develop talent. The mindset underlying the Power of Flexing contrasts starkly with how companies and their HR departments have traditionally handled leadership development.

A NEW MODEL FOR LEADERSHIP DEVELOPMENT BASED ON THE POWER OF FLEXING

Organizations care about leadership development—a lot! A 2014 McKinsey report describes the field this way: "For years, organizations have lavished time and money on improving the capabilities of managers and on nurturing new leaders. US companies alone spend almost $14 billion annually on leadership development."[1] Yet, despite this vast investment, leadership is still thought to be the number one talent issue facing organizations worldwide. In a Deloitte survey, 86 percent of respondents rated it urgent or important.[2] Moreover, when five hundred executives were asked to rank their top three human-capital priorities, nearly two-thirds of the respondents identified leadership development as their highest concern. And while organizational leaders cite the development of leaders at all levels as vitally important, only 13 percent of them claim that they do it well.[3]

The problems start with the basic methodology most organizations apply to their leadership development efforts. Most companies use a differentiate-the-few strategy, selecting a small proportion of their employees as high potential and investing in their development accordingly. While this strategy may work in the short run for recruiting and hiring the best programmers, marketers, and managers, it's a poor fit for building the cadre of leaders throughout the organization that is needed today. And yet it is the predominant strategy. In a recent study of eighty companies known for their commitment to leadership development, 42 percent indicated that high potentials represent between 1 and 9 percent of their total population—which means that these companies are writing off up to 99 percent of their workforce as "non-leaders" unworthy of leadership development. Another 35 percent of the companies studied set the percentage of high-potential workers at up to 15 percent. And although the results of such winnowing processes may never be publicly disclosed, "the vast majority of employees know their status whether they are formally told or not."[4] So more than three-quarters of organizations are saying to 85 percent of their employees: *Your leadership is not needed or encouraged.*

There may have been a time in history when this strategy made some sense. In the industrial-era economy, steeply hierarchical organizations created a competitive advantage. Decisions were made by a small group at the top and fed down the organization through a process of command and control. In a world where education, information, and managerial skills were limited to a relative handful of people, this approach often worked. But it fails in today's world, which is increasingly complex and dynamic. This new world demands that organizations respond to problems that are complicated, ambiguous, and rapidly changing. In such a world the organization needs input and initiative from people who are close to the action: IT professionals who are attuned to emerging technological innovations; customer service specialists who can sense emerging trends in customer preferences and demands; and frontline HR staffers who have their fingers on the pulse of employee discontent and can highlight small morale problems before they become big ones. In short, organizations today need more people who think like leaders and act like leaders, but the traditional, differentiate-the-few leadership development strategy makes developing such a broad cadre of leaders less likely to happen.

Making matters worse, evidence suggests that most companies don't even choose the right people for the selective development programs. Leadership development specialists Jack Zenger and Joseph Folkman recently analyzed data from three companies that had identified 5 percent of employees as having high potential for leadership. Based on a 360° assessment, these scholars found that 42 percent of the identified high potentials actually were below average in leadership effectiveness, and 12 percent were in their organization's bottom quartile.[5] They attributed these poor choices to the organization's tendency to select those who have great technical skills, who have a strong drive for results, who honor their commitments, and who fit the culture. While all of these attributes have some impact on a person's ability to lead, they are less important than more central skills of leadership such as the abilities to appropriately delegate, influence well, and drive necessary change. All companies that differentiate-the-many relegate to the leadership scrap heap countless employees who may actually have *greater* leadership potential than the handful of anointed ones. What a sad waste of human potential.

Allan Church, senior vice president of global talent assessment and development at PepsiCo, has been arguing for a different approach. He suggests that companies need to identify those with leadership potential by measuring the ability to learn and grow.[6] Perhaps it's time to put that ability at the center of our leadership development efforts. Rather than choosing a few and giving them opportunities to grow their leadership, let's help employees to learn to develop themselves and support the many rather than differentiating the few. Such an approach starts with the recognition that anyone can grow their leadership and their personal effectiveness no matter where they start the journey. It takes seriously the finding that only 30 percent of an individual's tendency to emerge as a leader is attributable to genetics, leaving a wide range of possible growth for most individuals.[7]

To give all employees their best shot at learning to lead, an approach based on the Power of Flexing teaches everyone a methodology for growing their own leadership potential. This approach makes leadership growth more democratic, opening the ranks of potential leaders to those who were once among the many "unchosen." It counteracts the effects of similarity bias, which encourages managers to select next-generation leaders who look, talk, act, and think like them.[8] Similarity bias tends to perpetuate a relatively homogeneous, non-diverse leadership team—exactly the kind of team that will struggle when confronted with quickly changing, unpredictable problems in an increasingly diverse world.

Because this approach relies on individuals' agency, an endorse-the-many approach to leadership development also enhances feelings of empowerment. Over time, employees learn to do for themselves, taking responsibility for their own development and overall growth. Research shows that "when individuals see themselves as the primary active agent in their growing, they take the initiative to grow on their own by seeking out opportunities themselves. When employees see the organization as the primary active agent in growing, in contrast, they may simply wait for opportunities to come to them, such as through a training program or a promotion." With a more active, agentic stance, they are more likely to take advantage of opportunities to lead.[9]

This approach also avoids some of the natural downsides of the traditional differentiate-the-few approach to leadership development. When 85 percent of employees are told that they are not worth investing in, they are more likely to become disaffected, less motivated, and less committed to the organization. Many will develop a healthy antagonism toward the anointed few. Conflict, resentment, and frustration are natural outcomes. Giving everyone the ability to develop themselves minimizes these problems.

For all of these reasons, a leadership and personal effectiveness program that invests in the many is attractive to employees. We live in an increasingly transient employment market in which people move from company to company and sometimes industry to industry throughout their careers. If individuals have to continually sell themselves in a competitive job market, learning how to grow and develop their leadership and personal effectiveness becomes an especially important survival skill. Companies that enable and support this ability will be more desirable employers than those that don't.

This new approach to leadership development requires a shift to what my colleague Krishna Savani calls a "universal mindset regarding leadership."[10] It also requires moving from thinking of leadership development as something that one does by stopping work and going somewhere else to learn, to something one learns on the job, within the experiences that one would be having anyway. HR departments can play an important role in fostering these shifts. They can take steps to involve employees, managers, and leaders in adopting the Power of Flexing, making its benefits available to everyone in the organization.

A BETTER WAY TO ON-BOARD NEW HIRES

Flexing can be instilled in employees from the very start while on-boarding new hires. Organizations often bring in many employees at once—for example, hiring a group of new college or business school graduates shortly after the end of the academic year. They then put them through a rotation program involving short stints in a variety of business functions. Such a program could be enhanced significantly by flexing. A company could bring these new hires together prior to their first rotation to have them learn about the importance of the growth mindset, identify personal flex goals that feel current and relevant for them to pursue (along with learning the content skills related to the functional area in which they'll be working), and articulate several experiments they might try in their first work rotations.

In addition, new hires could be grouped together in peer coaching teams or paired with peer partners with whom they could share their growth plans. Peer coaches could help their partners clarify their flex goals, generate ideas for experiments, and work on maintaining a learning mindset. The peer partners would also help keep accountability high through regular feedback and discussions.

After the first rotation, the entire group of new hires could regather to engage in systematic reflection, learning from one another about successful strategies and challenging barriers. In their second rotation they could continue to work on the same flex goal or switch to a new goal that now seems more relevant and important. This process of meeting together, going off into the rotations, and coming back together to reflect would be repeated for the third and fourth rotations as well.

At the end of the entire rotation program, this cohort of new hires will have learned a lot about the organization and the work it does, like employees in most rotation programs. In addition, however, they will also have leveraged their rotation program experiences to learn a lot about themselves—much more than is normal in a traditional employee on-boarding program. They will have identified some personal developmental opportunities, clarified ways they can be more effective and leader-like, observed role models in other new hires that they may want to emulate, and received feedback that they have processed carefully in reflection sessions.

Adding flexing to the on-boarding process will also reinforce from the start that employees are the owners of their own development, that their development is important to the organization, and that supports will be provided along the way.

It will also allow members of a particular cohort to develop significant intellectual, social, and psychological bonds with one another, having shared in an intimate way the learning and growth challenges they've faced. In the years to come, the resulting network of employees and leaders all trained in the Power of Flexing and conversant with the processes and benefits of self-growth can then play an important role in supporting further growth for the individuals in the network and, by their modeling, growth for others throughout the organization.

FLEXING FOR CAREER TRANSITIONS

In addition to helping new hires, flexing can also be a powerful tool for newly promoted leaders or employees moving from one division, subsidiary, or country to another.

As we've noted, transitions are a natural time for flexing—a point at which people are more open and attuned to their impact on others, the level of their personal competencies, and the need for new action and attitudes. Organizational support can reinforce and amplify these attitudes, prompting transitioners not just to master their new roles but also to deepen their self-knowledge.

Once an organization has decided on a promotion, transfer, or other transition, the HR department could take several steps to support employee growth through flexing. An ideal program might be one in which several transitioners could form a working group, learning more about what it means to lead well, the elements of personal effectiveness involved in transitioning to a new position, and the personal challenges they each face.

Then each transitioner might be asked to pinpoint a specific upcoming experience as a source for growth—for example, the first meeting with their new team, a strategy-setting retreat, or a difficult conversation that needs to be held. This kind of thinking ahead—also called *prospection*—has been shown to have a variety of positive outcomes. A study that tested this idea using a micro transition—going from home to work—found that employees prompted to engage in role-clarifying prospection during their morning commutes considered those commutes less onerous and experienced higher job satisfaction and lower turnover.[11] If prospection has these effects in such a micro transition, think what it might contribute to more major, organizational transitions.

Transitioners could also be supplied with a transition checklist that identifies recommended actions designed to increase their effectiveness—for example, "identifying and meeting with key stakeholders" and "getting agreement on how success will be measured in the new job." The checklist could also include the key elements of the Power of Flexing process: committing to a learning orientation, setting a flex goal, identifying experiments, seeking feedback, making time for reflection, and so on. The transitioning program could also incorporate the peer coaches and systematic reflection processes used in the on-boarding program described above.

You might wonder whether the effectiveness of such a transitioning program could be compromised by the fact that the transitioners will probably be moving into a wide variety of locations and situations. Actually, that's a feature, not a bug. Engaging in deep, reflective conversations with colleagues experiencing challenges much different than their own will allow transitioners to learn not just from their own experiences but from the experiences of others.

That's what we observed at the University of Michigan when we ran such a program for students who were on their way to do internships in various locations in the summer between program years. We introduced the students to the Power of Flexing prior to their summer placements and took them through the initial steps together. They were then grouped with others going into different industries and in different locations to maximize diversity of input and to lessen concerns about confidentiality. These student groups met together virtually during the summer and then gathered for a reflection session after their return to campus. They reported that the diversity of experiences they were exposed to greatly enhanced their learning.

HOW SENIOR LEADERS CAN BENEFIT FROM THE POWER OF FLEXING

When an organization on-boards a high-level executive hire, a lot is at stake. In a big firm, this kind of hire may be handling a business with thousands of employees and billions of dollars in revenues. Even in a smaller company, a newly hired executive will occupy a highly visible position, control important resources, and convey significant symbolic messages through each of their words and actions. The success or failure of the new leader's first few months on the job may have a critical impact on the long-term future of the business.

Given what's at stake, the best organizations often devote significant resources to this sort of high-level transition. One of my colleagues was involved in such a program as an HR executive at a large, innovative technology firm. In one on-boarding of a very senior hire, she, her manager, and the manager of the new hire were all involved in developing a plan for his integration. My colleague's job in particular was to be the "eyes and ears" of the department. During weekly meetings with the new hire, she would filter things that she'd heard from the new hire's direct reports and colleagues, including feedback that people were sharing but did not want to share directly with him, and deliver it to him in a useful form. This feedback was remarkably varied. Sometimes the new hire's colleagues offered valuable detailed suggestions about communications strategies or leadership tactics that might be useful to him. In other cases they offered comments as simple as "I wish he would sometimes ask about my kids!"

The senior-level on-boarding process that my colleague participated in featured the ideal cadence of activities for flexing: a periodic meeting followed by live action, followed in turn by another meeting for reflection. Intentionally implementing the Power of Flexing could turn those meetings into opportunities to identify flex goals, to brainstorm on experiments to meet those goals, and to share feedback on progress made and issues remaining. Yes, this is a resource-intensive approach that can be used only at the most senior level of a company, where dedicated HR professionals are available for one-on-one coaching. But it amps up the learning by using the experiences that the new hire is having anyway and turning them into opportunities for increased leadership and personal effectiveness growth as well.

FLEXING AS A TOOL FOR CROSS-CULTURAL ENGAGEMENT

Living and working temporarily in a culture quite different from your own features many of the attributes known to demand—and to encourage—

personal learning, development, and growth; it is challenging and requires the ability to communicate, cooperate, and lead despite unusually difficult interpersonal and cultural boundaries. It's not surprising that global companies have developed a range of methods for helping groups of managers prepare for and make the most of international assignments. These methods include:

- **Short-term simulations,** in which team members develop specific skills through role-playing and trial-and-error exercises;
- **Action learning,** in which team members practice techniques for situation analysis in order to ensure they enhance their personal effectiveness skills as much as possible; and
- **Volunteerism,** in which leaders engage in service projects in foreign cultures as a way of developing a global mindset and an appreciation for diversity.

The good news is that flexing can be used to supplement and enhance *all* of these approaches.

Kevin Thompson, a colleague of mine at the University of Michigan, introduced the idea of Service Corps to the top leadership of IBM. The concept was to send executives all around the world for four-week stretches to work on projects designed to help far-flung communities, along the lines of what Peace Corps workers do. When Kevin first presented the idea, he said he was "laughed out of the room." But then CEO Sam Palmisano set developing more of a global mindset throughout IBM's executive and managerial ranks as a major strategic priority. Suddenly the idea of having a team of executives devote time to service work in a foreign locale made a lot more sense.

The program began soon after that and continues to this day. Through Service Corps, IBM executives develop a broader understanding of the world that helps them overcome their often parochial mindsets. They also get a chance to work intensely in cross-cultural groups, addressing issues of team development and conflict resolution as well.[12]

Coca-Cola's Donald Keough Executive Leadership Academy, though not focused on volunteerism, offers some similar benefits to executives in need to greater global awareness. Coca-Cola leaders spend six weeks immersed in various aspects of the company's business around the world, developing new skills, learning more about their own strengths and weaknesses, and developing lasting bonds with the peers with whom they share the experience.[13]

Both IBM's Service Corps and Coca-Cola's Donald Keough Executive Leadership Academy are effective tools for enhancing managers' global capabilities. But consider how much more the participants in these programs might learn if they engaged in the flexing throughout the process. Suppose, for example, they came together for exercises that would put them into a learning mindset and help them to set flex goals for themselves—for example, to work on being more influential or listening better while they're doing the volunteer work. Imagine how they might bond and learn from one another if they served as one another's accountability partners, gave developmental feedback, and reflected together on lessons learned.

My experience helping people on their leadership journeys has shown me that many managers yearn for a more intimate commitment to others at work as well as for a deeper process of learning and growth about themselves and our world. Taking successful programs aimed at cultural enrichment and layering on the Power of Flexing would enhance their potential for personal skill development while solidifying a mindset shift that makes self-development a top priority.

HR'S ROLE IN CREATING TOOLS FOR FLEXING

Yet another key role the HR department can play is in creating tools that support flexing.

Leigha Kinnear, a learning design specialist with years of experience across several institutions, was perennially frustrated with the challenge of helping people learn how to learn. She knew that the ability to learn from experience and then to translate that learning into higher levels of effectiveness was a key competency that millions of people needed to develop. But she'd found that conveying these skills to others was incredibly difficult. "I know exactly how to convey the building blocks of leadership development," she says. "But teaching people how to learn is so amorphous." Kinnear struggled with this challenge for years.

Kinnear's encounter with the Power of Flexing framework finally gave her the structure she needed. A client who needed tools for talent development and was familiar with flexing hired Kinnear to build tool kits around each of the flexing competencies and to create a discussion guide that managers could use to help their direct reports with their flexing. The workbook Kinnear developed included exercises, recommended videos and articles, activities, suggestions for experiments, and more.

Kinnear's experience illustrates an additional way that HR departments can help their employees use flexing for personal growth and development—by becoming in-house sources of tools designed to make flexing part of workers' daily routines.

For example, HR departments commonly publish lists of competencies—"The ten things leaders need to do to be more effective in this organization," for instance. It would be a simple matter for such lists to include strategies derived from the Power of Flexing that can help leaders improve their competencies over time. These and other tool kits designed or customized by HR professionals could incorporate the complete Power of Flexing system or focus on selected elements of it: developing a learning orientation, identifying flex goals, designing experiments, seeking feedback, or reflection.

These concepts can also be built into the company's orientation program for new employees, the annual review and appraisal processes, and other traditional HR functions. The result will be to help ensure that continual personal development, with the support of the organization, is high on everyone's agendas.

Valuable training and support for flexing can be offered in settings other than for-profit businesses. Nonprofits, community groups, schools and universities, religious institutions, and many other types of organizations can develop and disseminate flexing programs and tools that their members and associates can use to foster their own personal growth.

This is happening right now at the Stephen M. Ross School of Business at the University of Michigan, where I teach. The Sanger Leadership Center supports research and practice dedicated to "accelerating leader development" and making it more broadly available. The staff at Sanger faced the same problem as do organizations: How do you get busy people to attend to their leadership when they're absorbed with, in Sanger's case, passing courses, searching for jobs, planning club events, and so forth? What they invented was an ingenious structure they call the Sanger Leadership Journey. This program encourages and enables students to take ownership over their own personalized leadership development journeys by taking advantage of their experiences during the MBA program not just to grow their conceptual and analytic tools but also to grow their leadership. The Sanger Leadership Journey is a five-step system that incorporates most of the basic ideas and practices that make up the Power of Flexing, including goal setting, experimentation, and reflection. Sanger staff have also developed supporting mechanisms like those I'm describing here to help students on their individual leader learning journeys. These include a journey workbook, a place for students to record reflections and log various assessments; an evidence-based leader behavior encyclopedia for students to find validated leader behaviors to try out as experiments; and year-round peer coaching groups to support students in their leadership journeys.

HR departments and leaders of various organizations might emulate such practices to help employees to shape and support their own journeys to become more effective leaders.

PEER-TO-PEER FLEXING INITIATIVES: HOW HR CAN HELP

When conditions are right, a company's HR department can support flexing by following rather than leading. Here's a story of one organization that suggests how it can happen.

Tommy Wydra is the kind of person others describe as a "go-getter." As an undergraduate student at the University of Michigan, he majored in neuroscience and served as president of his fraternity. After graduation, while working to complete a weekend MBA in preparation for a job in consulting at McKinsey, he embarked on a three-year financial development program (FDP) at Michigan Medicine, the university's medical center, The FDP was set up with a dual purpose: to contribute to the financial work of the health system while also enhancing the personal development of the program's participants.

When Wydra read about the Power of Flexing on my website, he asked to meet with me to learn more. He thought it could be a perfect tool to help those engaged in the FDP with their own personal development programs.

However, when Wydra first pitched the idea of the Power of Flexing to the other interns in his FDP cohort, not even his characteristic vibrant enthusiasm could animate the room. His colleagues responded with blank stares and a few eye rolls. When he pushed them a bit, asking each person in the room to set a personal development goal and share ideas about things they might do to achieve those goals, they made up goals and chatted with one another for a few minutes just to placate him. "It was really uncomfortable," Tommy recalls. The meeting ended quickly.

Asja Kepeš is one of Wydra's colleagues in the FDP and, like some of the others, was anxious when she'd heard about the Power of Flexing.

"It was pretty early on in the FDP program," she says, "and I wasn't necessarily comfortable sharing my areas of development with my peers in the group." It didn't help that Kepeš was the only woman in the FDP. "As a woman in finance," she explains, "I feel the need to constantly prove myself. So being vulnerable with my male counterparts isn't something I love to do." Wydra's idea struck her as a form of "forced vulnerability," and it made her very uncomfortable.

However, instead of simply writing off Wydra's pitch as a waste of time, Kepeš went to him to share her concerns. In response, Wydra asked for her help in creating an environment more conducive to sharing vulnerabilities. Together they developed another presentation to better frame the Power of Flexing within the context of their jobs. They also worked to design a flexing program that could provide an effective development space for the FDP participants. They set up the program to run quarterly, with interns selecting a goal for their development for each quarter, taking actions on those goals and seeking feedback during the quarter, then engaging in reflection at the end of the quarter.

They also reformatted the flexing process to fit the needs and temperaments of the FDP participants in their department, seeking to cultivate safety and deep conversations while assuring their colleagues that they could choose their own levels of vulnerability. They even created their own vocabulary to make the flexing concepts fit their "finance brains." *Experiments* were renamed *tactics*. The quarterly group meetings for setting goals were called *approach sessions*. They also added a one-on-one feedback component to the process, pairing each participant with a partner to provide accountability and support throughout the quarter. The partners could talk as often as they wanted, but they were asked to commit to holding at least two meetings, called *deep dives*—one at the midpoint of the quarter and one toward the end of the quarter, just before the approach session for the next quarter.

Wydra and Kepeš pitched the new concept to the team. Feeling they didn't have much to lose by trying it, the group agreed.

The results were gratifying. The attendees came to their end-of-quarter approach session prepared to share their goals for the next cycle. The goals were personal and varied, ranging from "improving my presentation skills" and "learning to be more concise in describing my ideas" to "mastering the programming language VBA" and "asking five people to lunch." During the approach session, the interns found real value in hearing about one another's experiences; for example, some discovered that others had already pursued a goal they now had, which provided insights they could use in designing their experiments for the upcoming quarter. Wydra and Kepeš watched with astonishment and pride. They could feel the energy brimming in the room: voices got louder, and people were feverishly taking notes as they talked with their colleagues. The meeting ran long, and most attendees left feeling equipped and energized.

Having engaged in the flexing process over the first year of their three-year program, the FDP participants say they have a better idea of themselves and their own development. They have also built a stronger sense of shared community, which helps these high-achieving individuals keep an eye on their personal goals. "In life, we set these big goals for ourselves," Kepeš says. "But sometimes, if you're not focused on them, they can fall by the wayside just from everyday work. The Power of Flexing helps us integrate our goals and launch small goals in our everyday lives."

Alex is a manager and an FDP alumnus who mentored some of that year's participants. As time passed, he noticed something was changing. His mentees had a different spark in them. They were approaching their jobs with a stronger sense of intention, and they seemed to take ownership of their own development. Even their ability to give feedback had improved. Alex decided to try the flexing practices himself. "I think I'm reaching more of my goals just by setting that strategic direction," he says.

"Setting a framework to get to a goal, and building it into your conversation on a day-to-day basis rather than reflecting back only every half a year or every quarter, makes it much easier to actually reach your goal."

The FDP flexing program created by Wydra and Kepeš relies heavily on peer-to-peer coaching rather than the help of experienced, credentialed coaches. Professional coaches often take a skeptical view of this approach—and it's true that it's no substitute for an ongoing one-on-one relationship with a trained coach. But as the FDP program shows, a lot of energy, direction, and development can be generated when peers engage with their colleagues.

Within organizations, HR departments can play an important role by supporting and guiding peer-driven flexing programs. They can encourage specific groups in the organization to launch such programs; provide live or online resources on critical coaching skills, such as listening well, creating safe spaces, and giving feedback; suggest topics and activities; and create opportunities for flexing groups to share stories of success or challenges that other groups can learn from.

In their best-selling book *Switch: How to Change Things When Change Is Hard*, the Heath brothers, Chip and Dan, argue that it can be a mistake to try to bring about change through centralized planning and organization. Instead, look for the bright spots—places where positive change is already happening—and then jump in to support and nurture them.[14]

Tommy Wydra and Asja Kepeš are two of those bright spots. Perhaps one of the best things an HR department can do is to identify such bright spots in the organization and help them to grow.

HR DEPARTMENTS HAVE SOMETIMES been criticized as a major stumbling block in the way of creating a more experience-based, individualized approach to leadership and personal-effectiveness development.[15] In a world where employee development is destined to become more personalized, self-initiated, and self-directed, HR departments need to figure out how best to facilitate and support such efforts if they hope to remain relevant. The payoff can be substantial in terms of individual learning, leadership development, and the facilitation of similar growth at the organizational level. We'll turn to that challenge in our next chapter.

CHAPTER 11

HOW FLEXING CAN HELP TO BUILD A LEARNING ORGANIZATION

Transforming an entire organization into a place where growth is encouraged poses significant cultural challenges. Organizations are often intensely attuned to achievement, have little tolerance for mistakes, and demand that individual insecurities, uncertainties, and emotions be left at the door. In such spaces, blaming and finger-pointing become common, and true individual growth becomes rare—a big problem for organizations that are striving to survive in an increasingly complex and dynamic world.

It gets worse! Contexts like these can push some bosses to become excessively controlling, even abusive, since they can gain a feeling of superiority by using blame to make others feel inferior. Over time, the corporate culture evolves in such a way that everything starts to revolve around pleasing upper management rather than extraordinary achievement and continual development. As everyone starts worrying about being judged, it's hard for courage and innovation to survive. Soon learning and growth grind to a halt.

Once your company culture gets mired in these sorts of attitudes, escaping from them can be difficult no matter how good your intentions or finely tuned your strategy. Fortunately, there are steps that organizations of every kind and size can take to inculcate the Power of Flexing into every division, department, and team. Making flexing and the learning mindset it nurtures into core features of your company culture can help to turn your company or nonprofit into a learning organization where both individuals and the organization as a whole are constantly growing.

True learning organizations do the following:

+ Find systematic ways to reinforce through words and actions that skills are learnable, rather than assuming they are innate talents or gifts that some people have and that others lack.
+ Have a top management that conveys consistently that the organization values and rewards learning and perseverance, not just ready-made genius or talent, and establishes policies and procedures in support of those attitudes.
+ Create feedback systems that promote a focus on learning and future success, rather than focusing on identifying failures, assigning blame, and punishing mistakes.
+ Treat managers as resources for learning rather than as taskmasters whose main role is to impose discipline and expose wrongdoing.

Many elements go into building a learning organization. Because it gives every employee a template for continual learning and personal development, the system you have been learning in this book helps to establish a cultural setting in which openness to new ideas is the norm.

CREATING A LEARNING ENVIRONMENT

To see how this works, let's consider how one big company has achieved culture change around the issue of growth.

The company is Microsoft, one of the biggest tech companies in the world. Like many successful companies, Microsoft had succumbed over time to the stultifying effects of enormous size, complexity, bureaucracy, and complacency. Now that has changed. Against all odds, under the leadership of CEO Satya Nadella, who replaced Steve Ballmer in 2014, Microsoft has managed to refocus its culture on learning and growth. As of this writing (2020), the company is once again attracting top engineering talent, it is helping to lead some of the most exciting technological innovations in the world, and its growth rate and profitability have recovered from the declines they'd suffered in recent years.

I learned about Microsoft's learning-centered turnaround from several sources, including journalistic accounts, published interviews with company leaders, a wonderful London Business School case on his leadership,[1] and Satya Nadella's own book, *Hit Refresh: The Quest to Rediscover Microsoft's Soul and Imagine a Better Future for Everyone* (New York: HarperCollins, 2017). But I also learned a lot from my conversations with Charley Marshall, an MBA graduate from the University of Michigan in 2020. Charley was an interesting and unusual MBA student. He grew up intending to be a pastor and majored in theology and philosophy in college but soon felt the world of business calling him. By the time he graduated, he was involved in three start-up companies, which put him on a steep learning curve about business. After detouring to spend time as a Peace Corps volunteer in Ecuador, he entered the dual degree program at Michigan, graduating with an MBA and an MS in sustainability.

As you may have surmised, Charley is an avid learner. When he spent the summer of 2019 working for Microsoft, I was excited to hear firsthand about his experiences there. There's an old saying, "Fish discover water last," that captures the truth that the culture surrounding us in a society or an organization is so pervasive that we often fail to notice it. Charley was new to Microsoft, which made him the perfect person to see its evolving culture clearly. The observations that follow owe a lot to Charley's observations.

SATYA NADELLA'S CHALLENGE

When Indian-born software engineer Satya Nadella took over as Microsoft's third CEO, he inherited a troubled business. Many of the company's most talented team members had fled to more dynamic companies like Google and Apple. Revenues and profits, while still huge, had stopped growing as quickly as before, and the stock price had begun to fall as outside observers realized that the company's innovative capacity had diminished. Microsoft had faded as an important tech player, and morale was at a low point.

Nadella was worried. He knew that the tech environment was on the verge of some dramatic new shifts, and he sensed that the company's fear-driven culture would make it hard for it to adapt to the coming changes. That culture encouraged people to behave in ways focused on internal politics, putting their energy into proving that they were good demonstrating how much they knew rather than experimenting with what they didn't know, and projecting confidence rather than asking questions that might reveal ignorance. As a result, Microsoft had largely stopped innovating.

Nadella recognized these problems but he was unsure how to tackle them. He spent his first year in listening and learning mode, as we saw recommended by tech entrepreneur Shishir Mehrotra (whose reflection practices we discussed in chapter 6). Nadella heard from Microsoft employees that they shared his dissatisfaction with the company's fear-driven culture. Software engineers told him they wanted Microsoft to become cool again—to be a company that would lead the world rather than follow. They also wanted to work for a Microsoft whose mission was meaningful and impactful. These aspirational, growth-oriented drives still existed within Microsoft's people, but they were latent; they needed to be encouraged and supported.

Nadella realized that his primary goal should be to inculcate a learning mindset into every Microsoft employee—to help people realize that innovation and growth are always within reach of every individual. It's the same conclusion that Peter Heslin, perhaps the most prominent researcher on the topic of how a learning mindset works in an organization, would have reached. To "create more of a growth-minded culture," Heslin says, "you need to take steps to present important competencies as learnable" and that "the firm values learning, perseverance, and efforts."[2] Nadella took this approach as his first and most urgent assignment, setting himself the goal of moving Microsoft from a "know-it-all" culture to a "learn-it-all" culture.

But making such a major cultural shift would not be easy. Like many organizations, Microsoft had created a *genius culture* rather than a *growth culture*.[3] Microsoft managers saw their first task as hiring "the best" and then using performance appraisal and promotion systems to weed out any less-than-superlative employees who had somehow slipped through the cracks. As a result, people within the company spent a lot of time wondering whether they "had what it takes" and avoiding any actions that might risk failure.

Two scholars, Bob Kegan and Lisa Lahey, have vividly described how cultures like this work: "In most organizations nearly everyone is doing a second job no one is paying them for—namely, covering their weaknesses, trying to look their best, and managing other people's impressions of them. There may be no greater waste of a company's resources. The ultimate cost: neither the organization nor its people are able to realize their full potential."[4]

The now defunct Enron—the once much-admired energy company that collapsed into bankruptcy in 2001 amid revelations of massive, systemic fraud—is perhaps the most extreme example of a genius culture. In their definitive book on the Enron saga, Bethany McLean and Peter Elkind described it as "a company that prized 'sheer brainpower' above all else, where the task of sorting out 'intellectual stars from the merely super bright' was the top priority when making hires and promotions."[5] That description brilliantly captures the essence of a genius culture.

A growing body of research shows exactly how and why genius cultures are so often dysfunctional. One team of researchers found that employees in growth-oriented companies felt more passion for their work and were more dedicated to performance improvement than those in companies with a genius culture. Genius-culture companies also exhibited less collaboration between employees, less risk taking, less innovation, and a weaker commitment to integrity and ethics.[6] The last-named quality, of course, was the one that ended up dooming Enron to an ignominious demise.

And as you can imagine, companies with a genius culture are not attuned to learning. They fail to create the zone of psychological safety necessary for learning.[7] Employees approach experience not with a learning mindset but rather as if girded for battle, intensely pursuing their productivity goals but ignoring the need to grow and develop as individuals, and regarding activities like pausing for reflection as a mere waste of time. In short, practicing the Power of Flexing within a genius culture is next to impossible.

IS YOUR COMPANY A LEARNING ORGANIZATION?

An organization's culture and the assumptions, beliefs, and values it inculcates are often subtle and difficult to recognize, especially for those who are immersed in it. (Again: "Fish discover water last.") Does your current organization have the characteristics of a learning organization? The following questions may help you to see. The more yes answers you tally, the *further* your organization is from being a true learning organization.

1. Does the company culture tend to lionize and honor the achievements of a handful of "rock stars" who are assumed to have special gifts that elevate them above their colleagues?

2. Are hiring decisions based largely on candidates' perceived cognitive ability or having a "brain" for technology, marketing, sales, people management, leadership, or other areas of activity (as opposed to their growth potential)?

3. When individuals or departments are singled out for praise (citations, awards, bonuses, and so on), is the emphasis mainly on quantifiable performance (as opposed to effort and dedication)?

4. When mistakes, errors, or failures occur, are time and energy expended on determining who is to blame and ensuring that the responsible parties are humiliated, ridiculed, fired, demoted, or otherwise punished (as opposed to learning useful lessons from the mistakes)?

5. Do employees make a noticeable effort to conceal their mistakes from others, to "doctor" the results of projects to make them appear more successful, or otherwise to "spin" their job performance in the eyes of their colleagues?

6. If an employee performs well in the wake of a failure, does an earlier performance appraisal reflecting the failure remain unchanged, as if it carries a stigma that can never be fully removed?[8]

FIRST STEPS IN PROMOTING CULTURE CHANGE AT MICROSOFT

Nadella worked hard on his program of culture change. Convincing 125,000 people to buy into something as squishy as a new mindset is a tough task, but Nadella tackled it enthusiastically.

One of the culture-change tools Nadella leaned on was top-down communication. He began giving speeches extolling the importance of lifelong learning. He sketched a vision of Microsoft as a company dedicated to providing people in every walk of life with the technological tools they needed to make the world a better place—an idealistic mission that many employees found inspiring. He also pushed managers to start spending more time listening to customers rather than assuming that they knew what users needed better than the users themselves did.

Little by little, Microsoft employees began to hear the message, and some started trying to apply it. One account manager decided to spend a week patrolling the streets with a team of police officers to get a better sense of how they could be helped by access to remote data—supported by technology tools from Microsoft, of course. Another manager spent two days with hospital workers to get a clearer sense of how paperless information flow should work for them, helping to make better health care available to more people.

As stories like these spread through the company, Microsoft employees began to realize that their new CEO was serious about making the company a learning organization, and they slowly began adopting similar attitudes and behaviors.

Nadella also took seriously the challenge of making sure that his own actions exemplified and supported his message of continuous learning. He knew that the behaviors of people at the top of any organization have an outsize influence on the organizational culture. Even words and actions that may seem insignificant in themselves can send powerful signals about what is and isn't important and valued, subtly shaping the assumptions and attitudes of people throughout the business.

Sensitive to these realities, Satya Nadella took several steps that sent strong cultural signals about the importance of instilling a growth mindset at Microsoft. His initial CEO letter to all employees expressed his personal commitment to continuous learning, and he reinforced the message through some of his first senior-level appointments. For example, Jill Tracie Nichols was named chief of staff because Nadella had seen how well she worked with others. "I want my office to be about the culture we are trying to create," Nadella declared, and Nichols embodied that intention.[9]

Perhaps the most dramatic symbolic action Nadella took involved his recovery from a frankly stupid mistake he made early in his tenure. During an onstage interview that was part of an annual event celebrating women in computing, Nadella was asked to address the difficulty many women in tech companies experience in being paid as well as their male colleagues. He shocked the mostly female audience by advising them *not* to be forthright about what they needed and deserved. "It's not really about asking for a raise," he said, "but knowing and having faith that the system will give you the right raise." He went on to say, "That might be one of the initial 'super powers,' that quite frankly, women [who] don't ask for a raise have. It's good karma. It will come back."[10]

Nadella's tone-deaf remarks were met with widespread outrage. He quickly realized the seriousness of his misstep. Rather than duck the issue or try to explain his comments away, he apologized publicly within a day, saying, "I answered that question completely wrong. Without a doubt I wholeheartedly support programs at Microsoft and in the industry that bring more women into technology and close the pay gap." He added, "If you think you deserve a raise, you should just ask."[11]

Nadella didn't stop there. Within a week he distributed a memo to Microsoft employees in which he apologized again for his gaffe, saying that he had "underestimated exclusion and bias—conscious and unconscious—that can hold people back." He went on to outline a three-pronged plan to enable Microsoft to address the widespread bias that his own remarks had reflected, including initiatives to ensure equal pay for equal work, a greater commitment to diversity in the hiring process, and expanded training for employees on "how to foster an inclusive culture."[12]

But Nadella also engaged in smaller actions that equally made a statement. When a young manager in charge of new employee orientation (Microsoft brings in 20,000 new employees a year) thought that her lineup of managers teaching "the Microsoft way" to these employees ought to include her iconic CEO, she (bravely) emailed him directly. To her surprise, Nadella quickly responded, "Yes this is important, let's get it on the schedule."

Through both large and small actions, Nadella modeled for all Microsoft employees how they could learn, change, and grow as a result of their own actions and the feedback those actions elicited—even when the process might be embarrassing or painful.

ALIGNING ORGANIZATIONAL SYSTEMS BEHIND THE CULTURE CHANGE YOU NEED

Symbolic words and actions from the top of an organization are important. But by themselves they can't generate truly pervasive and lasting cultural change. To achieve that, you need to institutionalize the changes you seek—to alter your organizational processes, procedures, policies, and rules so that they line up in support of the new culture you seek to create.

Mindful of this fact, Satya Nadella started pushing Microsoft to move in the direction of being a learning organization through changes to its human resource policies. Researcher Ben Schneider points out that organizational culture changes, in part, when new kinds of people begin joining the company and those with older value sets begin to leave.[13] As Nadella's gospel of the growth mindset spread at Microsoft, the processes of attraction, selection, and attrition began to move the company in the new direction. People like Charley Marshall began to be attracted to Microsoft because of the new values it was publicly espousing, such as its commitment to the mission of creating a more accessible, equitable world through technology and its culture. "The world that Microsoft is trying to create is the world I want to create," Charley told me. And he added, "Joining Microsoft is like a continuation of the learning I have done in school." Comments like this were strong evidence that Nadella's program of culture change was taking hold. Without ever hearing it, Charley was following the excellent advice offered by Tim Van Hauwermeiren, CEO of Argenx, in a commencement address at Vlerick Business School in Ghent, Belgium: "Care more about your learning curve than your salary curve!"[14]

Nadella also took steps to blow up the performance appraisal and promotion system, which is typically one of the most powerful cultural levers within any organization. Consider again the example of Enron. The company's leaders believed that money and fear were the only things that truly motivated people. They instructed managers to grade employees on a scale from 1 to 5, and they mandated that at least 15 percent had to receive the lowest score regardless of their actual level of performance, after which the unfortunate 15 percent were given two weeks to find new jobs. This ruthless system came to be known as "rank and yank." You can imagine the ways in which this process shaped behavior.

Nadella inherited a similar performance appraisal system at Microsoft, one that stacked employees into slots ranging from "top" to "poor" and required 10 percent to be squeezed into each slot. It was a system precision-designed to lock people into a performance-prove mindset and to kill any potential for collaboration among employees. Nadella shredded it, replacing forced rankings, annual review meetings, and even performance reviews and objectives with a system that put more influence in the hands of managers and emphasized coaching and continual feedback to employees.

My inside source, Charley Marshall, really resonated with Microsoft's new performance appraisal system. He felt that it clearly communicated that people trusted his capabilities and competence and ensured that he got high-quality feedback from his manager. Charley particularly appreciated the so-called pulse checks he received two or three times during his internship summer (quarterly for regular employees). In fact, when I talked to Charley nine months after his last pulse check, he could still recite the five questions he was asked:

1. Tell me about your current projects.
2. Describe the progress you've made on those projects.
3. In what ways have you built on the projects or successes of others at Microsoft?
4. In what ways have you embodied diversity and inclusion at Microsoft?
5. In what ways have you embodied a growth mindset at Microsoft?

Charley noted that question 3 vividly encapsulated the change from what he'd heard about the pre-Nadella era. "In Microsoft in 2008," he said, "no one would have had any incentive to build on the work of others." By having managers ask these questions at regular intervals, Microsoft further pushed its entire culture in the direction of learning, openness, and growth.

Under Nadella's leadership, Microsoft took other steps to reinforce the desired cultural change. For example, the company organized activities designed to facilitate and encourage cross-departmental collaboration, such as a weeklong summer "Hackathon" in which people were invited to form temporary groups to study and propose solutions to a wide variety of problems. Microsoft also created opportunities for employees to work on volunteer projects together, thereby getting to know colleagues from other departments.

To monitor and further incentivize collaboration, Microsoft used its own Teams tool, which helps people see how they are and are not working together. A weekly report tells employees how many hours they've spent on email during and after work hours, who they spent the most time with, and other patterns of network-building activities.

Microsoft also began offering employees a wealth of learning opportunities; in fact, Charley Marshall reported having so many chances to take on special learning projects that they ended up overlapping with one another. Not only did the company make such projects available, but it actually *encouraged* employees to take advantage of them—unlike the practice at some other firms, where subtle signs of disapproval are sent to people who accept such offers.

ENSURING CONSISTENT MESSAGING FROM FRONTLINE MANAGERS

The actions and reactions of those at the top of the organization are noticed and attended to, of course. But an individual's actions are even more powerfully affected by their local context—which means that the most important influence on the attitudes and actions of most employees is their immediate bosses. I always tell the executives I teach when they complain about the performance-prove cultures in which they work to remember that as you move up in an organization, you will soon be not only someone who reacts to the culture that exists around you but an important culture creator for the people who report to you. What kind of boss will you be? What role will you play in creating a culture that supports the growth and development of those who report to you and depend on you for important signals about what matters most? If the things that the boss says, does, encourages, discourages, rewards, and punishes are aligned with the values that the company seeks to inculcate, then the results the organization wants are likely to follow. But if frontline managers behave in ways that are inconsistent with the company's avowed values, employees are likely to ignore those values.

Research by psychologist Fiona Lee and her colleagues has explored the effect of messaging by managers on employees' willingness to experiment—an issue that is obviously directly relevant to the Power of Flexing. They found that what deters people from experimenting and innovating most is when managers send inconsistent messages. (These messages affected these outcomes even more than messages that were consistently discouraging.) Inconsistency makes the rules seem unpredictable and ambiguous, causing anxiety and fear that deters experimentation and drives employees to "freeze in place" rather than take the risks inherent in trying new things.[15]

Here are some steps any organization can take to help ensure that its frontline managers are speaking, behaving, and leading in ways that support learning and growth rather than erecting barriers to them.

Encourage Managers to Harness the Power of Questions

Questions direct attention and action. The researcher Morgan McCall, who has studied how newly promoted leaders grow—or fail to grow—in their jobs, once contacted a small number of newly promoted leaders every other week and asked them two questions: "What have you done since we last talked?" and "What if anything have you learned from it?" Fairly quickly, *because they knew he would be asking,* they started to pay more attention to what they were learning and were impressed by their growth.[16] Managers need to understand that they are models of behavior for those they supervise—and that questions in one-on-one meetings such as the ones McCall asked are one way to promote the continuous learning and growth that organizations need. Using such questions consistently will encourage employees to think about the topic, even between meetings, and thereby make self-development a personal priority. As we've seen, for young employees such as Charley Marshall, his manager's questions during regular pulse check meetings sent a strong signal about the importance of self-development for everyone at Microsoft.

Make Two-Way Feedback a Regular Activity Throughout the Organization

Charley reported that, during one-on-one meetings, his manager at Microsoft routinely offered him feedback on his performance. More unusually, she also routinely asked *him* for feedback as well. Think of the impact of having this kind of behavior multiplied across many frontline managers. Imagine a manager saying to peers and subordinates, "I'm currently working on being a better listener [or developing some other important skill]. Do you have any advice for me?" It seems likely that those on the receiving end of such a query would feel encouraged to be equally transparent about their own goals and equally willing to accept feedback that might lead to learning and growth.

Encourage personal-development goal setting at all times throughout the organization. Morgan McCall, whom we just met, observed, "Much of development is a matter of attention. If people can learn to keep learning in mind, more of it can happen." Companies can employ this principle by encouraging employees at all levels to continually set their own development goals—not just as part of an annual review process but as an ordinary feature of daily work life. Managers can play a helpful role by discussing such goals in routine group or one-on-one conversations, perhaps using questions like those included in the Microsoft pulse check system. Simply focusing people's attention on personal development in this way can go a long way toward ensuring that it happens.

Train Managers to Be Mindful of the Ways They Speak

The language used in everyday work often reflects differing attitudes toward growth and learning. Managers who tend to be locked into the achievement mindset are likely to use statements like "We need to stop tolerating screwups around here," "We've got to get our top people working on these problems," "It's time we separate the wheat from the chaff," and "Let's face it, it's all about the bottom line." By contrast, managers who appreciate the value of the growth mindset are likely to use statements like "We need to think through the underlying causes of our mistakes," "We need to put our people into positions where they can grow and learn,"

"It's time we get our whole team working together," and "If we don't get the processes right, we won't get the results we want."

Managers can be trained to recognize verbal patterns like these and encouraged to think about the signals they send to those around them. Managers can do a lot to ensure that the people they work with continue to grow, both as individuals and as a team—and the language they use is one simple but important tool for making this happen.

A MANAGER'S MOST IMPORTANT IMPACT: HOW THEY RESPOND TO FAILURE

In chapter 3, I noted that your view of failure and possible failure is one of the biggest barriers to experimentation. It turns out that how failures, errors, or mistakes are viewed in a culture is key to creating a learning organization more generally as well.

In a genius culture, when employees find that they have made mistakes, they spend more time kicking themselves and trying to hide their mistakes from others than they do trying to learn from them. The cost of this pattern may be substantial. In a culture where mistakes can't be recognized and learned from, employees become afraid to try anything new, and innovation suffers accordingly.[17]

By contrast, in a growth-centered organization, it's possible to instill a positive framing for failures and errors. And while some may worry that this perspective could lead to sloppy work and poor performance, other leaders recognize it as critically important.

David Kelley, founder of the widely admired design company IDEO, understands this dynamic quite well. He is said to wander the floor of his company, exhorting people with a smile, "Fail often in order to succeed sooner!" His goal is to send a clear message about the value of risking errors in the service of growth.[18] Ed Catmull, cofounder of the movie studio Pixar and author of several books on creativity, puts it this way:

"Failure isn't a necessary evil. In fact, it isn't evil at all. It is a necessary consequence of doing something new."[19] And as we've seen, Microsoft CEO Satya Nadella demonstrated through personal behavior how an embarrassing public mistake could be transformed into a positive learning experience—not just for him personally but for his entire organization.

Scientific research backs up these anecdotes. When trainees in one study were told that "errors are a natural part of the learning process!" or "the more errors you make, the more you learn!" they came to see errors more positively and therefore experienced fewer dysfunctional emotions such as frustration, guilt, and embarrassment. The new perception changed their cognitive processes as well, making them more likely to look for the causes of their errors and to explore the potential value of different solutions. A second study focusing on project failures similarly concluded that learning is enhanced when failures are viewed as a normal part of life and work rather than something to be avoided at all costs.[20]

In addition, other research shows that recognizing mistakes as "normative" encourages risk taking, experimentation, and learning. One study titled "Even Einstein Struggled," exposed ninth- and tenth-grade students to the stories of accomplished scientists such as Albert Einstein, Marie Curie, and Michael Faraday. Some students were shown how the scientists struggled intellectually and in their personal lives, while other students were exclusively shown how the scientists made significant scientific discoveries. Only those who had learned about the struggles of the historic scientists showed improved science learning post-intervention.[21]

As all these examples show, the cultural message that errors are acceptable supports individuals in their learning orientation and experimentation—which means it's one of the most important values for managers in an organization to internalize, act upon, and share with others. The result will be learning and growth—not just for individual employees but for the organization as a whole.

Bob Eckert is an organizational consultant whose company, New

& Improved, coaches organizations in becoming more innovative. In a 2015 article, Bob and his team offered the following advice about how managers can help their team members find value in the mistakes they make.

Here's what you do the next time there's a significant error, failure, or "bump in the road." Get the team together and debrief it by asking the following questions:

+ What worked well?
+ What would you do differently?
+ What did you learn or relearn?
+ What learnings will you apply next time?

Notice that the last two words of this reflection are *next time*. That means that you won't retreat to your cave and never try something new again but rather that you'll persist, persevere, push forward, and be tenacious in getting it to work.[22]

I like this list of questions, as well as the advice about "next time." It reflects a real growth mindset, which uses every experience in life, good or bad, as the basis for doing better in the future.

When bosses consistently ask those around them for feedback and information about problems, mistakes, and failures—not just successes—they uncover crucial data they might not otherwise discover. The issues that may be revealed—an emerging customer preference, an under-the-radar competitor, or a new technology that might impact the firm's future—could be vital to the future success of the organization. And the surfacing of such issues is highly context dependent. In a culture that is supportive of continual growth and learning, they will likely become known; in a genius culture, they will likely be suppressed and create bigger problems in the long run.[23] But in a learning organization, individuals are encouraged to raise issues and come clean with the mistakes they've made, enabling them and the entire company to learn from those mistakes.

ARE YOU A GROWTH-PROMPTING LEADER?

Leaders can be very important role models for growth. To be such a role model, try to do the following:

1. Acknowledge your own limitations, faults, and mistakes.
2. Model "teachability" by sharing stories of when you have learned and what you've learned.
3. Spotlight follower strengths and contributions. Let people know what they are contributing so that they can grow those strengths over time.
4. Legitimize uncertainty. Share when you don't necessarily know what's coming, but express confidence that together the team can face it.
5. Support follower development. Show that it's okay to make a mistake as long as something is learned from it.
6. Seek feedback. Show that you are open to their views of your leadership.

Research shows that these leader behaviors prompt subordinate growth and engagement, especially in contexts where the entire culture is focused around growth (like that created at Microsoft), there isn't extreme pressure, and the behaviors are done in a sincere manner.[24]

ACHIEVING CULTURAL CHANGE IS a long journey, and measuring success is often difficult. But from the vantage point of 2020, it seems clear that Satya Nadella's effort to transform the culture of Microsoft, shifting it from a know-it-all company to a learn-it-all company, has been paying significant dividends. No longer a laggard in the high-tech arena, Microsoft has spent the last two years alternating positions with Apple at the top of the list of the world's most valuable companies and is currently on track to achieve a market value of more than $2 trillion in the foreseeable future—a remarkable turnaround by any measure.

Forbes columnist and corporate culture analyst Caterina Bulgarella offered two insights into how it happened in a column written in November 2018, shortly after Microsoft overtook Apple for the top spot on the corporate value leaderboard. She first noted that Microsoft didn't just build a "nice culture" but rather "focused on capacities that are highly instrumental to its new strategy." She then pointed out that "these new culture assets provide Microsoft with a source of "renewable energy." As she put it: "If Microsoft is learning to learn . . . the value of this mindset has no expiration date."[25]

"Learning to learn"—what could be a better description of Satya Nadella's biggest contribution to the company he heads? And as Bulgarella suggests, this is one corporate asset that never gets worn-out, obsolete, or used up, because it offers the ability to continually reinvent the organization to meet whatever new challenges tomorrow may bring.

What could be more inspiring to the rest of us who are all striving, in our own ways, to make continual learning, development, and growth parts of our personal DNA as well as that of the businesses, civic organizations, families, and other communities to which we belong? After all, if an Indian-born, cricket-loving software engineer who learned empathy as he coped with the challenges of a son with special needs can get a huge company like Microsoft to reshape and rejuvenate its culture, the odds are great that the same thing can happen in the places and groups we care about.

It's a hopeful message for you to ponder as you continue your efforts to apply the Power of Flexing to both the personal challenges you may face and the organizations that you may be a part of or lead.

EPILOGUE:
A LIFE OF GROWTH

Call me biased, but I think the best thing you can say about someone is that they continued to grow, develop, change, improve, and evolve throughout their life. The growth to which you aspire may include what I have called content growth—learning to code, mastering a new language, starting a band, perfecting a craft, or becoming a poet. But I hope this book motivates you to find space in your life for personal growth as well. Personal growth is crucial if you want to be like that role model you most admire, to have more influence as a leader, to create better relationships with those joining you on a task, and, ultimately, to bring positive change into our troubled world. Personal growth doesn't benefit you alone—it empowers you to bring benefits to others, whether it is through listening well and encouraging others to speak, motivating others to follow a wise course of action, or helping to reconcile differences when others are in conflict. In this way, you can help fuel a positive cycle of change for all those whose lives you touch.

As I've stressed in the pages of this book, personal growth requires learning how to learn from the experiences life throws at you. A maxim often attributed to the eminently quotable John C. Maxwell says it well: "Change is inevitable. Growth is optional."[1] A life well lived tends to keep us off-center. Just when you think you have all the answers and have organized your life perfectly, something happens to unsettle your thinking and spoil your plans: Your company decides to assign you to a job overseas. A sudden illness or tragic death casts a pall over your family. An industry shift makes your current technological expertise obsolete. An unexpected promotion demands skills you never dreamed of needing. You find yourself thrust into a range of new experiences, feeling unprepared and overwhelmed.

How you'll respond to this kind of challenge is up to you. I hope you'll choose to make it an opportunity to learn and grow. Doing so takes courage, strength, and determination. But having a plan to follow and a system to use can help enormously—and that's what I hope this book has provided, in the form of the Power of Flexing.

Of course, learning and growth aren't only for times of severe dislocation or trauma. We can and should make time for self-development even when our work feels routine and our lives feel well ordered. Like physical exercise, the mental and emotional workout that flexing provides can enhance your strength, flexibility, agility, and adaptability in all kinds of circumstances. These qualities are so valuable that they deserve and reward a regular investment of time and energy. In the words of Ari Weinzweig: "People will say that they don't have time to work out, but the people who do it always make time—and they actually get more done because they feel better. It's the same for learning, which is like working out for your mind. It doesn't make you perfect, but as with working out, when you're learning, you're excited and you have good energy and you want to go do something about your learning. I work eighty, ninety hours a week some weeks, but I'm reading a lot of books all the time."

The most successful people find ways to incorporate learning and growth into their lives continually. The Power of Flexing helps make it possible.

The systemic approach to growth that flexing provides also helps us deal with another challenge that is inherent in growth—namely, the vulnerability that true growth demands. One of my favorite statements on this comes from the poet David Whyte, who may have the most profound insight into our current hustle culture:

> Speed has become our core competency, our core identity. We do not know what powers we would be left with if we stopped doing what we were doing in the busy way we were doing it. Besides, there is a deeper, older human intuition at play that knows any real step forward comes through our pains and vulnerabilities, which is the reason we began to busy ourselves in the first place, so that we could stay well away from them.[2]

Growing as a person requires us to explore more deeply who we are; to take the risks involved in making a commitment to improve; and to recognize and explore the places in our minds and hearts where we feel less than perfect. The learning mindset fostered by the Power of Flexing makes it easier to undertake these challenging, sometimes painful tasks—and to do so in a spirit of joyful curiosity and exploration.

The goal that animates my life is to help people to grow into their most effective selves, however they might define *effectiveness*. My greatest hope is that this book has given you some ideas about a path toward such growth and some practices that will keep you on that path no matter what life throws at you.

I wish you good growth.

ACKNOWLEDGMENTS

I have put off writing a book for several years, watching colleagues and former students producing books that have been well received and impactful, but not me. Instead, I would go through cycles of: "I think I might want to write a book," after which I would visit a bookstore and think, "The world has way too many books!" and then discard the idea. After several cycles, I finally realized that the world may have a lot of books, but it does not have my book yet, and that I have some things to say. Finally, I leaped in! And what a joyful journey it has been, full of so many people who have inspired and helped me along the way.

Starting most generally, I have the great good fortune of working for the bulk of my career in the wonderful Management and Organizations Department at the University of Michigan. This is a setting that continually stimulates growth. Over the years, my overarching goal has been just to try to "run with" my MO colleagues, who have been amazing role models for me. Whether it's expanding a leadership initiative at the school, creating a movement to bring a positive perspective into organization studies, or pushing for greater social responsibility in the business world, these are people who are trying to do something bigger than themselves and for others, and I've had the great good fortune of working most of my career among them.

I started this journey with one of those colleagues, Scott DeRue. Our early days of batting around ideas (many of which ended up in this book) and making them practical will always shine brightly as very happy memories. I was sorry to lose Scott as my close collaborator when he went from being a junior faculty hire in my department to the dean of the Ross School in record time!

We were aided in those early efforts by the enormous enthusiasm of four Michigan undergraduates: Sarah Blegen, Grace Gale, Nicole Jablon, and Maggie Mai. Those four (plus one interview from Tim Jezisek) interviewed "people they admired," whose stories of learning and growth were the seed corn for much that made its way into this book. Maggie Mai provided extra help in coding the interviews and setting up a system by which we could find these people later on, an effort that has paid dividends! I also thank the wonderful Ashlyee Freeman, who spent the summer after her MBA doing additional interviews and pushing the storyline further.

I am very grateful for the seventy-two people who shared their time and knowledge with us (some more than once!). While not every interview is described in this book, they all influenced the writing and thinking that went into it. I'm very grateful for their candor and generosity. I am especially grateful to Karin Stawarky and Shahnaz Broucek, two amazing coaches who helped me see how the Power of Flexing easily fit in with their coaching practice, and Chris Murchison and Tommy Wydra, for loving these ideas enough to bring them directly into their workplaces.

While the book story nominally started with my work with Scott, the Power of Flexing brings together ideas that I have been researching for decades. In feedback seeking, I thank Anne Tsui and Greg Northcraft, who joined me early in my career in trying to understand this interesting behavior, and Katleen De Stobbeleir, who came along later and revitalized my interest in it. In the area of growth mindset and learning orientation, I thank the indefatigable Peter Heslin and Lauren Keating and also Julia Lee Cunningham and Laura Sonday, as we applied these ideas to leadership. Finally, regarding reflection, I thank the amazing Maddy Ong for joining me on an extensive journey into better understanding reflection as it shows up at work, and to Uta Bindl and Henrik Bresman for joining later on. I so appreciate these colleagues for their intellectual companionship, drive, good ideas, and good humor over the years.

I also thank the many professionals who made this book possible. My developmental editor, Karl Weber, was a great mentor through the entire process as well as just a wonderful writer. It was always delightful to see how he would take my prose and translate it even more for a practitioner audience. In many places, he was a magician! I am also grateful to the phenomenal agent, Leila Campoli, who took a bet on this first-time author. Her knowledge, positivity, spirit, and excellent sales skills really made a difference in how this journey went. And part of how it went was to put me in the hands of the similarly wonderful Rebecca Raskin at HarperCollins! Early on, I asked Rebecca why she was so excited to be editing this book. She looked confused by the question, shrugged, and enthused, "I just think the world really needs this!" She couldn't have answered in a more meaningful way for me. Her light-touch editing was always thoughtful and helpful. A single line or question from her often led me to rethink paragraphs and sections. And her boundless enthusiasm for this project made every conversation with her a joy.

The manuscript was strengthened by the excellent copyediting done by David Chesanow. As Rebecca made a career pivot just after we copyedited the manuscript, I am extremely grateful to the amazing Hollis Heimbouch for stepping into her shoes and also to Nick Davies and Laura Cole for heading up the publicity and marketing for this book and David Koral, the senior production editor. I am very appreciative for their skill, enthusiasm, and help.

I'm also grateful for the marketing and communications department at the Ross School of Business and particularly Bob Needham, who always asked when the book was coming out, how it was going, and how he could help.

On the personal side, I was supported by an amazing group of women. These include my three daughters, each of whom appears in the book and who all supported me with their enthusiasm. I especially call out my youngest, Madeline, who believes so strongly in me and just loved the idea that her mom was writing a book. She pushed me hard to be my bravest self in my work and kept track of and celebrated every milestone! My good friend Jane Dutton was a stalwart in this book journey, an endless font of enthusiasm and support. I have been lucky to have this friendship since the very first days in my doctoral program and I do not take it for granted. Our periodic phone calls as I wrote in South Africa and as we weathered the COVID quarantine really helped keep me moving and pushed my writing in directions that I had not always anticipated. The wonderful Sally Maitlis has had an uncanny ability to be there for me at pivotal moments and made a huge difference with her humor and her insight. I also so appreciate my most recent partner in crime on so many projects, the delightful Brianna Caza, who really knows how to celebrate! I don't always feel that I deserve this level of interest, support, and enthusiasm, but I am deeply grateful for it.

I am also grateful for the help of those further along than me on this book journey. Prime examples are two former students, Scott Sonenshein and Adam Grant, who are way ahead of most of us in bringing research and science to the world of practice. The ways in which they showed up to tease me, encourage me, or offer advice at just the right moments meant a lot. I thank them, along with Jen and Gianpiero Petriglieri, Herminia Ibarra, and Katleen De Stobbeleir for their advice, introductions, support, and faith in me. The amazing Dolly Chugh also came into my life through this book-writing process and offered a seemingly endless willingness to meet and provide information, even though she has an enormously busy life herself! It was she who turned me on to Leila Campoli, so in essence, it was she who made this all happen! And then there's my local "book buddy," Ethan Kross, who was just ahead of me in this process. He has so generously shared all his knowledge and offered me unconditional support. I'm forever in debt to all these folks.

Book writing can be a lonely journey, and I was very grateful for anyone who ever asked about my progress. I held the rule that I wouldn't bring up the book unless people asked, not wanting to be "that person" who endlessly talks about something that takes forever to happen! My siblings, my book groups, my Ann Arbor friends, and my high school friends all would ask occasionally and every time I got to talk about the book, it helped.

The writing of this book took place over two unusual years—a sabbatical year and then a pandemic year. I'm grateful for all the places where I was able to make progress on this writing, including our very small apartment in Pretoria, South Africa; a series of cheap motels outside national parks during the "work-a-little, hike-a-little" part of our sabbatical; at my sister Pat's house in California; on a bed in the back bedroom of our home in Ann Arbor, where I wrote for the first five months of the pandemic; and from the office we finally set up on our sun porch, where I rode out the rest of the pandemic. Place really matters to me, and I love that this book will always bring back all these special times and places.

Finally, I am also grateful to my husband, Jim, my 24/7 companion throughout the long months of quarantine in 2020, and my partner for most of my life. You were the first (but certainly not the last) to tease me about flexing by engaging in biceps curls to demonstrate. Thanks for giving me the space to work on this book. *Now* you can read a draft!

NOTES

INTRODUCTION

1. Many of the cases and anecdotes in this book are based on real-life experiences shared by individuals who have been interviewed by the author and her students. To protect their confidentiality and the privacy of their work colleagues and others, in cases where anonymity has been requested, names and other identifying details have been changed.

2. The early development of the flexing model was done in conjunction with my wonderful colleague Scott DeRue, under the heading "mindful engagement" and applied narrowly to leadership development. You can find that work here: S. J. Ashford and D. S. DeRue, "Developing as a Leader: The Power of Mindful Engagement," *Organizational Dynamics* 41, no. 2 (2012): 146–54. This book and the Power of Flexing framework explore the broader use of these ideas for developing as a person, not just in service of being a better leader but for a wide variety of goals such as being a better spouse and parent, being the person you most want to be, and so forth. Because personal effectiveness is so essential to being a good leader, the Power of Flexing has great leadership relevance as well.

3. In agile product development, a sprint is a set period of time during which specific work has to be completed and made ready for review (see https://searchsoftwarequality.techtarget.com/definition/Scrum-sprint). Here, a sprint is a decision to focus on personal development for a specific length of time and in a specific area with intention and movement toward a particular goal.

4. Jerry Colonna, *Reboot: Leadership and the Art of Growing Up* (New York: HarperCollins, 2019).

5. A. H. Maslow, *The Psychology of Science: A Reconnaissance* (New York: Harper & Row, 1966), 22.

6. Andrew Nusca, "IBM's Rometty: 'Growth and Comfort Don't Coexist,'" Fortune.com, Oct. 7, 2014, https://fortune.com/2014/10/07/ibms -rometty-growth-and-comfort-dont-coexist/.

7. E. T. Higgins, "Beyond Pleasure and Pain," *American Psychologist* 52, no. 12 (1997), 1280.

8. Scott Sonenshein, Jane E. Dutton, Adam M. Grant, Gretchen M. Spreitzer, and Kathleen M. Sutcliffe, "Growing at Work: Employees' Interpretations of Progressive Self-Change in Organizations," *Organization Science* 24, no. 2 (2013): 552–70. Quote is from page 567.

9. Anne Lamott, *Dusk, Night, Dawn: On Revival and Courage* (New York: Riverhead Books, 2021), 136.

10. Sonenshein, Dutton, Grant, Spreitzer, and Sutcliffe, "Growing at Work," 567.

11. D. P. McAdams, "The Psychology of Life Stories," *Review of General Psychology* 5, no. 2 (2001):100–122.

12. Sonenshein, Dutton, Grant, Spreitzer, and Sutcliffe, "Growing at Work," 565.

CHAPTER 1: EXPERIENCE IS THE BEST TEACHER . . . BUT ONLY WHEN YOU FLEX

1. G. S. Robinson and C. W. Wick, "Executive Development That Makes a Business Difference," *Human Resource Planning* 15, no. 1 (1992): 63–76.

2. M. Wilson and J. Yip, "Grounding Leadership Development: Cultural Perspectives," *Industrial and Organizational Psychology* 3 (2010), 52–55.

3. Cynthia D. McCauley, Marian N. Ruderman, Patricia J. Ohlott, and Jane E. Morrow, "Assessing the Developmental Components of Managerial Jobs," *Journal of Applied Psychology* 79, no. 4 (1994): 544.

4. Lisa Dragoni, Paul E. Tesluk, Joyce E. A. Russell, and In-Sue Oh, "Under-

standing Managerial Development: Integrating Developmental Assignments, Learning Orientation, and Access to Developmental Opportunities in Predicting Managerial Competencies," *Academy of Management Journal* 52, no. 4 (2009): 731–43.

5. D. Scott DeRue and Ned Wellman, "Developing Leaders via Experience: The Role of Developmental Challenge, Learning Orientation, and Feedback Availability," *Journal of Applied Psychology* 94, no. 4 (July 2009): 859–75.

6. Excerpts from M. McCall Jr., "Peeling the Onion: Getting Inside Experience-Based Leadership Development," *Industrial and Organizational Psychology* 3, no. 1 (March 2010): 61–68.

7. Ellen J. Langer, *Mindfulness* (Reading, MA: Addison-Wesley, 1989). Quote is from page 15.

8. This advice is based on the wonderful work of Ellen J. Langer. Two places to follow up if you are interested: Ellen J. Langer, *Mindfulness* and *The Power of Mindful Learning* (Boston: Da Capo, 2016).

9. Bryan E. Robinson, "The 'Rise and Grind' of Hustle Culture," *Psychology Today*, Oct. 2, 2019, https://www.psychologytoday.com/us/blog/the-right-mindset/201910/the-rise-and-grind-hustle-culture.

10. James E. Loehr and Tony Schwartz, *The Power of Full Engagement: Managing Energy, Not Time, Is the Key to High Performance and Personal Renewal* (New York: Simon & Schuster, 2005).

11. D. Day, "The Difficulties of Learning from Experience and the Need for Deliberate Practice," *Industrial and Organizational Psychology* 3 (2010): 41–44. Quote is from page 41.

12. Bannon Puckett, "Morehouse's President Discusses the Seeds and the Soil of Cultivating Diversity on EDU: Live," 2U, March 2, 2021, https://2u.com/latest/morehouse-president-david-thomas-discusses-seeds-soil-cultivating-diversity-edu-live/.

CHAPTER 2: MINDSET MATTERS

1. In Dweck's groundbreaking work *Mindset: The New Psychology of Success* (New York: Ballantine, 2007), these two contrasting ways of viewing

oneself and the world are referred to as *the achievement mindset* and *the growth mindset*. Other experts have used differing terms for similar concepts. As noted, my preference is for the terms *performance-prove mindset* and *learning mindset* because the "performance-prove" label better captures the preoccupation of folks with this mindset to show and demonstrate their achievement to others.

2. Peter A. Heslin and Lauren A. Keating, "In Learning Mode? The Role of Mindsets in Derailing and Enabling Experiential Leadership Development," *Leadership Quarterly* 28, no. 3 (2017): 367–84. This wonderful article begins to show how a learning mindset affects all of the practices identified in the mindful engagement process described in S. J. Ashford and D. S. DeRue, "Developing as a Leader: The Power of Mindful Engagement," *Organizational Dynamics* 41, no. 2 (2012): 146–54. Though I talk about setting a learning mindset as a separate practice in the flexing system, I also discuss the importance of this mindset for every other practice as well, based on Peter and Lauren's work.

3. For a recent review of this research, see Don Vandewalle, Christina G. L. Nerstad, and Anders Dysvik, "Goal Orientation: A Review of the Miles Traveled and the Miles to Go," *Annual Review of Organizational Psychology and Organizational Behavior* 6 (2019): 115–44.

4. Laura J. Kray and Michael P. Haselhuhn, "Implicit Negotiation Beliefs and Performance: Experimental and Longitudinal Evidence," *Journal of Personality and Social Psychology* 93, no. 1 (2007): 49.

5. Aneeta Rattan, Catherine Good, and Carol S. Dweck, "'It's OK—Not Everyone Can Be Good at Math': Instructors with an Entity Theory Comfort (and Demotivate) Students," *Journal of Experimental Social Psychology* 48, no. 3 (2012): 731–37.

6. Lisa Dragoni, Paul Tesluk, Joyce E. A. Russell, and In-Sue Oh, "Understanding Managerial Development: Integrating Developmental Assignments, Learning Orientation, and Access to Developmental Opportunities in Predicting Managerial Competencies," *Academy of Management Journal* 52, no. 4 (2009): 731–43.

7. Juliana G. Breines and Serena Chen, "Self-Compassion Increases Self-Improvement Motivation," *Personality and Social Psychology Bulletin* 38, no. 9 (2012): 1133–43.

8. K. Lanaj, R. E. Jennings, and S. J. Ashford, "When Self-Care Begets Other Care: Leader Role Self-Compassion and Helping at Work" (working paper, University of Florida, 2020).

9. Jennifer S. Beer, "Implicit Self-Theories of Shyness," *Journal of Personality and Social Psychology* 83, no. 4 (2002): 1009.

CHAPTER 3: SETTING A LEARNING FOCUS

1. James E. Maddux and June Price Tangney, eds., *Social Psychological Foundations of Clinical Psychology* (New York: Guilford Press, 2011), 122.

2. G. T. Dora, "There's a S.M.A.R.T. Way to Write Management's Goals and Objectives," *Management Review* 70, no. 11 (1981): 35–36.

3. T. Matsui, A. Okata, and T. Kakuyama, "Influence of Achievement Need on Goal Setting, Performance, and Feedback Effectiveness," *Journal of Applied Psychology* 67, no. 5 (1982): 645–48.

4. G. H. Seijts and G. P. Latham, "Learning Versus Performance Goals: When Should Each Be Used?," *Academy of Management Perspectives* 19, no. 1 (2005): 124–31.

5. G. Oettingen, H. J. Pak, and K. Schnetter, "Self-Regulation of Goal Setting: Turning Free Fantasies About the Future into Binding Goals," *Journal of Personality and Social Psychology* 80, no. 5 (2001): 736–53.

6. Charles S. Carver and Michael F. Scheier, *On the Self-Regulation of Behavior* (Cambridge, UK: Cambridge University Press, 2001).

7. Check out these titles by Ari Weinzweig: *A Lapsed Anarchist's Approach to Building a Great Business; A Lapsed Anarchist's Approach to Being a Better Leader; A Lapsed Anarchist's Approach to Managing Ourselves;* and *A Lapsed Anarchist's Approach to the Power of Beliefs in Business.* He has some amazing insights into business and leadership.

8. Check out these wonderful articles by Drew Carton on how company leaders can articulate better visions: A. M. Carton, C. Murphy, and J. R.

Clark, "A (Blurry) Vision of the Future: How Leader Rhetoric About Ultimate Goals Influences Performance," *Academy of Management Journal* 57, no. 6 (2014), 1544–70; A. M. Carton and B. J. Lucas, "How Can Leaders Overcome the Blurry Vision Bias? Identifying an Antidote to the Paradox of Vision Communication," *Academy of Management Journal* 61, no. 6 (2018): 2106–129; A. M. Carton, "'I'm Not Mopping the Floors, I'm Putting a Man on the Moon': How NASA Leaders Enhanced the Meaningfulness of Work by Changing the Meaning of Work," *Administrative Science Quarterly* 63, no. 2 (2018): 323–69.

9. Henk Aarts, Peter M. Gollwitzer, and Ran R. Hassin, "Goal Contagion: Perceiving Is for Pursuing," *Journal of Personality and Social Psychology* 87, no. 1 (2004): 23.

10. You can find information on the exercise at https://positiveorgs.bus .umich.edu/cpo-tools/rbse/.

11. See https://blog.whil.com/performance/mindful-perfectionist.

12. Oettingen, Pak, and Schnetter, "Self-Regulation of Goal Setting."

13. H. G. Halverson, *Succeed: How We Can Reach Our Goals* (New York: Penguin, 2010).

14. S. C. Huang and J. Aaker, "It's the Journey, Not the Destination: How Metaphor Drives Growth After Goal Attainment," *Journal of Personality and Social Psychology* 117, no. 4 (Oct. 2019): 697–720.

15. Oettingen, Pak, and Schnetter, "Self-Regulation of Goal Setting."

16. Ibid.

17. M. S. Pallak and W. Cummings, "Commitment and Voluntary Energy Conservation," *Personality and Social Psychology Bulletin* 2, no. 1 (1976), 27–30.

18. C. S. Dweck and D. Gilliard, "Expectancy Statements as Determinants of Reactions to Failure: Sex Differences in Persistence and Expectancy Change," *Journal of Personality and Social Psychology* 32, no. 6 (1975): 1077–84.

19. John R. Hollenbeck, Charles R. Williams, and Howard J. Klein, "An Empirical Examination of the Antecedents of Commitment to Difficult Goals," *Journal of Applied Psychology* 74, no. 1 (1989): 18.

CHAPTER 4: UNLEASHING YOUR INNER SCIENTIST

1. J. C. Maxwell, *The Maxwell Daily Reader: 365 Days of Insight to Develop the Leader within You and Influence Those around You* (New York: Harper-Collins, 2007), 123.

2. G. Oettingen, H. Pak, and K. Schnetter, "Self-Regulation of Goal Setting: Turning Free Fantasies about the Future into Binding Goals," *Journal of Personal and Social Psychology* 80, no. 5 (May 2001): 736–53. These authors are quoting Allen Newell and Herbert Alexander Simon, *Human Problem Solving* (Englewood Cliffs, NJ: Prentice-Hall, 1972).

3. Fiona Lee, Amy C. Edmondson, Stefan Thomke, and Monica Worline, "The Mixed Effects of Inconsistency on Experimentation in Organizations," *Organization Science* 15, no. 3 (2004): 310–26; and R. Rosenthal and R. L. Rosnow, *Essentials of Behavioral Research: Methods and Data Analysis*, 2nd ed. (New York: McGraw-Hill, 1992).

4. J. Dahl, *Leading Lean: Ensuring Success and Developing a Framework for Leadership* (Sebastopol, CA: O'Reilly Media), 65.

5. You can read Chris's blog post at https://blog.whil.com/performance/mindful-perfectionist.

CHAPTER 5: IT TAKES A VILLAGE TO GROW

1. Kent D. Harber, "Feedback to Minorities: Evidence of a Positive Bias," *Journal of Personality and Social Psychology* 74, no. 3 (1998): 622; and Loriann Roberson, E. A. Deitch, A. P. Brief, and Caryn J. Block, "Stereotype Threat and Feedback Seeking in the Workplace," *Journal of Vocational Behavior* 62, no. 1 (2003): 176–88.

2. The Dunning-Kruger effect is clearly and entertainingly explained in an episode of the NPR radio series *This American Life* titled "In Defense of Ignorance," April 22, 2016, https://www.thisamericanlife.org/585/in-defense-of-ignorance.

3. David Dunning, Judith A. Meyerowitz, and Amy D. Holzberg, "Ambiguity and Self-Evaluation: The Role of Idiosyncratic Trait Definitions in

Self-Serving Assessments of Ability," *Journal of Personality and Social Psychology* 57, no. 6 (1989): 1082.

4. William R. Torbert, *Action Inquiry: The Secret of Timely and Transforming Leadership* (San Francisco: Berrett-Koehler, 2004).

5. Steven P. Brown, Shankar Ganesan, and Goutam Challagalla, "Self-Efficacy as a Moderator of Information-Seeking Effectiveness," *Journal of Applied Psychology* 86, no. 5 (2001): 1043.

6. The best place to learn more about this app is on its main site: https://kaizen.app.

7. Brené Brown, "Taken for Granted: Brené Brown on What Vulnerability Isn't," *WorkLife with Adam Grant*, February 22, 2021, https://podcasts.apple.com/us/podcast/taken-for-granted-bren%C3%A9-brown-on-what-vulnerability-isnt/id1346314086?i=1000510270643.

8. https://kaizen.app.

9. Douglas Stone and Sheila Heen, *Thanks for the Feedback: The Science and Art of Receiving Feedback Well (Even When It Is Off-Base, Unfair, Poorly Delivered, and Frankly, You're Not in the Mood)* (New York: Penguin, 2015).

10. You can hear Lisa's story in her own words: "Learning from a Mistake," video, Stanford Graduate School of Business, https://drive.google.com/file/d/1U5fGyYMzJawMkwYFC6fBuRr_VGWlVK43/view.

CHAPTER 6: WRINGING MEANING FROM EXPERIENCE

1. John William Gardner, *Self-Renewal: The Individual and the Innovative Society* (New York: W. W. Norton, 1995), 13.

2. David Whyte, *Crossing the Unknown Sea* (New York: Riverhead Books, 2002), 128.

3. Jerry Colonna, *Reboot: Leadership and the Art of Growing Up* (New York: HarperCollins, 2019).

4. Ari Weinzweig, *A Lapsed Anarchist's Approach to the Power of Beliefs in Business* (Ann Arbor, MI: Zingerman's Press, 2016).

5. Adam L. Alter, and Hal E. Hershfield, "People Search for Meaning When They Approach a New Decade in Chronological Age," *Proceedings of the National Academy of Sciences* 111, no. 48 (2014): 17066–70.

6. Karen Brans, Peter Koval, Philippe Verduyn, Yan Lin Lim, and Peter Kuppens, "The Regulation of Negative and Positive Affect in Daily Life," *Emotion* 13, no. 5 (2013): 926–39.

7. D. Scott DeRue, Jennifer D. Nahrgang, John R. Hollenbeck, and Kristina Workman, "A Quasi-Experimental Study of After-Event Reviews and Leadership Development," *Journal of Applied Psychology* 97, no. 5 (2012): 997.

8. Aldous Huxley, *Texts and Pretexts: An Anthology with Commentaries* (New York: W. W. Norton, 1962).

9. Peter A. Heslin, Lauren A. Keating, and Susan J. Ashford, "How Being in Learning Mode May Enable a Sustainable Career Across the Lifespan," *Journal of Vocational Behavior* 117 (March 2020): 103324.

10. William Burnett and David John Evans, *Designing Your Life: How to Build a Well-Lived, Joyful Life* (New York: Knopf, 2016).

11. Amir Erez, Trevor A. Foulk, and Klodiana Lanaj, "Energizing Leaders via Self-Reflection: A Within-Person Field Experiment," *Journal of Applied Psychology* 104, no. 1 (2019): 1.

12. Ethan Kross and Ozlem Ayduk, "From a Distance: Implications of Spontaneous Self-Distancing for Adaptive Self-Reflection," *Current Directions in Psychological Science* 20, no. 3 (2011): 187–91; Igor Grossmann and Ethan Kross, "Exploring Solomon's Paradox: Self-Distancing Eliminates the Self-Other Asymmetry in Wise Reasoning About Close Relationships in Younger and Older Adults," *Psychological Science* 25, no. 8 (2014): 1571–80. You might also want to take a look at Ethan's recent book: Ethan Kross, *Chatter: The Voice in Our Head, Why It Matters, and How to Harness It* (New York: Random House, 2021).

13. Heather C. Vough and Brianna Caza, "Where Do I Go from Here? Sensemaking and the Construction of Growth-Based Stories in the Wake of Denied Promotions," *Academy of Management Review* 42, no. 1 (2019).

14. Heslin, Keating, and Ashford, "How Being in Learning Mode May Enable a Sustainable Career Across the Lifespan."

15. Reverend James Wood, ed., *Dictionary of Quotations* (London, New York:

Frederick Warne & Co., 1899), and Bartleby.com, 2012, https://www
.bartleby.com/345/authors/110.html#2. Accessed February 21st, 2021.

16. Lanaj, Foulk, and Erez, "Energizing Leaders via Self-Reflection: A Within-Person Field Experiment."

17. Joyce E. Bono, Theresa M. Glomb, Winny Shen, Eugene Kim, and Amanda J. Koch, "Building Positive Resources: Effects of Positive Events and Positive Reflection on Work Stress and Health," *Academy of Management Journal* 56, no. 6 (2013): 1601–27.

CHAPTER 7: MANAGING YOUR EMOTIONS TO ENHANCE YOUR LEARNING

1. These ideas were embellished by listening to the wonderful Robin Ely teach women executives as part of the Leading Women Executives program based in Chicago. You can find out more about this extaordinary organization dedicated to accelerating the advancement of female executives at https://leadingwomenexecutives.net/. Find out more about Robin Ely here: https://www.hbs.edu/faculty/Pages/profile.aspx?facId=7287.

2. For work-related results, see Bono et al., "Building Positive Resources: Effects of Positive Events and Positive Reflection on Work Stress and Health." For a review, see Alex M. Wood, Jeffrey J. Froh, and Adam W. A. Geraghty, "Gratitude and Well-Being: A Review and Theoretical Integration," *Clinical Psychology Review* 30, no. 7 (2010): 890–905.

3. Noelle Nelson, Selin A. Malkoc, and Baba Shiv, "Emotions Know Best: The Advantage of Emotional Versus Cognitive Responses to Failure," *Journal of Behavioral Decision Making* 31, no. 2 (Sept. 2017): 40–51.

4. See Nolen-Hoeksema's many articles examining the downside of rumination. Here is one starting point: Susan Nolen-Hoeksema, "The Role of Rumination in Depressive Disorders and Mixed Anxiety/Depressive Symptoms," *Journal of Abnormal Psychology* 109, no. 3 (Aug. 2000): 504–11.

5. Elizabeth Baily Wolf, Jooa Julia Lee, Sunita Sah, and Alison Wood Brooks, "Managing Perceptions of Distress at Work: Reframing Emotion

as Passion," *Organizational Behavior and Human Decision Processes* 137 (Nov. 2016): 1–12.

6. See, for example, C. M. Barnes, J. A. Miller, and S. Bostock, "Helping Employees Sleep Well: Effects of Cognitive Behavioral Therapy for Insomnia on Work Outcomes," *Journal of Applied Psychology* 102, no. 1 (2017): 104; A. T. Beck, *Cognitive Therapy and the Emotional Disorders* (Oxford, UK: International Universities Press, 1976); A. C. Butler, J. E. Chapman, E. M. Forman, and A. T. Beck, "The Empirical Status of Cognitive-Behavioral Therapy: A Review of Meta-Analyses," *Clinical Psychology Review* 26, no. 1 (2006): 17–31; Byron Katie, *Who Would You Be Without Your Story?: Dialogues with Byron Katie* (Carlsbad, CA: Hay House, 2008); F. Hanrahan, A. P. Field, F. W. Jones, and G. C. Davey, "A Meta-Analysis of Cognitive Therapy for Worry in Generalized Anxiety Disorder," *Clinical Psychology Review* 33, no. 1 (Feb. 2013): 120–32; and K. M. Richardson and H. R. Rothstein, "Effects of Occupational Stress Management Intervention Programs: A Meta-Analysis," *Journal of Occupational Health Psychology* 13, no. 1 (Jan. 2008): 69.

7. B. L. Fredrickson, "Positive Emotions Broaden and Build," *Advances in Experimental Social Psychology* 47 (2013): 1–53.

8. Klodiana Lanaj, Trevor A. Foulk, and Amir Erez, "Energizing Leaders via Self-Reflection: A Within-Person Field Experiment," *Journal of Applied Psychology* 104, no. 1 (Jan. 2019): 1–18.

9. Ibid.

10. B. L. Fredrickson and T. Joiner, "Reflections on Positive Emotions and Upward Spirals," *Perspectives on Psychological Science* 13, no. 2, 194–99, https://doi.org/10.1177/1745691617692106. Citation on page 196.

11. Bethany E. Kok, Kimberly A. Coffey, et al. "How Positive Emotions Build Physical Health: Perceived Positive Social Connections Account for the Upward Spiral between Positive Emotions and Vagal Tone," *Psychological Science* 24, no. 7 (2013): 1123–32; Bethany E. Kok and Barbara L. Fredrickson. "Upward Spirals of the Heart: Autonomic Flexibility, as Indexed by Vagal Tone, Reciprocally and Prospectively Predicts Positive

Emotions and Social Connectedness," *Biological Psychology* 85, no. 3 (2010): 432–36.

12. C. Vázquez, P. Cervellón, P. Pérez-Sales, D. Vidales, and M. Gaborit, "Positive Emotions in Earthquake Survivors in El Salvador (2001)," *Journal of Anxiety Disorders* 19, no. 3 (2005), 313–28.

13. J. V. Wood, S. A. Heimpel, and J. L. Michela, "Savoring Versus Dampening: Self-Esteem Differences in Regulating Positive Affect," *Journal of Personality and Social Psychology* 85, no. 3 (2003), 566–80; F. B. Bryant, "Savoring Beliefs Inventory (SBI): A Scale for Measuring Beliefs About Savoring," *Journal of Mental Health* 12 (2003): 175–96.

14. Lanaj, Jennings, Ashford, "When Self-Care Begets Other Care: Leader Role Self-Compassion and Helping at Work" (working paper).

15. Lanaj, Foulk, and Erez, "Energizing Leaders via Self-Reflection: A Within-Person Field Experiment."

16. Dalai Lama, Desmond Tutu, and Douglas Carlton Abrams, *The Book of Joy: Lasting Happiness in a Changing World* (New York: Avery, 2016), 83.

CHAPTER 8: THE POWER OF FLEXING IN A VARIETY OF CIRCUMSTANCES

1. Nigel Nicholson and Michael West, *Managerial Job Change: Men and Women in Transition* (Cambridge, UK: Cambridge University Press, 1988).

2. Blake E. Ashforth, David M. Sluss, and Alan M. Saks, "Socialization Tactics, Proactive Behavior, and Newcomer Learning: Integrating Socialization Models," *Journal of Vocational Behavior* 70, no. 3 (2007): 447–62; and Blake Ashforth, *Role Transitions in Organizational Life: An Identity-Based Perspective* (New York: Routledge, 2012).

3. If you are interested in identity change during transitions, please see the wonderful work by Herminia Ibarra at the London Business School: Herminia Ibarra, "Provisional Selves: Experimenting with Image and Identity in Professional Adaptation," *Administrative Science Quarterly* 44, no. 4 (1999): 764–91. You also might take a look at how Ibarra applies

these ideas to leadership in the following wonderful book: Herminia Ibarra, *Act Like a Leader, Think Like a Leader* (Boston: Harvard Business Review Press, 2015).

4. Herminia Ibarra and Roxana Barbulescu, "Identity as Narrative: Prevalence, Effectiveness, and Consequences of Narrative Identity Work in Macro Work Role Transitions," *Academy of Management Review* 35, no. 1 (2010): 135–54.

5. See https://www.espn.com/college-sports/columns/story?columnist= hays_graham&id=2924051.

6. These descriptions come from the coach Karin Stawarky, whom we first met in chapter 2.

7. Scott Sonenshein, Jane E. Dutton, Adam M. Grant, Gretchen M. Spreitzer, and Kathleen M. Sutcliffe, "Growing at Work: Employees' Interpretations of Progressive Self-Change in Organizations," *Organization Science* 24, no. 2 (2013): 552–70.

8. Source: Shahnaz Broucek.

9. Lawrence G. Calhoun and Richard G. Tedeschi, "The Foundations of Posttraumatic Growth: An Expanded Framework," *Handbook of Posttraumatic Growth: Research and Practice* (Mahwah, NJ: Lawrence Erlbaum, 2006): 3–23. You might also look at the following paper for how this growth occurs in work settings: Sally Maitlis, "Posttraumatic Growth: A Missed Opportunity for Positive Organizational Scholarship," *The Oxford Handbook of Positive Organizational Scholarship*, edited by Kim S. Cameron and Gretchen M. Spreitzer (New York: Oxford University Press, 2012), 909–23.

10. This claim aligns closely with recent thinking on the role that a growth mindset plays in successful aging. For a fuller perspective on this issue, see Peter A. Heslin, Jeni L. Burnette, and Nam Gyu Ryu, "Does a Growth Mindset Enable Successful Aging?" *Work, Aging and Retirement* 7, no. 2 (April 2021), 79–89.

11. Glenn Affleck, Howard Tennen, and Katherine Gershman, "Cognitive Adaptations to High-Risk Infants: The Search for Mastery, Meaning, and

Protection from Future Harm," *American Journal of Mental Deficiency* 89, no. 6 (1985), 653–56.

CHAPTER 9: COACHING TEAM MEMBERS IN THE POWER OF FLEXING

1. Jane E. Dutton, Laura Morgan Roberts, and Jeffrey Bednar, "Pathways for Positive Identity Construction at Work: Four Types of Positive Identity and the Building of Social Resources," *Academy of Management Review* 35, no. 2 (2010): 265–93.

2. Ibid.

3. You might find yourself venturing into complicated psychological territory that involves deep-seated problems beyond those an amateur is equipped to address. In such cases, a coachee may want to engage the help of a professional therapist.

4. K. E. Weick, "Small Wins: Redefining the Scale of Social Problems," *American Psychologist* 39, no. 1 (1984): 40–49, https://doi.org/10.1037/0003 –066X.39.1.40.

5. You can find information on this exercise, its development, and how to use it at the following link: https://positiveorgs.bus.umich.edu/cpo-tools /rbse/I.

6. Julia Lee Cunningham, Francesca Gino, Dan Cable, and Bradley Staats. "Seeing oneself as a valued contributor: social worth affirmation improves team information sharing." *Academy of Management Journal* ja (2020).

7. Thanks to Karin Stawarky for her help on an early draft of this guide.

CHAPTER 10: FLEXING YOUR COMPANY

1. Pierre Gurdjian, Thomas Halbeisen, and Kevin Lane, "Why Leadership-Development Programs Fail," *McKinsey Quarterly* 1, no. 1 (2014): 121–26.

2. Adam Canwell, Vishalli Dongrie, Neil Neveras, and Heather Stockton, "Leaders at All Levels: Close the Gap Between Hype and Readiness," *Global Human Capital Trends: Engaging the Twenty-First-Century Workforce*, edited by Cathy Benko, Robin Erickson, John Hagel, and Jungle Wong (West Lake, TX: Deloitte University Press, 2014).

3. Ibid.

4. Allan H. Church, Christopher T. Rotolo, Nicole M. Ginther, and Rebecca Levine, "How Are Top Companies Designing and Managing Their High-Potential Programs? A Follow-up Talent Management Benchmark Study," *Consulting Psychology Journal: Practice and Research* 67, no. 1 (2015): 17.

5. Jack Zenger and Joseph Folkman, "Companies Are Bad at Identifying High-Potential Employees," *Harvard Business Review*, Feb. 20, 2017, https://hbr.org/2017/02/companies-are-bad-at-identifying-high-potential-employees.

6. See, for example, Allan Church and Sergio Ezama, "PepsiCo's Formula for Leadership Potential," ATD (Association for Talent Development), *TD Magazine*, https://www.td.org/magazines/td-magazine/pepsicos-formula-for-leadership-potential.

7. Richard D. Arvey, Zhen Zhang, Bruce J. Avolio, and Robert F. Krueger, "Developmental and Genetic Determinants of Leadership Role Occupancy Among Women," *Journal of Applied Psychology* 92, no. 3 (2007): 693.

8. This bias has been shown in many studies, including in the selection of managers and board members. Geoff Eagleton, Robert Waldersee, and Ro Simmons, "Leadership Behaviour Similarity as a Basis of Selection into a Management Team," *British Journal of Social Psychology* 39, no. 2 (2000): 301–8; and James D. Westphal and Edward J. Zajac, "Who Shall Govern? CEO/Board Power, Demographic Similarity, and New Director Selection," *Administrative Science Quarterly* 40, no. 1 (March 1995): 60–83.

9. David V. Day and Hock-Peng Sin, "Longitudinal Tests of an Integrative Model of Leader Development: Charting and Understanding Developmental Trajectories," *Leadership Quarterly* 22, no. 3 (2011): 545–60.

10. Paper presented at the Mindsets & Organizational Transformation conference, London Business School, March 15, 2017.

11. Jon M. Jachimowicz, Julia Lee Cunningham, Bradley R. Staats, Francesca Gino, and Jochen I. Menges, "Between Home and Work: Commuting as an Opportunity for Role Transitions," *Organization Science* 32, no. 1 (Oct. 2020): 64–85.

12. See the wonderful case on Kevin's efforts at IBM: Christopher Marquis and Rosabeth Moss Kanter, "IBM: The Corporate Service Corps," *Harvard Business Review* (March 27, 2009), Harvard Business School Case 409-106, 22 pp.

13. R. Wartzman, "Coke's Leadership Formula: Sending Its Rising Star Execs Away for Six Weeks," *Fortune*, May 14, 2015, https://fortune.com/2015/05/14/coke-leadership-program/.

14. Chip Heath and Dan Heath, *Switch: How to Change Things When Change Is Hard* (New York: Random House, 2010).

15. Morgan W. McCall Jr., "Recasting Leadership Development," *Industrial and Organizational Psychology* 3, no. 1 (2010): 3–19.

CHAPTER 11: HOW FLEXING CAN HELP TO BUILD A LEARNING ORGANIZATION

1. These insights into Microsoft draw heavily on this wonderful case written by colleagues at London Business School: Herminia Ibarra, Aneeta Rattan, and Anna Johnston, "Satya Nadella at Microsoft: Instilling a Growth Mindset," London Business School, June 2018, https://krm.vo.llnwd.net/global/public/resources/WIN_Engage/143/LBS128p2_SR_CS_20181024.pdf.

2. Peter A. Heslin, Donald Vandewalle, and Gary P. Latham, "Keen to Help? Managers' Implicit Person Theories and Their Subsequent Employee Coaching," *Personnel Psychology* 59, no. 4 (2006): 871–902.

3. Material on a "culture of genius" was drawn from: Mary C. Murphy and Carol S. Dweck, "A Culture of Genius: How an Organization's Lay Theory Shapes People's Cognition, Affect, and Behavior," *Personality and Social Psychology Bulletin* 36, no. 3 (2010): 283–96; and Elizabeth A. Canning, Mary C. Murphy, Katherine T. U. Emerson, Jennifer A. Chatman, Carol S. Dweck, and Laura J. Kray, "Cultures of Genius at Work: Organizational Mindsets Predict Cultural Norms, Trust, and Commitment," *Personality and Social Psychology Bulletin* 46, no. 4 (2020): 626–42.

4. Robert Kegan and Lisa Laskow Lahey, *Immunity to Change: How to Over-*

come It and Unlock Potential in Yourself and Your Organization (Boston: Harvard Business School Publishing, 2009).

5. As quoted in B. McLean and P. Elkind, *The Smartest Guys in the Room: The Amazing Rise and Scandalous Fall of Enron* (New York: Penguin, 2003).

6. Canning et al., "Cultures of Genius at Work."

7. Amy C. Edmondson and Zhike Lei, "Psychological Safety: The History, Renaissance, and Future of an Interpersonal Construct," *Annual Review of Organizational Psychology and Organizational Behavior* 1, no. 1 (2014): 23–43.

8. P. A. Heslin, G. P. Latham, and D. Vandewalle, "The Effect of Implicit Person Theory on Performance Appraisals," *Journal of Applied Psychology* 90, no. 5 (2005): 842–56, https://doi.org/10.1037/0021–9010.90 .5.842.

9. From an interview with Jill Tracy Nichols, quoted in Ibarra, Rattan, and Johnston, "Satya Nadella at Microsoft: Instilling a Growth Mindset."

10. Selena Larson, "Microsoft CEO Nadella to Women: Don't Ask for a Raise, Trust Karma," *ReadWrite*, October 9, 2014, https://readwrite.com /2014/10/09/nadella-women-dont-ask-for-raise/.

11. Eugene Kim, "Microsoft CEO Satya Nadella Apologizes: 'If You Think You Deserve a Raise, You Should Just Ask,'" *Business Insider*, October 9, 2014, https://www.businessinsider.com/satya-nadella-apologizes-women -pay-2014-10#:~:text=Microsoft%20CEO%20Satya%20Nadella%20 Apologizes,Raise%2C%20You%20Should%20Just%20Ask'&text= %22Without%20a%20doubt%20I%20wholeheartedly,and%20close%20 the%20pay%20gap.%22.

12. "Microsoft CEO Satya Nadella Apologizes Again in Internal Memo," *NBC News*, October 17, 2014, https://www.nbcnews.com/tech/tech -news/microsoft-ceo-satya-nadella-apologizes-again-internal-memo -n228211.

13. Benjamin Schneider, "The People Make the Place," *Personnel Psychology* 40, no. 3 (1987): 437–53.

14. As quoted in this wonderful book: Marion Debruyne and Katleen De

Stobbeleir, *Making Your Way: The (Wobbly) Road to Success and Happiness in Life and Work* (Tielt, Belgium: Lannoo, 2020).

15. Lee et al., "The Mixed Effects of Inconsistency on Experimentation in Organizations."

16. Morgan W. McCall, "Recasting Leadership Development," *Industrial and Organizational Psychology* 3, no. 1 (2010): 3–19.

17. Elliott and Dweck (1988) have shown that when people adopt performance goals—which they are likely to do in an entity environment (Bandura and Dweck [1985]; Dweck and Leggett [1988])—they fear that they might reveal evidence of their potential inadequacies and they worry about being identified as an imposter in the setting. Elaine S. Elliott and Carol S. Dweck, "Goals: An Approach to Motivation and Achievement," *Journal of Personality and Social Psychology* 54, no. 1 (1988): 5; M. Bandura and Carol Sorich Dweck, "The Relationship of Conceptions of Intelligence and Achievement Goals to Achievement-Related Cognition, Affect and Behavior," unpublished manuscript, Harvard University (1985); Carol S. Dweck and Ellen L. Leggett, "A Social-Cognitive Approach to Motivation and Personality," *Psychological Review* 95, no. 2 (1988): 256.

18. This *Economist* article talks about this slogan: https://www.economist.com/business/2011/04/14/fail-often-fail-well.

19. E. Catmull and A. Wallace, *Creativity, Inc.: Overcoming the Unseen Forces That Stand in the Way of True Inspiration* (New York: Random House, 2014).

20. Dean A. Shepherd, Holger Patzelt, and Marcus Wolfe, "Moving Forward from Project Failure: Negative Emotions, Affective Commitment, and Learning from the Experience," *Academy of Management Journal* 54, no. 6 (2011): 1229–59.

21. Xiaodong Lin-Siegler, Janet N. Ahn, Jondou Chen, Fu-Fen Anny Fang, and Myra Luna-Lucero, "Even Einstein Struggled: Effects of Learning about Great Scientists' Struggles on High School Students' Motivation to Learn Science," *Journal of Educational Psychology* 108, no. 3 (2016): 314.

22. "Finding the Value in Your Mistake," *New & Improved*, January 16, 2015, https://newandimproved.com/2015/01/16/learning-value-mistakes/.

23. See the research on how to "sell" issues within an organization. For example: Jane E. Dutton, Susan J. Ashford, Regina M. O'Neill, Erika Hayes, and Elizabeth E. Wierba, "Reading the Wind: How Middle Managers Assess the Context for Selling Issues to Top Managers," *Strategic Management Journal* 18, no. 5 (1997): 407–23; and Susan J. Ashford and James Detert, "Get the Boss to Buy In," *Harvard Business Review* 93, no. 1 (2015): 16.

24. Bradley P. Owens and David R. Hekman, "Modeling How to Grow: An Inductive Examination of Humble Leader Behaviors, Contingencies, and Outcomes," *Academy of Management Journal* 55, no. 4 (2012): 787–818.

25. Caterina Bulgarella, "Learning, Empathy and Diversity Have Put Microsoft on a Path of Unstoppable Growth," *Forbes*, December 4, 2018, https://www.forbes.com/sites/caterinabulgarella/2018/12/04/learning-empathy-and-diversity-have-put-microsoft-on-a-path-of-unstoppable-growth/#2694c5ea4d8f.

EPILOGUE: A LIFE OF GROWTH

1. J. C. Maxwell, *The Maxwell Daily Reader: 365 Days of Insight to Develop the Leader within You and Influence Those around You* (New York: HarperCollins Leadership, 2007), 123.

2. David Whyte, *Crossing the Unknown Sea: Work as a Pilgrimage of Identity* (New York: Riverhead, 2002).

INDEX

ABOUT THE AUTHOR

SUSAN (SUE) J. ASHFORD holds the Michael and Susan Jandernoa Professorship and is chair of the Management and Organizations group at the Ross School of Business at the University of Michigan. Her academic work has been published in all the top journals in her field and she has been recognized with two lifetime achievement awards for her scholarship from the Academy of Management. Her academic work has been published in the *Academy of Management Review*, *Academy of Management Journal*, *Administrative Science Quarterly*, *Strategic Management Journal*, and the *Journal of Applied Psychology*. She lives in Ann Arbor, Michigan.